Naturally Chinese

Healthful Cooking from China

Naturally Chinese

by Ruth Rodale Spira

Book and jacket design by John K. Landis
Photographs by T. L. Gettings and Robert Griffith

Rodale Press, Inc.
Book Division
Emmaus, Pa. 18049

Printed in the United States of America on recycled paper

Library of Congress Cataloging in Publication Data

Spira, Ruth Rodale.
   Naturally Chinese.

   Bibliography: p.
   1. Cookery, Chinese. I. Title.
TX724.5.C5S64   64'.5'951   73-20862
ISBN 0-87857-080-2 (Hardcover)
ISBN 0-87857-219-8 (Paperback)

4   6   8   10   9   7   5

Dedication

To my husband, Joel, who has always
encouraged my writing and cooking.
To my daughters who, along with my husband,
consumed a great variety of Chinese dishes
with patience and a sense of high adventure.

Acknowledgments

I want to thank my old friend Vernie Lee, who
first gave me a feeling for good Chinese
cooking, who introduced me to family-style
Chinese cuisine, and who graciously gave me
valuable suggestions to improve this book.
The following staff members at Rodale Press
deserve special mention: Charles Gerras, Book
Editor, for his invaluable help and advice in
preparing the manuscript, Joy Robinson and
Sara Mammen for aid in researching material
in the Rodale Press library, Mark Schwartz, PhD,
for technical assistance in understanding food
chemistry, Joan Bingham and Joanne Moyer
for great service in readying the
manuscript, and Tom Gettings for his fine
photographic coverage.
I am also indebted to John and Hannah Fang
of the Empire China Restaurant in Allentown,
Pennsylvania, for help in mastering special
Chinese cooking techniques.
My appreciation to the following business
establishments who provided materials for
photographs used in this book: Homespun
Weavers, Emmaus, Pennsylvania; and The
China Barrel, Wescosville, Pennsylvania.

Preface

Ruth Spira and I first met some 15 years ago, when her interest in Chinese foods and cooking methods was quite new. She had recently finished her studies at New York's China Institute. Since I am Chinese and was raised in a typical Chinese family, Ruth's enthusiasm for my culture kindled our friendship.

We spent many pleasant hours together touring the Chinese markets of New York, and I taught her the traditional methods of selecting ingredients for Chinese recipes. (I am pleased to note she included that shopping information in her book.) Often she would question me about foods and cooking practices that I had always taken for granted, and I would provide her with answers. But that was many years ago. Today Ruth Spira's knowledge of Chinese cooking exceeds my own in many ways.

Her book explains to me exactly what some of the ingredients I have always used contribute to a recipe, both in terms of flavor and nutrition. We Chinese are extremely health-minded—discriminating about what we eat. We subconsciously categorize foods according to their healthfulness. It seems that there is some special Chinese dish for every human malady and some malady that can be helped by every dish. Many of these Chinese recipes have always seemed much too complicated for any but an expert cook to prepare. Ruth has removed much of the mystery and the work from Chinese cooking without destroying either the flavor or nutritional benefits. You don't even need special utensils to make Ruth's recipes.

I'm proud of my friend, Ruth Spira. Her book proves that Chinese cooking can be easy and fun, as well as practical and creative.

Vernie Lee

李趙凌雪

Contents

Chapter 1

Chinese Cooking
Is Fun--
and Easy

I am hooked on Chinese cooking and very glad of it. No matter how far afield I range into other cuisines, I keep returning to the pleasures of my *wok*. Cooking with this round-bottomed Chinese pan brings out my deepest creative urges. I always experience a feeling of excitement when the ingredients are all assembled, the pan is heating and some favorite stir-fry dish is about to be reborn.

Even better, as I toss about a treat like *moo goo gai pan* until the chicken and mushrooms are succulently tender and the vegetables are crisp, but no longer raw, I know that I'm not having all this fun at the expense of my family's health. To the contrary, fast stir-frying, one of the main Chinese techniques of cooking, keeps the freshness and nutrients in food better than any other method. Vitamin-rich vegetables predominate in these dishes, in which perhaps only one-third is meat. Meats sliced in the Chinese manner are fully cooked in one or two minutes, losing no food value in boiling liquid or wasted pan juices. Lean meat, well stripped of fat, is usually preferred. The cooking is done mostly with peanut oil, an unsaturated fat.

Stir-fried dishes are very harmonious mixtures, exceptionally well-flavored, full of texture surprises and color appeal. The combinations are often simple, but they excite the palate by playing tender meat slices against crisp pieces of vegetables, white meat and mushrooms against bright green scallions, green peppers or snow peas. Both appetite and eye are pleased by the creation.

In other words, you can nourish your family inexpensively and in grand style through the fine art of Chinese cooking.

Why not learn the food secrets of a nation with a great health record? Over the years scientific observers have reported that heart disease resulting from cholesterol-clogged arteries is uncommon in China. The blood-cholesterol level of the average Chinese runs little more than half that of most Americans. The Chinese do not assault their stomachs with over-processed, over-preserved foods as Americans do, and this may be one reason that cancer of the digestive tract occurs much less frequently in mainland China than in many so-called modern countries.

If we were to search out the ideal diet, and especially a diet for a healthy heart, it would probably come amazingly close to most Chinese cuisines.

Here are the dietary basics, evolved during more than 2,000 years of civilization:

1. Eat small quantities of meat, often mixed with a high proportion of vegetables. Lean meats are preferable to the fatty cuts, which are higher in cholesterol.

2. Emphasize fresh fish.

3. Use no milk products. These high in cholesterol foods are a rarity, even for babies.

4. Cook mainly with unsaturated oils.

5. Eat soybeans (known to reduce cholesterol levels) in many forms as a protein source.

6. Eliminate desserts. What we consider dessert is virtually non-existent in China, keeping sugar consumption to a minimum. (Sugar has been implicated in certain types of heart disease.)

7. Stir-fry or steam as many foods as possible. These cooking methods are best suited to preserving nutrients, flavor and the increasingly scarce fuel supply.

8. The Chinese, it seems, have explored every living plant and animal as a food possibility. This has led to the discovery of some highly-nutritious but unorthodox diet items, such as black mushrooms, lily buds and seaweed.

It is surprising that this country, which was always haunted by poverty, has been able to make so much out of so little. Instead of subsisting on simple, monotonous cereal fare, the Chinese made their cuisine into a true art form, containing many elements usually associated with painting or architecture. Even more remarkable, the art is practiced three times a day by millions of Chinese cooks.

This sense or artistry was cultivated by generations of wealthy Chinese noblemen at the Imperial Court, well over 3,000 years ago. They were intellectually curious as a class, searching out all possible edible materials, whether on land or in the sea, wild or cultivated, that might contribute to a higher cuisine.

Foods from the sea must have been especially appreciated since they were a bounty, free from the limitations of land. Even today, a Chinese banquet is hardly complete without one or two exotic seafood dishes like shark's fin soup or sea cucumber, both highly prized for their unusual textures.

Each dish has an artistic pattern:

1. The ingredients are cut into a uniform geometric shape: sliced, slivered, diced or minced. They should harmonize with each other.

2. A variety of meats and vegetables is combined in exciting color and texture contrasts.

3. Flavorings may be exceptionally delicate or highly aromatic and hearty. Variety is the keynote.

4. Cooking time is usually very short and timing is crucial. The success of the creation depends upon a good understanding of the "medium" and its limitations.

When the dish is served it is perfect for immediate enjoyment, with no cutting or seasoning needed—a work of art.

This very practical art form began to fascinate me when I lived in New York some years ago and became familiar with The China Institute. The Institute included courses in Cantonese and Mandarin cooking along with courses in brush painting and the other fine arts. I enrolled in the cooking school and felt that I too was an art student, learning the proper techniques to apply in perfecting my art.

Having grown up on The Organic Farm in Allentown, Pennsylvania, as the daughter of J. I. Rodale, I knew that food was more than just a means to stave off hunger. But here was a new dimension for me, a cuisine that nourished both body and soul. No wonder it is so popular throughout the world.

You may be asking yourself, "Can I really cook authentic Chinese food? Do I need special ingredients or equipment to make it taste really Chinese?"

What do you really need?

Many delicious and unquestionably Chinese dishes can be prepared using ingredients which are readily available. Stir-fry works wonders with broccoli, cabbage, string beans, onions, celery, green pepper, Chinese cabbage, and many other highly nutritious, common vegetables. Chicken parts, particularly the breasts, fresh fish, lean pork, flank or sirloin steak and beef shin are the chief meat ingredients called for in most Chinese recipes. Soy sauce, garlic, dry sherry and scallions are the basic flavoring agents.

A large, black, cast iron pan will substitute nicely for the traditional *wok*, especially if your stove is heated by electricity. (The *wok* works best fired by the direct-contact flame of gas.) A fine steamer can be devised easily by placing a high rack in a roasting pan that has a lid.

You can experiment with Chinese recipes for months without leaving your neighborhood to shop for an ingredient or a utensil. For those more adventurous cooks who want to buy ingredients that are specifically Chinese, I recommend a trip to the gourmet section of your local department store as a start. In my area of Pennsylvania, I found such delicious staples as cellophane noodles, purple laver seaweed, canned bean curd, water chestnuts, dried black mushrooms and bamboo shoots.

The health food stores provide good quality soy sauce, mung beans and soybeans for sprouting and brown rice.

A very simple way to supply yourself with Chinese ingredients is by mail. Companies that will ship oriental ingredients anywhere in the United States are listed in this book (see index). Pick out the one closest to you to keep the postage low. Most will send catalog sheets upon request, listing many dried or canned (as a last resort) ingredients, which will last for months.

If you want the pleasure of cooking with fresh Chinese vegetables, arm yourself with a well-thought-out marketing list and plan a trip to a nearby Chinatown. You will find that the grocery stores there stock a good selection of fresh vegetables, special meats and fish, dried and canned items, and small, useful equipment, such as cleavers.

When spring comes, try your hand at raising Chinese vegetables, if you have a spot of land available. We have had good success for a number of years growing our own sugar peas (snow peas) and celery cabbage (see index) at the Organic Farm.

Winter or summer, it is always easy to supplement the vegetable supply with freshly-sprouted mung beans or soybeans. Mung beans can be sprouted, without any trouble, in a few days. Soybeans need a bit of coddling, but far outstrip mung beans in nutrition and, in my opinion, flavor.

Once the basic ingredients are assembled, you need only add a little attention to detail and proper timing to prepare superb Chinese dishes, that are the equal of many *haute cuisine* French or Italian specialties, and far faster and easier to prepare than most.

Start simply. It will be very tempting to cook a complete Chinese meal when you begin. Resist the impulse. While most of the dishes are not difficult or time-consuming to prepare, they do require a certain feeling for the Chinese way in the kitchen. Choose a simple soup or a stir-fry meat dish, with one or two vegetables as a start. Most Chinese soups blend well with a steak or roast chicken dinner. By increasing the portions of the ingredients to suit your family's size, a stir-fry dish becomes an outstanding main course, served with rice and a salad.

For dining at home, I usually select a maximum of four dishes regardless of the number of guests. Like most people, I must make-do with a four-burner range, plus an oven. Rice and soup each need a burner; that leaves one for a last-minute stir-fry dish, and another for a steamed or braised dish. A stew or roast can occupy the oven. An appetizer that consists of a cold meat, fish or vegetable can sometimes be prepared a day or more in advance.

Timing and careful menu planning are all-important. Non-critical stews and soups can be cooked hours ahead of time but stir-fried dishes, especially those that include sliced meats, fish and fresh vegetables, must be cooked at the last minute and served immediately. Green vegetables will turn a drab, gray-green shade if reheated, losing much of the appeal of the freshly-prepared dish.

For your own convenience, don't attempt more than one stir-fry dish at a meal, unless the recipe specifies that it can be reheated without harm. I have particularly marked such recipes, so that you can construct menus with the proper timing in mind.

The preparation of a steamed dish can dove-tail nicely with one that is stir-fried. All the ingredients of the former can be assembled on the steaming platter somewhat in advance. The actual steaming, which takes seven to thirty minutes, generally needs no attention and can progress during the stir-fry operation.

The Chinese are fond of certain deep-fried fish or meat dishes, which require last-minute preparation. The deep-frying technique is not as simple as the stir-fry, nor as healthful, but anyone who plans to cook in the Chinese manner should be familiar with it. The flavor rates "excellent" and the nutrition can be "reasonably good," *if the food is handled with special care.* The high temperatures required to deep-fry take their toll in heat-sensitive nutrients such as vitamin C, however. If you do want to deep-fry, let me suggest that you choose foods whose important nutritional values are not so readily affected by a high heat — high-protein fish or chicken livers, for example.

Avoid planning a menu with both a stir-fried and a deep-fried dish, unless you are willing to spend extra time in the kitchen as dinner proceeds.

All traditional Chinese meals are accompanied by large quantities of white, highly polished rice. It wasn't always this way. For thousands of years the Chinese used partially-brown rice, polished "imperfectly" between grinding stones. Not until the beginning of the twentieth century did really white, machine-milled rice become available. The most healthful parts of the grain, the germ and the bran, were then completely removed, mainly for cosmetic reasons.

Nutritionally speaking we are much better off using simple brown rice, quite in keeping with centuries-old Chinese cuisine. More than that, the flavor of brown rice is more definite—rich and nutty. If you want to use a blander rice occasionally, perhaps with delicate chicken and fish dishes, try converted or parboiled rice. It is nutritionally superior to white rice, and easier to cook.

Chapter 2

The Beautiful Balance
of a
Chinese Meal

A first-class cook in any country checks for what foods are in season when planning a dinner. To the Chinese it is especially important since the ingredients are cooked so naturally with only the simplest of sauces.

During the winter it is harder to find fresh, young produce. Since the Chinese never had a well-developed marketing system, in the winter months they survived, to a large extent, on sprouted vegetables, dried items, and their own summer vegetables and meats that had been heavily salted down.

Soybeans and mung beans manufacture vitamins as they sprout; what a fortunate discovery for the nutrition of the Chinese people! Drying is another healthful means of preserving home-grown summer produce. We would do well to add these methods to our own year-round Chinese cooking. However, salting produce to preserve it is a stop-gap measure, at best. Salt is not really a food, but a chemical compound, which has been implicated in strokes, high blood pressure, cancer, colds, and even falling hair.

Contrasts of tastes and textures should always be kept in mind when deciding on a menu. The cook can achieve an exciting, yet balanced, selection with these choices:

1. Contrast a "heavy" meat or fish dish (a high proportion of meat or fish to other ingredients) with a "light" meat dish (mostly vegetables, with a small quantity of meat).

2. Combine a meat with vegetables dish with a dish that is predominantly egg (a steamed custard, for example).

3. Varying the cuts of meat will change its flavor to a surprising extent. The Chinese have wonderful ways with tender sirloin or a flank steak, as well as with their favorite long-simmered shin, oxtail or short-rib dishes. Vitamin-rich kidneys and heart taste especially good when cooked in the Chinese manner. The meat and fish chapters discuss the great number of cuts suitable for Chinese cooking.

4. Add variety by cubing, dicing, slicing or shredding—cutting the ingredients into different shapes for each dish.

5. Balance a highly flavored dish, seasoned with star anise and soy sauce, for example, with a delicate dish that depends only on the natural taste of its ingredients.

6. Combine hot dishes with a refreshing, lightly-chilled appetizer, especially in summer.

7. Include a light, clear soup with filling main dishes. Save the rich, multi-ingredient soups to accompany simple dishes, especially when "light" meat dishes predominate, or use them for a banquet-type feast.

If you are cooking for young children, try to choose Chinese dishes that are in keeping with their previous exposure to different or unusual foods. They seem to love noodle and noodle-like dishes, especially mung bean threads (cellophane noodles), either in soup or combined with slivered meats and vegetables. Most children do not appreciate salty or highly spiced foods. Go easy on garlic, star anise, and fermented black beans at first.

Soybean sprouts were a great success with every member of my family, much to my amazement. I was grateful that so healthful a vegetable needed no salesmanship on my part. My girls found the sprouts as much fun as noodles and they appreciated the added treat of a crunchy texture.

Any dish with lots of bones and chewy cartilage is given an automatic top rating by the girls. Suzy, my twelve-year-old, has devised a scale of preference that goes from one (for yecch! dishes) up to five, a rating given sparingly for all-time greats. My two other children, Lily, six, and Juno, four, join Suzy in ranking each dish decisively. Spareribs and oxtail reign supreme, in company with soybean sprouts and agar-agar seaweed salad (again the noodle syndrome, I guess).

It is a tradition in our family to provide a drumstick at meals as a teether for every baby. As children we always fought for the chewy bones, quite unaware of their great reserves of calcium and phosphorus. We just couldn't resist their superb, firm texture, contrasting with soft, juicy meat.

My mother cooked the foods that were mainly traditional to her Lithuanian heritage. These were hearty peasant dishes, using the less expensive cuts of meat. Ironically, these meats often contain more nutrition than the costly, tender cuts. Nana Rodale still whips up her favorite bean soup with veal bones, which her grandchildren relish. This is a classic of textural contrasts, to be eaten en famille without great regard to appearances.

Not all families have the benefit of a heritage of honest peasant cooking. Perhaps your family is enamored of great hunks of tender beef, too expensive and too rich in cholesterol and calories for a steady diet. Chinese cooking will introduce you delightfully, to the flavorsome, nutritious, economical cuts which peasants all over the world have learned to use—first because they were forced to use them, then they came to enjoy them, and finally, in many cases, they came to prefer them.

Coming as she does, from a family background where eating was always an adventure, Suzy readily took to even the more exotic Chinese ingredients. She is completely fascinated with the design and taste of lotus stem, and relishes the crunchy texture of the delicate fungus called "cloud ears."

All the girls are especially fond of that most talked-about of all Chinese specialties, "thousand-year-old eggs," or "ancient eggs." We serve them quartered, to be dipped in soy sauce mixed with clear stock. Perhaps we are also getting the benefit of some newly-activated organisms which aid digestion, like those we get in unpasteurized yogurt.

We find that certain Chinese dishes are ideal for the dieter. Although many of the Chinese recipes are prepared with small amounts of oil, the overall fat and oil content of the foods is probably much less than that of American foods.

We have come to depend on clear broths, absolutely fat-free, served with a few slices of vegetables or lean meat. For dieters in the family, clear soup intake is unlimited. I always make a large quantity of it in the hope that there will be some left (a rarity) which can be "recycled" as a snack or to enhance another meal. For stir-fry dishes, the Chinese *wok* with its rounded bottom allows for fast frying with less oil than with a flat-bottomed pan. The continual dieter, especially, will find it worth having. Calories can also be cut by preparing dishes that consist predominantly of vegetables. Many recipes can be adjusted to turn a "heavy" meat dish into a "light" meat dish.

The great choice of chicken and fish recipes will delight the calorie-counter. Many of the steamed dishes are prepared with very little oil, or none at all. They depend on soy sauce for their rich flavor. Steamed whole fish or flounder fillets should be part of every dieter's regular fare.

Two cautions for those watching calories: your intake of brown rice, or any other rice, should be limited; the same is true of salt and soy sauce. Some rice is needed to balance the richly-flavored meat-vegetable dishes, but don't overdo it. Eating highly-salted foods will cause your body to hold weight-producing liquids. Nothing is more discouraging than dieting day after day with no discernible weight loss.

Remember that it is not necessary to cook complete or elaborate Chinese meals, even after you feel familiar with the oriental scheme of cooking. You will discover that certain single dishes enter your family's own culinary hall of fame, to be recreated by popular request time and again. For example, we always return to simple egg drop soup and "multi-ingredient" fried brown rice as a favorite Sunday night supper. Or whenever I find a fresh, crisp bunch of watercress, I tend to include watercress soup in the dinner menu, regardless of what else I am cooking. The clear, rich, high-vitamin broth is an asset to even the finest continental meals.

Chapter 3

The Regional Cooking of China

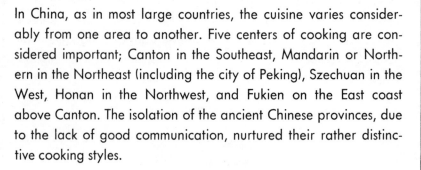

In China, as in most large countries, the cuisine varies considerably from one area to another. Five centers of cooking are considered important; Canton in the Southeast, Mandarin or Northern in the Northeast (including the city of Peking), Szechuan in the West, Honan in the Northwest, and Fukien on the East coast above Canton. The isolation of the ancient Chinese provinces, due to the lack of good communication, nurtured their rather distinctive cooking styles.

The type of Chinese food most Americans are familiar with is Cantonese. This greatly varied style of cooking excels in the stir-fry. The first Chinese to emigrate came from the coastal area of Canton, in the Southeast. Many came to the United States to help build the transcontinental railroad during the mid-1800's. Some who remained in the United States set up restaurants specializing in their native Cantonese cooking.

In addition, they introduced the novel *chop suey* and *chow mein* (served with deep-fried noodles). Both dishes were devised to appeal to the Western palate, as mixtures of familiar ingredients. While not actually un-Chinese, they don't meet the Chinese standard of freshly stir-fried, crisp cooking. *Chop suey* is usually served warmed over, limp and gray, but it is still beloved by many Americans. Surely this is testimony to the flavor of Chinese cooking even under adverse conditions.

Cantonese

Cantonese dishes are more varied than those of any other school of cooking. The area's long coastline provides a wealth of seafood. The Canton Province is blessed with fertile soil and a benign, semi-tropical climate, which insures fresh vegetables in great variety. Food is simple but rich, depending to a great extent on its own flavor, and accompanied by few spices. Typical Cantonese dishes available in restaurants are steamed sea bass, chicken with snow peas and black mushrooms, barbecued spareribs, shrimp with black bean sauce, and *lo mein,* a dish made up of stir-fried fresh noodles with slivered meat and vegetables, perhaps the prototype of *chow mein.*

Mandarin

The aristocracy of China, centered for many years around the Emperor's court in Peking, helped to evolve a delicate, inventive cuisine. Sauces and wines are used frequently. Garlic and the onion family are popular. Favorite Mandarin dishes are *Mo-Shu-Ro* (slivered pork with cloud ear mushrooms, lily buds and bean sprouts, served rolled in a thin pancake), sweet and sour fish, and Happy Family, a seafood melange.

A banquet dish renowned throughout all of China is Peking Duck, whose crisp skin is served wrapped in a pancake with scallion and sweet-pungent *hoisin* sauce.

The Mongolians in the North favor lamb, barbecued or prepared in a chafing pot. Elsewhere in China lamb does not figure in cooking; its strong flavor does not blend well with other ingredients, especially in stir-fry.

Szechuan

Cooking from Szechuan is invariably highly seasoned. This is an inland province with a hot climate, the kind of environmental conditions that usually produce a peppery cuisine. Dishes are often oily, but tasty. Cloud ear mushrooms grow profusely here and are found in many dishes. The most famous specialty is Szechuan duck, steamed with hot peppers and aromatic spice, then deep-fried.

Honan

An inland area Northeast of Szechuen, Honan has developed a limited but unusual cuisine favoring sweet-and-pungent dishes. Hot peppers are used lavishly, often with garlic and wine. A well-known feature of Honanese cooking is sweet-and-sour carp from the Yellow River, deep-fried several times to achieve a crisp crust.

Fukien

As a coastal province, Fukien makes much use of its plentiful sea-food. Red-cooking is popular with its famed soy sauce. Clear, light soups are served frequently, often several at one dinner. Dishes are, in general, lightly spiced, like the foods of most other coastal areas.

Chapter 4

Achieving the Chinese Taste

Certain characteristic ingredients are important in achieving the "Chinese" taste. Although not every one is used in every dish, each contributes to the flavorful heartiness of Oriental cooking. All can be purchased locally, in supermarkets, health food stores, or liquor stores.

Many of these essentials, as well as some of the less common ingredients, are considered by the Chinese to have definite health-giving qualities. Lin Yutang, in *The Importance of Living*, published by John Day in 1937, writes of the Chinese "confusion" between food and medicine. Frequently, their medicine is a nourishing, well-flavored soup, containing up to twenty ingredients—mushrooms, cinnamon bark, herbs, wine, sea cucumbers, which are considered a banquet delicacy, horns of young deer (the Chinese appreciate bones), beaver kidneys, etc. The Chinese look upon such mixtures as a general tonic for the whole body, not necessarily as a treatment for a specific ailment.

Let's start with the foremost Chinese cooking ingredient, so characteristic of the Chinese flavor.

Soy Sauce

The distinctive flavoring you notice in most Chinese food is soy sauce. This dark brown liquid is made from soybeans, wheat, yeast, molds and salt. Over a period of months, sometimes years, soybeans and wheat are naturally fermented with special cultures, maturing into a hearty brew, rich in enzymes and basic amino acids.

You will find the American soy sauce that is sold in supermarkets rather bitter and excessively salty; the fermenting process is speeded up chemically to the detriment of flavor. A naturally-aged soy sauce, called *Tamari,* is sold in most health food stores. Chinese soy sauce can be found in some department stores or can be ordered through the mail. A "light" Chinese soy serves for most cooking and for dipping sauces. A thick, "heavy" soy, to which molasses has been added, is used to darken certain beef and pork dishes. Avoid Japanese *shoyu* sauce, as it generally contains the chemical preservative, benzoate of soda. The Chinese use soy sauce to improve flavor in most, but not all dishes. Its pungent taste is especially good with fish and liver.

Rice

Natural brown rice is preferable to polished white rice, which has been stripped of its rich outer bran and germ. Although the required enriching of white rice restores thiamine, niacin and iron, it fails to consider the full spectrum of vitamins, minerals, amino acids and polyunsaturated fats that have also been lost.

For all-around cooking, oval-grain brown rice is favored for its rich, nutty taste. Long-grain types, less sticky after steaming, are ideal for preparing fried rice.

Also nutritionally better than white rice is the cream-colored type known as parboiled or converted, used for centuries in parts of India and the Far East. It is subjected to steam, often under pressure, before it is dried, and finally polished. This procedure drives up to 70 percent of the valuable nutrients present in the bran and germ into the center kernel. This was enough to protect Orientals from beri-beri (a vitamin B deficiency disease) in contrast to those who switched to the "modern" polished rice at the turn of the century.

Remember, you save time when you cook with either brown or parboiled rice. No washing is necessary to take off the excess starch.

Oil

The Chinese prefer to cook with oils, usually soybean or peanut oil, rather than solid fats, like butter. If stirred often, oils lubricate the foods well without burning.

Soybean oil is of outstanding value nutritionally, containing high levels of polyunsaturates, vitamins E and K, and the important lecithin, which helps control cholesterol buildup.

Peanut oil has a somewhat blander flavor and is often used with delicate dishes. It provides polyunsaturated acids and vitamin E.

The most natural and healthful oils are prepared by the cold-pressed method, in which the oil is extracted simply with strong pressure, but without heat. These oils are available at specialty shops, health food stores and occasionally at supermarkets.

If you can't locate cold-pressed oils, choose the brands that are bottled without preservatives and additives.

Sherry

Dry sherry is a good substitute for the traditional rice wine of China, which is difficult to buy in the United States. Ask for a *fino* or *Amontillado*, rich, golden brown and well flavored, but not sweet. Meats and poultry are often marinated in a small amount of sherry before cooking. It helps to tone down any strong odors.

Wine is especially important in fish cookery. Most, if not all, of the alcohol evaporates in cooking, leaving a mysteriously delicious flavor.

Dry wine helps to control excess sugar levels for diabetics. Wine in small amounts is also believed to aid in digestion.

Scallion

Be sure to use the whole stalk of the scallion, white and green leaves, unless instructed differently. It serves as a flavoring in cooking as well as a color garnish on a finished dish, and is a good source of vitamin C. Chives and leeks may be substituted, when available.

Garlic

Garlic serves to heighten the flavor of many meat and fish dishes. Use fresh, very firm cloves. Discard those that are somewhat soft, since off-flavors may have developed which might be detected in the finished dish.

Frequently used as a flavoring for foods, garlic has also been regarded as an important medicine-food for thousands of years. It is used mostly as an aid to digestion. Current medical research shows that garlic regulates the bacterial activity of the stomach, encouraging the beneficial organisms. Garlic stimulates a good flow of gastric juices, and is considered valuable for use after antibiotic treatment to help restore the proper climate for bacteria in the stomach. Since garlic dilates the blood vessels slightly, it is also being investigated as a control for high blood pressure.

Cornstarch

Before cooking, meats and fish are frequently mixed with cornstarch. This acts to preserve flavor and to increase tenderness.

Soups and sauces are often thickened with cornstarch just before serving. Cornstarch is first mixed thoroughly with a small amount of cold water before being added to the simmering liquid.

Honey

Small quantities of sweeteners are often added to Chinese dishes to balance off the saltiness of soy sauce. A traditional food of old China, honey surpasses sugar in nutritive value, especially minerals, and I have substituted it for sugar wherever possible. There is little, if any, perceptible difference in taste; if anything, honey harmonizes with soy sauce better than sugar does. It is convenient to keep honey in a glass syrup dispenser for measuring out small amounts easily.

The darker the honey, the more likely it is to be unprocessed, still unclarified, and higher in food value. These honeys are often available at roadside stands.

Honey, long a favorite ingredient in Chinese health tonics, is believed to help preserve youth and strength.

Salt

Soy sauce is not a complete substitute for salt in cooking. A small quantity of salt is sometimes desirable to bring out the full flavor of the ingredients.

Monosodium Glutamate

Formerly considered an essential seasoning in Chinese food, monosodium glutamate, or MSG has come under fire as a rather toxic substance, suspected of causing brain and eye damage in test animals. Baby food manufacturers have voluntarily removed it from canned baby foods.

MSG has been named as the culprit in a common allergy called "Chinese Restaurant Syndrome," which causes a vise-like tightness and throbbing in the head, numbness in the back of the neck, and severe heart palpitations. I have been cursed with these symptoms when eating out in Chinese restaurants from time to time. But it never happens when I cook Chinese food at home.

I thought I was alone with my problem until Dr. Robert Kwok, of the National Biomedical Research Foundation in Maryland issued a call for help in finding the cause of these symptoms (*The New England Journal of Medicine*, 1968). The allergy was apparently familiar to many doctors, judging by the ensuing letters to the editor. A research project was set up and within a few months, some brave volunteers had dined their way to scientific truth. They proved that the high amounts of MSG, used particularly in soups, were responsible for the symptoms. A generous hand with MSG was customary in some commercial establishments, to save on flavorful ingredients, or to increase taste in bland dishes.

The best way to avoid the need for using MSG is to use good meats and fresh young produce.

Chapter 5

Chinese Cooking Techniques

When you begin to cook in the Chinese manner, allow yourself enough time to plan in advance and to concentrate on learning the important techniques, as you would with any new style of cooking.

I strongly recommend using a postage scale at home to weigh out ingredients for cooking until you become a good estimator. A Chinese chef would laugh me out of the kitchen, but it can be hard to tell quantities by sight, especially for light-weight ingredients like "cloud ears" and agar-agar. Sometimes you may decide to whip up a Chinese meal with just what you have in the refrigerator. However, when you have time to think ahead, you can work out harmonious dishes, plan a more elegant menu and do your marketing in advance. Furthermore, what you buy at the store should relate closely to the cooking techniques you will use to prepare the meal.

Stir-fry

First, prepare all ingredients before any cooking is started. Soak dried ingredients. Slice the meats and vegetables. Dry all washed ingredients, to avoid splashing when they are added to hot oil.

Keep the necessary seasonings at hand and, if the dish calls for thickening with cornstarch, prepare the thickening in advance with a few tablespoonfuls of cold water in a small dish.

The actual stir-fry cooking goes so fast that there is little time for last-minute preparations. The cook is very much involved in the stir-fry operation, so read the recipe carefully several times before beginning to cook. Then take to your pans and enjoy, enjoy.

Whether you use a *wok* or a heavy frying pan, heat the utensil well, then pour in cooking oil. Vegetables are usually fried first, starting with the hardest and proceeding to the tenderest. Keep the heat as high as possible while stirring continually with a wide spatula or cooking spoon. Turn the heat down if the ingredients begin to burn. This may happen if you are stir-frying small amounts. If the recipe calls for meat, transfer the vegetables to a dish while you prepare the meat. Pour a bit more oil into the utensil, then heat well.

Meat should also be stir-fried on high heat. When the meat is no longer raw, but not quite finished, return the pre-cooked vegetables to the pan and reheat. Usually some stock or water is added at this point to provide a sauce. Reduce the heat to medium and stir a mixture of cornstarch and water into the cooking meat and vegetables. Continue to stir until the sauce becomes clear and slightly thickened. Add a few more tablespoonfuls of liquid if the sauce should over-thicken, that is, become thicker than heavy cream.

Finally, taste for proper seasoning and adjust if necessary. Serve as soon as possible to preserve the lovely fresh colors and crispness achieved in stir-fry. Some dishes, those not dependent upon a bright green look, can be reheated briefly, within an hour or two, with a minimum of flavor loss.

Timing is especially important in perfecting the delicious stir-fry technique. With a little experience, you will learn when to add each vegetable without having to rely on written instructions; you will get to know the right shade of green for properly-cooked green peppers, broccoli or snow peas.

Sirloin steak and broccoli are seen ready for slicing with a cleaver. The heavy skin of the broccoli stems has been pared off. (See index for *Stir-Fried Beef and Broccoli*)

Slight freezing of steak makes the slicing job far easier.

It is best to allow the meat to defrost before proceeding with cooking or marinating.

Cut broccoli in diagonal slices to speed up the cooking.

In a *wok*, the broccoli is steamed in a few tablespoons of water to soften the vegetable.

The steamed broccoli is transferred to a dish for later use.

Beef is added to heated oil in the *wok*. On a high heat, the beef is stirred constantly until most of its redness is gone.

After steamed broccoli is returned to *wok* and heated briefly with meat, meat or vegetable stock is added to the mixture and heated to boiling. The beef and broccoli are rapidly stirred; the cornstarch in the marinated meat lightly thickens the sauce.

Handy tips:

To keep a supply of meats and fish in a convenient form for stir-fry, buy in quantity and freeze them. Chicken breasts, flank or sirloin steak (a whole flank steak may be quartered before freezing for easier cutting later), tender boneless pork, and fish fillets all freeze well. Place the meat or fish on a cookie sheet that is lined with wax paper, and freeze until firm. Then store in freezer bags and return to the freezer. When you are ready to cook, take out as many pieces of meat or fish as required, thaw them slightly and dice, slice, shred or mince. This method is also helpful in preparing meats for soups and steamed egg custards.

Steaming

The beauty of steaming is in presenting meats, poultry or fish simply, relying mainly on their own pure flavor. A steamed, fresh chicken is uniquely rich in the taste of its own juices, so perfectly preserved. A lightly seasoned fish is ideal for steaming. Freshness is important here, since any deficiency in texture or flavor is quickly apparent. Frozen fish won't do.

A steamed dish is a particularly good foil for a stir-fry, because the steamed dish is all assembled in advance. One can tend to the last-minute cooking of the stir-fry dish while the steaming is in progress.

The Chinese use a fast method known as "wet" steaming; full circulation of steam is allowed around the cooking ingredients.

A good steamer can be improvised by placing the cooking plate on a two-inch high rack in a wide-mouthed pot. Allow enough room inside the pot to permit removing the plate without upsetting it or burning yourself. If you have stove space to spare, try steaming in a large, oval roasting pan with an oval cooking platter. Use as small a platter as possible to avoid undue condensation of water in the food. Always have the water boiling when preparing to steam a dish.

Wet-steaming is a technique that requires certain equipment, but very little skill. Because it is so simple and one of the ways to cook meats, fish and vegetables most healthfully and deliciously, it is high on the list of important reasons why I enjoy Chinese cooking.

Generally, green vegetables don't fare well in steaming. It is too difficult to catch that emerald shade of green before it declines into grayness.

Deep-Frying

Properly done, the Chinese method of deep-frying produces some of the most delectable cooking products possible. The food is juicy inside and crisp on the outside. This is in the Chinese spirit of contrasting textures, to say nothing of succulent flavor.

Care must be taken to use fresh peanut, corn, safflower or soybean oil. To avoid wasting a large quantity of oil, choose a pot that is not too wide. Heat the oil to 375° and try to maintain this temperature throughout the cooking. Should it drop much lower, the frying food absorbs a disagreeable amount of oil; fried at temperatures significantly above 375°, the food tends to burn before the inside is fully cooked. Frying small amounts of food at a time tends to keep the temperature relatively stable. When the food is golden brown, remove it with a slotted spoon or strainer, set it on paper toweling to drain, then serve at once.

Oil for deep-frying should be discarded after reheating it once or twice. Prolonged high temperatures and reheating change the chemical structure of healthful vegetable oil, causing it to become dangerously carcinogenic.

Red-Cooking

Large pieces of meat and less tender cuts are usually braised or stewed, and richly flavored with soy sauce. The dark color of the gravy gives dishes made this way the name "red-cooking." A whole chicken, duck, large fish, shoulder of pork or leg of lamb may be red-cooked, often with spices, to be served hot with gravy, or cold with its delicious jellied sauce. For stewing, the Chinese favor cuts of meat that contain gelatinous parts, like shin of beef and oxtail, which do not become stringy from long cooking.

Always prepare red-cooked foods in a heavy pan to avoid scorching. Cover and simmer on a low heat until very tender. Let the food cool, then chill it in the refrigerator to congeal the fat, which should be removed before reheating. Any braising liquid left need not be wasted. The Chinese reuse it in red-cooking another dish, or dilute it and use it as the base for soup.

Clear-Simmering

Sometimes a chicken or fish is poached gently in clear liquid without soy sauce; this is known as clear-simmering. The cooking broth is usually served as a soup separate from the chicken or fish. But steaming over simmering water is ordinarily preferred to clear-simmering to conserve flavor in the food being cooked.

Parboiling

Parboiling is occasionally required either to soften a hard vegetable or to remove a disagreeable taste. In the former case, I suggest instead that vegetables be steamed with a few tablespoons of water in a covered pot. The water will virtually evaporate. This method saves nutrients that would ordinarily migrate into the parboiling liquid and be thrown away.

Roasting

When roasting meat, the Chinese chef strives for a juicy, well-flavored interior and a very crisp exterior. Poultry or pork is often marinated in a soy-based sauce for several hours or gently cooked with a marinade for a short time as a preliminary to roasting. To achieve a crisp skin, place the meat on a rack to allow good air circulation, or cook it on an oven rotisserie. The latter method can produce spectacularly successful Chinese roasting.

Stir-Frying with Pan or *Wok*?

Good Chinese cooking can be managed with Western pots and pans, especially when the kitchen stove is electric. For faster stir-frying, a heavy, black cast-iron frying pan makes better contact with electric heating coils than does the round-bottomed *wok*. Trace amounts of iron are released into foods as they fry in the black skillet; this is true of the cast iron *wok* as well. In fact, some scientists believe that the trend away from cast iron pans has contributed to iron deficiency in the United States.

I compromise by using *woks* and black frying pans almost interchangeably. Having a gas stove as I do, I find a small *wok* (12-inch diameter) the ideal size for preparing average portions of meats and vegetables. When braising a large whole fish or steaming a custard, I turn to the larger *wok* (14-inch diameter), a little clumsier to handle, but worth the effort.

If you go shopping for a *wok*, you will notice that the complete pan (and pot, for it can do the jobs of both) consists of three parts; the round-bottomed pan, a metal ring with draft holes, and a high-domed lid. Why the ring under the pan? The *wok* is an ancient, highly versatile cooking pan, developed to use over a charcoal or wood-burning stove made of tiles. The Chinese builder cut a number of holes in the top of the stove into which the various-sized *woks* were to be placed. The metal ring is an adaptation for Western stoves to prevent the *wok* from rocking.

Anyone who intends to master Chinese cooking will find pleasure in the engineering perfection of the *wok*. It was especially designed with high sloping sides for stir-frying chopped pieces of food. The cook can speedily toss the ingredients (no corners in the pan) without risk of spilling any. Fired with an intense heat centered on the bottom, the cooking proceeds at a very fast pace, but the food must be constantly stirred. Only a small amount of oil is needed; this bathes the food pieces as they fall back into the center of the pan. A very efficient tool for stir-frying is a wide spatula, about 3 inches square.

Another unique role played by the *wok* is that of a wet steamer. Here the cooking dish rests on a rack 2 inches above boiling water. The Western cook who is familiar with dry steaming in a double boiler will find that the technique of *wok* steaming works exceptionally fast, probably its *raison d'etre*. Fish fillets, for example, need only seven minutes of cooking by this method. The sloping sides of the *wok* make it easy to remove the plate when cooking is finished.

This fresh porgy, decorated with lily buds and sliced scallions, is ready for steaming.

As a deep-fryer, the *wok* cooks with an even heat and requires less oil because of its rounded bottom. Since oil should be thrown away after several fryings, this can save you money. The wide surface of the *wok* allows more pieces to cook freely without sticking together, particularly when batter-coated. The Chinese remove fried foods from the cooking pan with a wide, round, brass strainer, available by mail order and in Chinatown stores.

Braising and "red simmering" of meats and seafood in soy sauce, and poaching a whole fish in soup can all be done admirably in the same *wok*. I do keep stressing fish cooking since the Chinese are so very adept at handling seafood. Their treats almost invariably derive from the sea, like shark's fin soup, sea cucumber, or fish tripe.

Buying a *wok* used to entail a trip into Chinatown. Today, oriental mail-order houses, restaurant supply stores and even department stores regularly stock them. Recently I bought a new *wok* at Hess's Department Store in Allentown, Pennsylvania. What was only a novelty a few years ago has become a common and very convenient cooking tool.

Woks can be ordered from:

The Bridge Company
212 East 52 Street
New York, New York 10022

Katagiri
224 East 59 Street
New York, New York 10022

Cathay Hardware
49 Mott Street
New York, New York 10013

Kwong On Lung Importers
680 N. Spring Street
Los Angeles, California 90012

Oriental Import and Export
2009 Polk Street
Houston, Texas 77003

Do not cook with your new *wok* until you have conditioned it properly. The protective oil coating must be removed with hot water and soap, and this is the last time any soap should touch the *wok*. Rinse and dry it well. Pour enough oil into the *wok* to coat the complete inner surface and heat it moderately for a minute or two. Allow the oil to cool in the *wok*. Then pour it out and wipe the *wok* with paper toweling, leaving a very thin coat of oil on the surface. This seasoning gives the pan a relatively non-stick performance, which improves with use.

The easiest way to clean a *wok* is as follows: rinse it with very hot water, then scour it if necessary with a plastic sponge or a stiff brush. Rinse the *wok* again and dry with a towel or by heating it on a burner until the water evaporates. Never use soap or detergents for cleaning your *wok*; never scrub it with cleanser or a metal sponge. Such treatment will destroy the natural protective, non-stick seasoning so valuable for stir-frying. Your *wok* will eventually turn black, since it is made of cast iron. This is perfectly natural and in no way affects the taste of the food cooked in it.

Chapter 6

The Shape of Things: Cutting Foods for Chinese Cooking

The cutting of Chinese foods is performed entirely by the chef, either before or after cooking. The diner is completely spared the use of a knife at the table.

All Chinese cooking starts with a sharp knife for chopping. A Chinese chef prizes his cleaver, with which he slices, chops, smashes, and minces. The cleaver is a rectangular utensil made of tempered carbon steel, not as hard as stainless steel, but capable of being finely sharpened for proper cutting. It must be dried thoroughly after each use, or it will rust.

A Chinese cleaver is, of course, not a necessity. The French and Germans make a fine, large triangular knife of carbon steel that will substitute nicely. But I enjoy the feel of the cleaver; I appreciate its great versatility and I like its low cost. Also its wide blade is handy for carrying chopped ingredients directly to the stove, eliminating the bother of using a plate.

Most mail-order houses that feature Chinese foods sell small utensils such as cleavers. A light cleaver chops vegetables and meats nicely; a heavy cleaver cuts through most bone, so it is especially useful for preparing braised or steamed chicken dishes. It takes special care to avoid nicking your fingers when handling a cleaver. Brace the knuckles of the hand holding the food against the upper part of the blade, cut down, then push the food into the cleaver as you cut. Do not raise the cleaver above your knuckles. The knife is heavy enough to do most of the cutting without a strong downward thrust on your part.

A heavy bone cleaver is the ideal tool to chop a chicken Chinese style.

First disjoint the chicken into pieces, then chop pieces into 2-inch sections.

Another essential is a strong, thick cutting board or chopping block. Chinese kitchens were customarily provided with a round slice of a tree trunk, six inches thick. In American kitchens, the heavy cleaver used for chopping through bones should not be wielded over a decorative wooden block unless there is no objection to large nicks on the surface. I keep a small wooden board to put on top of my built-in block for bone chopping.

For dishes that are to be stir-fried, the ingredients may be diced, sliced, shredded or minced first. A chicken or duck may be cooked whole, then chopped with a bone cleaver, bone and all, into bite-sized pieces. If you do not have a bone cleaver, merely disjoint the fowl as usual and serve Western style, with a knife and fork.

The energy crisis reached the Chinese centuries ago. In fact, their whole cuisine was shaped by the pressures born of a wood shortage. The pre-cutting saves fuel by speeding up cooking time. And far from producing a bland or dull diet, cutting up ingredients before cooking allows a wonderful mingling of flavors and improves the penetration powers of the seasonings.

The Chinese consider it harmonious to cut all ingredients into the same shape in preparing a single dish. There may be great variety in the foods used, but a common denominator is created by equal design treatment. Also, it is easier to pick up similarly-cut ingredients.

Essentially, the Chinese are geometric in their gastronomy—that is, their cuisine is dominated by foods cut into cubes and shapes rectangular and linear. Food diced for stir-fry is preferred in ⅓-to-½-inch cubes, called *ding* in Chinese. Larger cubes are used in red-cooked stews (those flavored with soy sauce).

When slicing, cut ingredients into rectangles 1½ inches long, 1-inch wide and as thin as you can manage. This is called *pan* or *peen*. Meat is generally frozen lightly to allow easier slicing. Al-

ways cut off all fat, and cut across the grain, for greater tenderness.

Soft vegetables, such as scallions and cucumbers, are sliced vertically. Harder vegetables, celery and carrots for example, benefit from diagonal slicing; their tough fibers cook more quickly. A
rolling or oblique cut is sometimes used for hard thick vegetables
such as asparagus, carrots or broccoli. First cut the vegetable
diagonally, then make a quarter turn, cutting again diagonally.
Continue cutting in this manner. A vegetable sliced in the rolling
cut has a much more artistic appearance than the ordinary chunky
look of a vegetable ready for stew.

Cut celery, scallions, green pepper and boiled chicken for *Chicken Fried
Rice* (see index) into uniform small dice. Complete all cutting before beginning to cook.

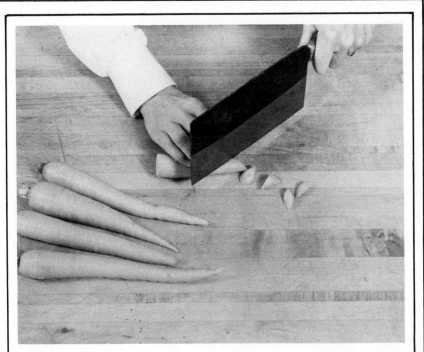

The decorative rolling cut is shown above. Make a quarter turn of the vegetable after each cut.

Linear cutting or shredding is best done by cutting the food into thin slices first, then stacking the slices and cutting them into thin strips. This method is called see and is especially popular because the flavors are diffused so well among ingredients.

Mincing, or *soong*, means chopping into fine cubes, preferably with the cleaver. Meat may be ground instead of chopped, but there is a loss of lightness, particularly when preparing meatballs.

How do you choose whether to dice, slice, shred or mince? Dicing is the quickest way, but slicing, and particularly shredding brings out more flavor. Chinese chefs decide by considering the ingredients they want to use. Some foods are naturally geometric. Linear foods like bean sprouts, noodles or lily buds suggest a shredded dish. Peas look best with diced ingredients.

Avoid cutting up ingredients more than an hour or two in advance. Vitamins are gradually lost from the many exposed surfaces. Flavor and consistency also suffer. Place the prepared ingredients on a plate, cover tightly and refrigerate until you are ready to cook them.

Chapter 7

How To Serve
a
Chinese Dinner

After learning the basic techniques of Chinese cooking and kitchen management, the next stop is to prepare a dinner to be enjoyed as the Chinese do—a friendly community affair. A native Chinese cook will serve several meat, poultry, fish, egg or vegetable dishes, usually one dish for each person, plus a soup and rice, with no single dish predominating. All, including the soup, are brought to the table at the same time, which allows the cook to enjoy her dinner without interruption. Each diner receives his own bowl of soup, to be drunk throughout the meal, and his own bowl of rice, but the rest of the foods are eaten from common dishes. Chopsticks fly into each dish as the diners choose succulent bits to eat with their rice.

This sharing of food seems strange to Americans brought up on individual portions. Even in Chinese restaurants, each diner expects to order his own dish, possibly to be tasted but not to be shared by the group. Because few restaurateurs were prepared to take on the job of teaching Westeners how to eat a proper meal, the combination plate was invented for the novice. It provides him with tastes of egg roll, *chow mein,* spareribs and fried rice, without the necessity of sharing.

A typical family meal in mainland China shows the customary sharing of all dishes among the diners, each with his own rice bowl. (Credit Robert Rodale.)

In the American home, we can adapt the basic Chinese mealtime pattern to our busy lives. Most American cooks would find it unnecessary and cumbersome to prepare more than three Chinese dishes for a meal, regardless of the number of people being served. It is simpler to increase the quantity of each dish. Serving spoons should be provided; the balancing act of selecting morsels from the serving bowls with chopsticks might prove too much for most of us.

Setting a Chinese Table

Using Chinese dishes and utensils adds a great deal to the pleasure and practicality of eating Chinese food. Besides being beautiful, they are eminently suited to the Chinese style of eating.

This dining table is set for a festive dinner for four, showing the proper positions for soup bowl, rice bowl, teacup and chopsticks.

The deep soup bowl keeps the liquid warm throughout the meal as the diner dips into other dishes. Rice is served in a similar deep bowl, very practical for use with chopsticks, or with a fork, for that matter. If you are going to eat with chopsticks, don't try to pick up rice from a flat plate; even the Chinese don't attempt that.

By all means, learn to eat with chopsticks. We have noticed that a fork can impart a metallic taste to the food; bamboo or ivory chopsticks don't interfere with food flavors.

For soup the Chinese use a porcelain spoon. This is very practical because it does not burn the mouth from hot liquid as a metal spoon can.

Dishes and Utensils

A medium-sized plate is in the center of each place setting. A deep soup bowl, about 4½ inches in diameter rests on the plate. A porcelain soup spoon is placed in the plate, to the right of the bowl. The chopsticks are placed to the right of the plate, often leaning on chopstick rests. A small teacup without handles is set directly above the chopsticks.

If soup is served with the main body of dishes, a deep rice bowl sits at the upper left of the center plate. Otherwise, the soup bowl can double as a rice bowl. A very small dish for condiments or sauces is placed above the center plate, if needed, or it can be placed between diners to be shared.

To complete the service, a 4 to 6 cup china teapot is required plus several serving bowls, a few flat dishes, an oval platter for fish, and a straight-sided serving bowl for soup. Any style of serving dishes will do, although the Chinese type is suggested for interested sinophiles.

This basic set of service, while essentially Chinese, is not limited to Chinese cooking. My family prefers all kinds of soup in the deep Oriental bowl rather than the shallow plate type. Chinese-style tea can accompany a Western meal with perfect harmony. The large serving china, too, is attractive for any type of cooking.

Because of the growing popularity of Chinese cooking, many of these special dishes can be found in local department stores, especially in large and medium-sized cities. If not, a trip to the nearest Chinese community will supply all these items quite inexpensively.

Chapter 8

Mastering the Art
of Nimble Chopsticks

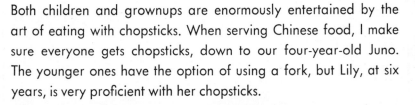

Both children and grownups are enormously entertained by the art of eating with chopsticks. When serving Chinese food, I make sure everyone gets chopsticks, down to our four-year-old Juno. The younger ones have the option of using a fork, but Lily, at six years, is very proficient with her chopsticks.

Chopsticks work on an entirely different principle than a fork. Food is grasped between the two chopsticks in a pincers action. One stick remains stationary, the other is moved to hold or release the food. Pick up one chopstick, pointing the thinner end toward the food. Place it loosely between the thumb and index finger, allowing it to rest on the last knuckle of the fourth finger, which is curved toward the palm. This chopstick does not move. The second chopstick is held with the tips of the thumb, index and third fingers. It is moved towards or away from the first chopstick. Now, holding the first chopstick down firmly with the middle of the thumb, practice on a small object that is not slippery.

Unless you are very dexterous, you will probably alternate with a fork for a time, but keep at it because using chopsticks adds to the Chinese experience.

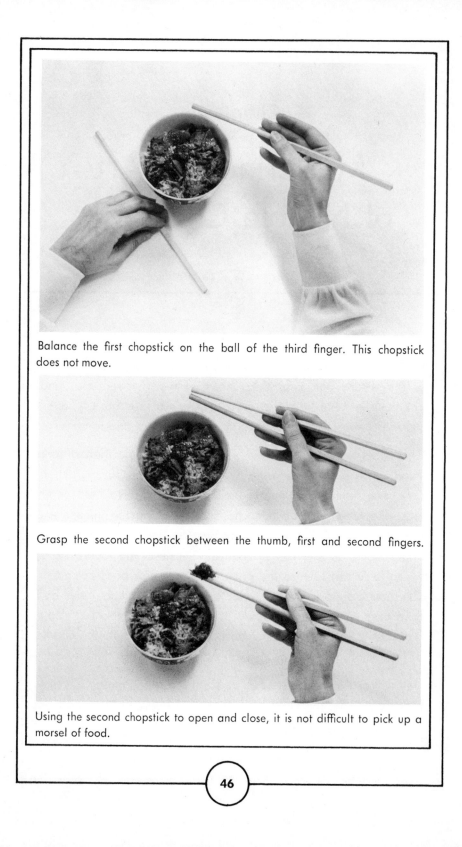

Balance the first chopstick on the ball of the third finger. This chopstick does not move.

Grasp the second chopstick between the thumb, first and second fingers.

Using the second chopstick to open and close, it is not difficult to pick up a morsel of food.

Most single food objects are held firmly between both chopsticks and then popped into the mouth. Minced food or rice may be lifted in its dish and shoveled into the mouth, rather than grasped. A large object like a shrimp is held tightly while the diner bites off pieces. Steamed fish, or any other very soft food, is pinched off with the chopsticks.

Be sure to keep the ends of the chopsticks even, or it will be difficult to pick up any food. Correct the lengths by tapping lightly against the plate.

Chapter 9

Tea,
Elixir of the Orient

Tea is to the Chinese what wine is to the French, a beloved beverage savored for its fine aroma, distinctive flavor and pleasing aftertaste. Several hundred types of tea, ranging from delicate green tea to rich and full-bodied black tea, are produced in the Orient. All have their devotees.

The tea plant, *Thea sinensis,* is an evergreen shrub belonging to the camellia family. As with the grape, the flavor differences among the beverages made from various species relate to soil types, the amount of sunlight and rain received by the plant and, particularly with tea, land elevation.

Tea time in China can be any time, but most often tea is served as a refreshing drink after or between meals. The Cantonese are the exception, for they customarily drink tea with their meals.

Tea is brewed from loose leaves in a china teapot, and can be kept hot with a tea cozy for several hours. Tea bags have not caught on in China despite their convenience, because the constriction of tea leaves in the bag precludes the use of delicate, high-quality teas, whose full flavor could not be released. For anyone who is familiar only with "broken" black tea in bags, a pleasant surprise awaits in the first tasting of fine tea brewed loose in a pot.

Tea is the world's most popular beverage. From its earliest use over 4,000 years ago, man has appreciated the psychological lift and mental stimulation tea provides without depressing side effects. Mildly brewed tea does not lead to insomnia nor does it interfere with digestion.

Originally, tea was prescribed as a medicinal beverage. Early Chinese physicians recommended it for colds, headaches, flatulence, dysentery, coughing and eye weakness. Japanese folk medicine claimed that green tea was effective against diabetes, anemia and scurvy. Tea gained its popularity when it was realized that a boiled drink could provide protection against certain diseases now known to be waterborne. Interesting modern research documents a number of these claims.

Although tea is a commonplace beverage, it is a highly complex one. In recent years, scientists have become interested in its complicated chemical structure and wide-ranging physiological effects. Tea is composed of tannins, caffeine, volatile oils, vitamins, trace elements, chlorophyll, protein and carbohydrates.

The tannins in tea, mainly responsible for its aroma and flavor, are very active biologically.

Properly-brewed tea can be a nutritious as well as delectable beverage. Small quantities of the trace minerals magnesium, flourine, zinc and aluminum are released into the brewing liquid. Tea also contains some of the B vitamins—riboflavin, thiamine, nicotinic acid, and pantothenic acid. Fresh green tea has a fair amount of vitamin C, but this is lost in producing black tea.

When tea is brewed, a portion of the calcium in the water is absorbed by the leaves, thereby becoming unavailable to the consumer. The loss is minimal, and heavy tea-drinkers can counteract the loss by including some extra calcium-rich foods in their diets—soybean products, nuts, seafood and cheese, or bone meal tablets.

Since green tea and black tea can be produced from the same plant, it is obvious that the processing makes the difference. To make green tea, the leaves are heated to soften them, then rolled and dried until they become crisp and turn a gray-green. Black tea is prepared by withering the leaves first to soften them. Then the leaves are passed through rolling machinery, where the leaf structure is broken up. Some liquid is lost in this stage. Next the leaves are fermented and they undergo a chemical change—oxidation—which turns them a reddish brown. The last step is drying with hot air, which stops further oxidation.

The brew from green tea is unusually delicate and aromatic, light green-gold in color. Black tea produces a rich, reddish-brown liquid, robust, but with a somewhat diminished aroma. Semi-fermented tea, called *oolong,* has characteristics midway between the two.

Buying Tea

The choice of teas from the Orient is abundant and varied; delicate green tea, more robust semi-fermented (*oolong*) tea, hearty black tea, and the unusual flower-scented teas.

China virtually has ceased exporting teas since the 1940's, but Formosa, Hong Kong and Japan export a reasonable selection. Hopefully, the opening of trade with the People's Republic of China will eventually bring us its great teas, especially the superb greens from the Canton area.

The following teas can be purchased from gourmet food shops, fine supermarkets or from Chinatown groceries.

Green Tea

Dragon Well (*Lung Ching*), a fine light tea from Chekiang, along the Eastern coast.

Eyebrows of Longevity (*Sow Mee*), grown in Kwangtung.

Gunpowder, from Northern China.

Silver Needle (*Gon Jim*), a light but slightly astringent tea from Kwangtung.

Water Nymph (*Suy Sen*), a lusty fragrant green from Kwangtung, in the Southeast.

Semi-fermented Tea

Black Dragon (*oolong*), rich and fragrant, from Formosa.

Black Tea

Iron Goddess of Mercy (*Iron Kwan Yin* or *Tit Koon Yum*), unusually superb, rich tea, grown in Fukien in the Southeast.

Keemun, a full-bodied, heady tea, grown in Anhwei Province in Eastern China.

Orange Pekoe, good-quality tea from small leaves, brewing a dark, strong liquor.

Prince of Wales, a blend of black teas.

Grand Yunnan (*Po Nay* or *Pu Erh*), a wine-like smooth tea from the interior Yunnan Province.

Lapsang Souchong (*Su Tang*), a spicy, smoked tea from Hunan in Central China.

Scented Teas

Chrysanthemum, Dragon Well green tea with dried blossoms of chrysanthemums or white aster, offers a full-bodied bouquet.

Jasmine, *Oolong* or black tea with Jasmine flowers, is delicately fragrant.

Lychee (*Lay Jee*), black tea with Lychee flowers, is rich and aromatic.

Other famous teas of China are listed below. Some of them may be available in the United States by the time you read this book.

Green Tea

Cloud Mist (Wun Mo), a very fine tea, grown in the high country of Kiangsi, in the central East.
Dragon's Beard (Lung So), a delicate tea from Kwangtung.

Black Tea

Clear Distance (Lu An or Ching Yuen), robust tea from Kwangtung.

Green tea is available from Japan in Japanese markets, the finest grade being Gyokuro, prepared from shaded shrubs.

When buying tea, keep in mind that the flavor will deteriorate in time, especially if the tea is exposed to air. Try some unusual types, but buy quantities you can use up within six months.

Purchase tea in tins or transfer tea that comes in a box or bag into a tin or tightly-closed jar immediately.

For the economy-minded, the same amount of green tea will go two to four times farther than black tea, because fewer leaves are needed in brewing.

Preparing Tea

Brewing tea can be a very pleasant ceremony, and only a few basic rules are necessary.

1. Heat fresh water, drawn cold from the tap.

2. Rinse a china teapot with boiling water (best, but not essential).

3. Measure tea leaves into the teapot: 1 heaping teaspoon of green tea for 6 cups of water; 1 to 2 tablespoons of black tea for 6 cups of water.

4. When water comes to a boil, pour it over the tea leaves immediately. Allow 3 to 5 minutes for brewing and serve tea at once.

A second infusion will be just as good, often better. Tea experts sometimes throw away the first liquor, relishing the high quality of the next brew. Those who want to avoid caffeine may want to drink only the second infusion. Virtually all the caffeine is released within 3 minutes of the first brewing.

An inveterate tea drinker myself, I brew a pot early in the morning and pour it into a large thermos, to be enjoyed all through the day.

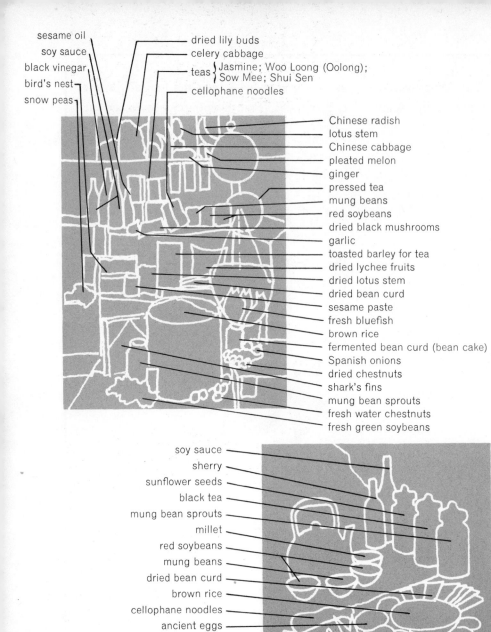

sesame oil
soy sauce
black vinegar
bird's nest
snow peas

dried lily buds
celery cabbage
teas { Jasmine; Woo Loong (Oolong); Sow Mee; Shui Sen
cellophane noodles

Chinese radish
lotus stem
Chinese cabbage
pleated melon
ginger
pressed tea
mung beans
red soybeans
dried black mushrooms
garlic
toasted barley for tea
dried lychee fruits
dried lotus stem
dried bean curd
sesame paste
fresh bluefish
brown rice
fermented bean curd (bean cake)
Spanish onions
dried chestnuts
shark's fins
mung bean sprouts
fresh water chestnuts
fresh green soybeans

soy sauce
sherry
sunflower seeds
black tea
mung bean sprouts
millet
red soybeans
mung beans
dried bean curd
brown rice
cellophane noodles
ancient eggs
raw shrimp
dried black mushroom
fresh bluefish
scallions
dried lotus stem
dried lychee fruits
dried chestnut

The Selection

The Choice

The Preparation

Dishes for a Dinner Party

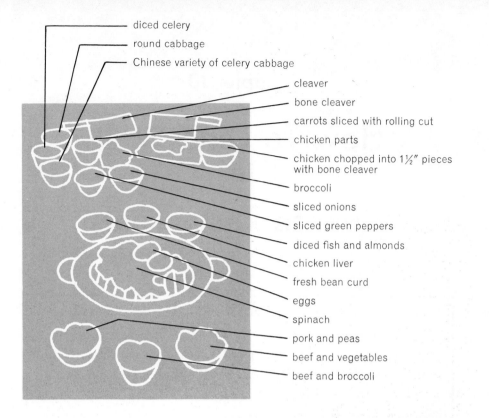

diced celery

round cabbage

Chinese variety of celery cabbage

cleaver

bone cleaver

carrots sliced with rolling cut

chicken parts

chicken chopped into 1½" pieces
with bone cleaver

broccoli

sliced onions

sliced green peppers

diced fish and almonds

chicken liver

fresh bean curd

eggs

spinach

pork and peas

beef and vegetables

beef and broccoli

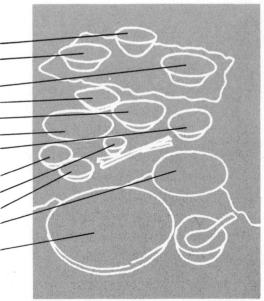

chicken fried rice

diced fish and peppers
in black bean sauce

egg foo yung

ancient eggs

bean curd with scallions

barbecued spareribs

bean sprouts with
snow peas and tomatoes

plum sauce

soy sauce

mustard

diced cut chicken
and broccoli

bean curd and greens soup

Chapter 10

How To Dine Well in Chinese Restaurants

Once in a while you may want to dine in a Chinese restaurant—to enjoy new tastes, to be inspired in your cooking efforts or to relax while the cooks whip up a series of dishes that you simply couldn't stage-manage.

When eating in the authentic Chinese manner, all diners share all of the dishes ordered, savoring the well-balanced variety of flavors and ingredients. One dish is usually ordered for each guest, in addition to soup. First, the types of meats are chosen—a chicken, pork, shrimp and beef dish, for example, for four people. Then the types of cooking are decided upon—stir-fried, steamed, roasted, deep-fried or braised (if available). Further variety is possible in methods of cutting, that is, diced, sliced, shredded or minced. Finally, one can diversify with sauces and seasonings—a delicate "white" dish without soy sauce combines well with a heartier meat dish, perhaps beef, with soy sauce, and a highly flavored dish using a sweet-and-sour sauce or five-spice seasoning. The object is to achieve a great variety of taste, texture, and color that will excite the senses.

The headwaiter in a Chinese restaurant can be prevailed upon to make these choices for you. Just let him know in advance how much you wish to spend.

Chinese Banquets

Can the ultimate in Chinese cuisine be enjoyed in this country? Perhaps the restaurant you choose will not be able to duplicate the elegance and grandeur experienced by President Nixon on his historic visit to Peking, but, generally, Chinese restaurants are prepared to create a complete and impressive banquet with a few days notice. The custom is to invite ten people to whom ten or more special banquet dishes will be leisurely served. An unusual soup, such as shark's fin, bird's nest, or winter melon, appears after the first few dishes, never at the beginning. Usually, rice does not accompany the banquet, but may be served near the end as a multi-ingredient fried rice.

In China, strong yellow rice wine is traditional at banquets and dinners. It is offered in very small amounts, served warm in cups with *hors d'oeuvres* or cold meats.

The Chinese wines that I have bought in Chinatown liquor stores have been disappointing. They tasted both strong and harsh, perhaps because of insufficient aging. So if you wish something more stimulating than tea with a Chinese meal, I suggest a dry, white wine, champagne, very dry sherry, or beer.

The Cantonese banquet listed below was arranged for us by Mrs. Vernie Lee in New York's Chinatown:

Shrimp chips
Fish balls in oyster sauce
Miniature shrimp with peas
Sweet-and-sour pork
Deep-fried shrimp patties
Shark's fin soup
Peking duck
Steamed squab with five-spice salt
Chicken, Virginia ham and broccoli
Lobster and ham fried rice

Abalone with sea cucumber
Beef fillet with Chinese vegetables (Steak Kew)
Lobster and chicken with vegetables
Fish maw with mushrooms and pork
Lychees and loquats

The following is a Northern Chinese banquet, which always starts with a large platter of thinly-sliced cold meats and fish.

Aniseed beef
Marinated abalone
White-cut chicken
Jellyfish
Ancient eggs
Diced chicken with nuts
Shark's fin soup
Sweet-and-pungent pork
Happy Family (fish maw, shrimp balls, abalone, sea cucumber, chicken, ham)
Beef with snow peas
Deep-fried fish fillets with chopped almond breading
Bok choy with black mushrooms
Peking duck
Stir-fried shrimp
Steamed fish in brown sauce
Eight precious rice pudding

Enjoying yourself fully at a Chinese banquet does require a talent for holding back your appetite. It may be tempting to fill up on the first few dishes, but *resist,* even if it means sending some delicacies back to the kitchen. The big, really great delights often appear toward the end of the banquet.

This is a good opportunity to sample exotic, nutritious treats like shark's fin, bird's nest or sea cucumber that might at first, seem too complicated to cook at home.

Chapter 11

Grow
Your Own
Chinese Vegetables

It is a natural step from cooking oriental style to raising authentic Chinese vegetables in your own garden. Western vegetables are often used interchangeably with oriental varieties by the Chinese, but Western vegetables cannot always replace crisp snow peas, *bok choy* and celery cabbage. These and other unique vegetables answer the demand for crunchy texture and bright color in Chinese cuisine.

A number of mail-order houses stock seeds of oriental vegetables:

W. Atlee Burpee Co., Philadelphia, Pennsylvania 19132, has sugar peas (or snow peas), celery cabbage, soybeans, and kohlrabi.

Nichols' Garden Nursery, 1190 North Pacific Highway, Albany, Oregon 97321, offers sugar peas (or snow peas), *bok choy* (or Chinese cabbage), celery cabbage, kohlrabi, both yellow and black varieties of soybeans, coriander, and white winter radishes. The owners claim that their soybean seeds have been grown with natural fertilizers in Japan. Some unusual oriental varieties of Western vegetables are also available. A small Japanese eggplant which has an especially delicate flavor, returns a very early crop. Look for oriental varieties of extra long cucumber, winter squash, leek and turnips.

Kitazawa Seed Co., 356 West Taylor Street, San Jose, California 95112, will send a price list for oriental vegetable seeds, including a number of celery cabbages, *bok choy*, sugar peas, and soybeans. They also stock seeds of lesser known Chinese vegetables such as bitter melon, similar in culture to cucumbers, and Chinese long beans, grown like green snap beans. Extending one and a half feet in length, the long bean often needs more cooking than its Western counterpart, but is used in the same recipes.

Burgess Seed & Plant Co., P.O. Box 218, Galesburg, Michigan 49053, lists soybeans, sugar peas, and a tremendously large winter radish called *Sakurajima*.

The Oriental Country Store, 12 Mott Street, New York, New York 10013, sells a complete assortment of Chinese vegetables seeds, though they are not listed in the mail-order catalogue. Snow peas, *bok choy*, winter melon, hairy melon, pleated melon, bitter melon, Chinese parsley and Chinese long string beans are available.

Snow Peas

First choice for the home garden has to be snow peas—the elegant, bright green, edible-podded variety featured so often in fine Chinese cooking. While snow peas can be bought in Chinatowns and, infrequently, in local farmers' markets during the spring, the price may run over four dollars a pound. But the supreme taste of home-grown freshly-picked snow peas is a reward in itself, regardless of the saving.

Snow peas require no shelling! Picking is done before the peas have formed in the pod. Whether prepared in a Chinese dish or boiled American style, the whole, tender pod is consumed. This is the variety *macrocarpon* of *Pisum sativum*, which lacks the fibrous inner lining of the regular pod. As a novice, I once grew shelling peas with the idea that very young pods, picked before the seed peas formed, might double for snow peas. It just doesn't work; we couldn't chew through the tough lining.

For use in Chinese cooking, I recommend the small variety of snow peas, called Dwarf Grey Sugar Peas, which matures in 65 days. The pod is just bite-sized, from two to three inches long. Larger varieties, like Mammoth Melting Sugar Peas grow rather unwieldy pods, four inches long. You will note that seed catalogs refer to them as sugar peas, or edible-podded peas.

A luxuriant producer, sugar pea plants can yield almost double the quantity of those for shelling peas, and the sugar peas have half the calorie count.

Before planting sugar peas, prepare the soil with finely-ground limestone (very long-lasting) to neutralize some of the acidity. Applications of ground phosphate rock and wood ashes or granite dust are helpful in replenishing phosphorus and potash. It is usually unnecessary to provide nitrogen, since the plants capture nitrogen from the ground air and "fix" it on their roots, as do all legumes. A generous application of compost will help hold moisture in the soil, a prime need of the developing pods.

All peas produce best in cool weather, so planting should be timed to have them mature enough to pick before the sizzling heat arrives. The rule of thumb is to plant six weeks before the last killing frost is expected, or as early as the ground can be worked thereafter. A fall crop can be put in during late July or early August. Be sure to water the plants during periods that lack a good, soaking rain once a week.

One package will handle fifteen row feet; one pound is needed for 100 row feet. If there has been too little rain, sprouting can be speeded up by soaking the seeds overnight before planting. A seed treatment of nitrogen-fixing bacteria is also helpful in enriching the nitrogen supply of the soil. A commercial product called Legume-Aid is available for this purpose.

All peas are much easier to pick if the plants are given some support. A common method is to plant a double row of seeds, three inches apart, placing the support between the rows. Prepare a trench two inches deep for each row. Then place the seeds one inch apart. Cover with earth and tamp down well. Sprinkle gently but thoroughly with the hose.

Right after planting, prepare a support of well-branched tree brush, chicken wire or strings hung between sturdy stakes. When pea plants are two inches high, thin them to three inches apart for dwarf varieties. Encourage growth by mulching with a six-inch layer of straw, hay or other disease-free plant material. Unless the season is unusually dry, extra watering should not be necessary. When the reddish blossoms drop and the pods are forming, make sure that the plants are receiving enough moisture.

Check the plants regularly; harvest when pods are mature but peas have not yet developed inside. Avoid letting sugar peas fill out, since this variety usually does not have the sweetness of shelling peas.

Cook fresh sugar peas within a few hours of picking, to preserve their natural sugar. Should there be a bumper crop, more than is wanted for Chinese dishes, steam them briefly with a small amount of water and serve with butter and a touch of salt.

The vines remaining after harvesting can be saved for a nitrogen-rich mulch or for enriching the compost heap.

Celery Cabbage (Pei Tsai)

A leafy vegetable of the mustard family, celery cabbage has been popular in China for over 1,500 years. One variety *Brassica pekinensis*, grows as a large cylindrical, light green head, needing seventy-five to eighty days to mature. A very good producer is the variety *Michihli,* although the Kitazawa Seed Company carries other excellent ones worth trying. Types bought from oriental seed suppliers and those bought fresh in Chinatown are more compact and a lighter green in color than celery cabbage found in supermarkets.

To grow luxuriant full heads of celery cabbage, fertilize the soil generously with an organic nitrogen fertilizer like soybean, cottonseed, or fish meal. Liming the soil is important as well. To help retain moisture during dry periods, turn under some two to three inches of compost before planting. An application of dried cow manure once the seedings emerge will help produce full large stalks.

Celery cabbage requires a cool, moist growing season to mature properly. A hot spell just before harvest will stunt growth as plants go to seed prematurely and will give them an undesirably-strong cabbage flavor. A fall crop often proves more successful since the heads are forming during the rainy (hopefully) autumn.

Plant seeds directly in the garden between July 1 and August 15. One package of seeds will be needed for 100 feet of rows, producing at least sixty-five heads. Prepare a trench one-inch deep and half fill it with sifted compost. Place the seeds in the trench, three inches apart; fill the trench with compost, tamp down and soak gently with the sprinkler or hose. Some watering may be needed should there be little rain while the seedlings are small.

When the celery cabbage is several inches high, thin out the plants to stand six inches apart. The tender, young thinnings are flavorful stir-fried and in soups. They need very little cooking, just enough to wilt the leaves. Slice them raw into salads, as well.

Thin the plants again to twelve to sixteen inches apart when they are six inches high. Apply a six-inch mulch at this time to protect the soil against the drying winds and sun.

Harvest as the stalks thicken into compact heads. Remaining heads may be picked when frost comes and stored in a cool, moist spot for up to two months.

Chinese Cabbage (Bok Choy)

Bok choy, a dark green leafy mustard plant with pure white stalks, is probably familiar to most fans of Chinese restaurants. It is served in *wonton* soup and in meat with Chinese vegetables. Known as *Brassica chinensis*, it has a somewhat stronger flavor than its cousin, celery cabbage, but is popular for its crispness and dramatic contrast of green leaf and white stem.

The culture of *bok choy* is identical with that of celery cabbage. When it is planted as a fall crop to mature in cool weather, an enormous yield can be expected. Harvest before, or just as, its yellow flowers come into bloom.

Coriander

A highly aromatic member of the parsley family, the flat leaves of coriander serve as a tasty garnish for numerous Chinese dishes.

Ordinarily grown for its pungent seeds, *Coriandrum sativum* thrives in ordinary, unfertilized soil. The flavor and aroma of herbs is lessened if fertilizer is applied, but finely-ground limestone can be mixed in to neutralize some of the soil acidity.

Choose a sunny exposure for coriander. Plant after all danger of frost has passed. Prepare a one-inch deep trench and sow seeds thinly. When the plants are two-inches high, thin them out to nine inches apart. Use the leaves as needed for flavoring, chopped or in sprigs. Another name for coriander is cilantro, or Chinese parsley.

Soybeans

Known as meat of the orient, soybeans have been cultivated in Asia since before 2,800 B.C. Their high-protein content has encouraged their varied use—as a fresh green bean, dried and cooked in soups; for soy milk and its products; and for sprouting. Highly recommended as a dried bean is *Kanrich*, a mildly-flavored variety. For eating as a fresh green bean and for sprouting, try *Hakucho*. Both varieties are available from Nichols' Garden Nursery.

Soybeans, *glycine max,* are native to the tropics. They need 100 warm days to mature. One package will plant a twenty-five foot row. Allow one pound for 150 row feet.

Feed the soil generously with finely-ground limestone, ground phosphate rock and granite dust (or wood ashes) before planting. Extra nitrogen is not necessary because soybeans, as legumes, fix nitrogen from the soil air.

After the hard frosts, plant seeds of the early, smaller varieties every two inches in rows two feet apart. Sow larger, late varieties three to four inches apart, in rows three feet wide. Seeds of all varieties of soybeans are planted one-inch deep.

Mulching is helpful for soybeans to conserve moisture and to avoid weeding, which is often damaging to these shallow-rooted plants.

Insects and plant disease rarely attack soybeans. Japanese beetles may find them attractive but these pests can be controlled for a long term through soil applications of milky spore disease.

Milky spore disease is a bacterial organism that creates a fatal disease in the grub. The disease is caused by a germ not harmful to man and is available commercially. It can be obtained from Fairfax Biological Laboratory, Clinton Corners, New York 12514.

Avoid weeding or walking through the crops when plants are wet with dew or rain. Disease spores that are harmful to soybeans may be spread on contact.

Green soybeans may be picked as soon as the pods are fully filled out. Harvesting of dried beans starts as soon as pods have turned brown. Without delay, pull the pods from plants and keep them in a dry, warm place until the pods split open.

Count on about fifteen pounds of shelled beans from a 100 foot row of soybeans.

By all means, turn under the nitrogen-rich vines after harvesting, or use them as a mulch for a late crop.

To shell green beans easily, pour boiling water over them. Let them stand for five minutes, then squeeze the beans out of one end of each pod. Add one cup of water and half a teaspoon of salt to each two cups of shelled soybeans. Boil for 15 to 30 minutes and serve lightly sprinkled with soy sauce, if desired.

To freeze fresh soybeans, simply shell them as described above and pack them into containers.

White Winter Radishes

Both the Chinese and Japanese appreciate this large, crisp type of radish (Raphanus sativus), either mild or quite pungent, which is grown as a fall crop.

Chinese radishes are served stir-fried or braised with meats, cooked in soups or chilled as an appetizer. Substitute them for water chestnuts.

A mild variety, known as Chinese white celestial radish, is recommended for its subtle flavor. It matures in sixty days to about three inches in diameter and six to eight inches long. The more spectacular Sakurajima grows to enormous size in seventy days, weighing up to thirty pounds.

To allow harvesting during cool weather, planting in late summer rather than spring is recommended. During prolonged heat large radishes become very strong in flavor, and hard and stringy.

Turn under several inches of compost before planting. Sow seeds three-quarters of an inch deep in rows eighteen to twenty inches wide. Thin to six inches between plants, wider apart for the larger radishes. Mulch with three to six inches of hay, straw or grass clippings to conserve moisture. Harvest as needed before frost is expected. Winter radishes may be stored in a cool, but frost-free place for several months.

Fresh wood ashes, lightly turned under, are helpful in controlling soil-born insects like root maggots or wire worms. Otherwise these radishes are generally untouched by insects or disease.

Kohlrabi

Crisp, turnip-like kohlrabi is a common sight in Chinatown groceries. Popular in Europe, it is still considered a "gourmet" vegetable to most Americans.

A member of the cabbage family, *Brassica oleracea caulorapa*, or kohlrabi, grows a ball-like swelling on its stem, just above ground. When raised and harvested properly, its flesh is remarkably sweet and tender.

A good variety for home plantings is Early White Vienna, which matures in sixty days. One package serves a forty-foot row, producing eighty bulbs. Plant seeds in the spring as soon as the frost is gone or in the late summer, sixty days before the first frost is expected. Kohlrabi matures best during the cool weather; a hot spell produces woody, strongly-flavored bulbs.

To prepare the bed for planting, spread it with finely-ground limestone and a two to three-inch layer of compost. Turn both under lightly. Sow seed half an inch deep in rows eighteen inches apart. Successive plantings may be made every two weeks until sixty days before midsummer. When seedlings appear, thin them to six inches apart. Then apply a thick mulch of hay, straw or grass clippings to keep the soil moist, and to avoid having to weed. Water the plants once a week if rain is sparse; this is especially important when bulbs are forming.

If the plants are troubled with aphids, spray them with a hard stream of water from the hose. Cabbage loopers are checked by applying a spray containing a special virus disease, which infects the loopers but is harmless to plants and to humans. The virus, *Bacillus thuringiensis*, is a high-potency biological control produced by a naturally-occurring bacterium that has received permanent Federal registration for control of the cabbage looper. The commercial name for this product is Biotrol, and it can be obtained from Thompson-Hayward Chemical Company, P.O. Box 2383, Kansas City, Kansas 66110.

When bulbs reach two to two and a half-inches in diameter, they are best for picking. Serve kohlrabi in stir-fry dishes, in soups or marinated in cold appetizers. Larger bulbs are especially crisp and may also be cooked in the same manner, but they will not taste as sweet as the smaller bulbs.

Harvested kohlrabi may be stored in a cool, frost-free spot and used as needed. Pull up the plants with the roots, stack them upside down on a bed of straw, and cover with a one-foot layer of more straw.

The culture of Chinese vegetables can be a fascinating project, and it requires no great expertise. I do suggest that a drawing be made of your garden, showing where each crop will be planted. It should be saved and consulted the following year to work out a successful rotation. Any type of vegetable that is plagued with plant disease should not be planted in the same spot more than one time every five years. A written gardening plan is advisable for both Chinese and Western vegetables.

Chapter 12

Gardening without a Garden

Have you ever wished you had room to grow your own fresh vegetables? Would you like to plant a crop that you could harvest in three to six days? Do you yearn to grow something fresh to eat in the winter?

Bean sprouts, the wonder crop of the Orient, will answer your needs. The land-starved Chinese developed the technique of bean sprouting many centuries ago to help feed, a bulging population. Here is the perfect year-round crop for the Chinese-food lover to grow, especially if he is also a would-be gardener without a garden.

The most popular bean for sprouting is the mung bean, really a tiny pea, which produces a good sprout in about three days. This is the bean sprout commonly served in Chinese restaurants. Mung bean sprouts combine well with chicken and fish because they are delicately flavored.

Sprouts from soybeans, although uncommon in restaurant cooking, are greatly appreciated in Chinese home-cooking for their rich, nutty flavor. They are best when cooked with hearty meats like beef and pork, in a full-bodied soup, or in a cold Chinese appetizer.

When a bean sprouts there is a tremendous jump in vitamins, especially B and C. Niacin levels double and riboflavin values quadruple. Soybean sprouts will even double their vitamin C content after a week of refrigeration.

Nutritionally, mung bean sprouts provide fairly good amounts of vitamins A, B and C. In comparison, sprouts of soybeans have more than 18 times the vitamin A content of mung beans and more than double the amount of most of the B vitamins. Soybeans also contribute outstanding amounts of protein, iron and calcium to the diet.

Some Chinese cooks recommend removing the beans from the sprouts before cooking. In Hong Kong I noticed people meticulously picking off the tiny green mung bean from the sprout. Perhaps it makes for a more elegant presentation, but what a waste of fine food value.

Home-grown soybeans may be sprouted easily if a few simple rules are followed. Grow a variety that is recommended for sprouting; there is a small-seeded type that sprouts quickly. Allow seeds a one-to-two months rest after harvesting.

Soybeans and mung beans for sprouting may be purchased at health food stores or ordered by mail from one of the Chinatowns (see mail-order sources). Request fresh beans from the current year's crop. Old beans have a lower germination rate and tend to rot, sometimes spoiling the rest of the crop.

How To Sprout

Carefully wash half a cup of beans for sprouting. Throw away all imperfect beans. Place the remaining ones in a two-quart glass jar, fill it with lukewarm water and let the beans soak overnight.

Discard the soaking water the next morning, then rinse and drain the beans. Cut out a square of cheesecloth and attach it with a rubber band across the mouth of the jar. Place the jar in a bowl, top down, and tilted. Keep the bowl and jar in a dark spot, perhaps a kitchen cabinet.

Three times a day or more, run water over the beans several times and let them drain. This frequent washing helps to remove molds and bacteria that might spoil the sprouts. Then invert the jar in the tilted position in the bowl again and return it to the dark cabinet.

After five or six days, three days for mung beans, sprouts will have grown one-and-a-half to two inches long, ready to eat. One-half cup of seeds should grow about two or three cups of sprouts.

Sprouts covered with water in a bowl or jar and refrigerated will keep well for up to a week. Just rinse them well, drain them thoroughly and cover the sprouts with fresh water each day.

It is possible to freeze bean sprouts, but the result is a soggy vegetable, quite unlike the crunchy delight of fresh sprouts.

Suggested Menus

The menus listed below can be prepared using ingredients available in most communities. The only exception is mung bean sprouts, which may be grown easily at home (see "Gardening without a Garden").

The menus use fewer dishes than one would expect at an authentic Chinese dinner; the recipes will usually serve two or more people, rather than the individual portions common in Chinese restaurants. In some menus, portions may allow for more than the number of people being served, especially when cooking a large piece of meat or fowl, like tongue, duck or chicken. In true Chinese fashion, any leftovers can be the basis for fried rice or egg *foo yung* at a subsequent meal.

One or more dishes from these menus can, of course, be included in a Western-style dinner.

Menus To Serve Four People

Beef and watercress soup
Shredded chicken and bean sprouts
Steamed eggs with minced pork
Rice
Tangerines

Chicken and cucumber in sesame sauce
Red-cooked beef tongue
Stir-fried broccoli
Rice

Chicken soup with egg ribbons
Lion's head (pork balls with celery cabbage)

Sweet and sour chicken livers
Rice
Steamed sponge cake

Sautéed wontons
Roast duck
Spinach in soy sauce
Rice
Steamed pears

Menus To Serve Six People

Mung bean sprout salad
Beef and green peppers
Steamed eggs
Rice
Sweet peanut soup

Egg drop soup
Diced chicken and broccoli in cream sauce
Steamed fish fillets
Rice
Sliced apples

Squash soup
Braised whole fish
Chicken egg *foo yung*
Rice

Tomato egg soup
Diced pork with peas
Roast chicken, marinated
Rice
Almond float

Suggested Menus

The following suggested menus need some special Chinese ingredients, most of which can be purchased at specialty stores or by mail order.

Menus To Serve Four People

Bean curd and greens soup
Walnut chicken
Mo *shu ro* pork
Chinese pancakes or rice
Canned longans

Shredded pork soup with celery cabbage
Deep-fried fish with almonds
Minced beef and bean curd
String beans and cloud ear mushrooms
Rice

Seaweed egg drop soup
Braised chicken with mushrooms and lily buds
Round cabbage with green peppers
Rice
Steamed apples

Abalone soup
Shredded beef with cellophane noodles and soybean sprouts
Steamed whole fish
Rice
Watermelon slices

Suggested Menus

Menus To Serve Six People

Braised black mushrooms
Barbecued spareribs
Sliced fish fillets with Chinese vegetables
Rice
Canned lychees

Lotus stem soup with beef
Steamed green peppers stuffed with fish and pork
Sliced chicken with mushrooms
Rice

Sliced fish soup with cellophane noodles
Red-cooked oxtail
Chicken *chop suey*
Rice
Fresh pineapple slices

Hot-and-sour soup
Diced chicken gizzards with almonds
Minced beef with watercress
Rice
Canned loquats

Suggested Menus

Shrimp egg rolls
Curried chicken
Stir-fried beef, snow peas and black mushrooms
Rice
Sliced oranges

Skewered chicken livers
Winter melon soup
Diced fish and peppers in black bean sauce
Shredded pork and dried bean curd
Rice

Appetizers

Chapter 14

Preliminary dishes, especially those introducing banquets in North China, often consist of a beautifully-arranged assortment of cooked meats and fish, served as a cold plate. Some appetizers are prepared simply, with little seasoning, to be eaten with a dipping sauce. Others are well-flavored dishes with aromatic spices in their ingredients. Lightly-cooked vegetables, seasoned with a soy dressing may also be served.

In the South of China, hot dishes are customarily taken as appetizers, perhaps tidbits of chicken livers, shrimp balls or mushrooms. A diversion of nuts may also be offered—spiced peanuts, pinenuts, melon seeds or the toasted soybeans that are now available in most markets.

In planning *hors d'oeuvres* for home entertaining, choose those that are easy to eat with the hands, or foods that can be managed on a small plate.

At the dining table, an appetizer may precede the main dishes or it may be served at the same time. What Westerners think of as appetizers (egg roll, barbequed spareribs, etc.), the Chinese usually consider part of the main course, or a snack.

Some Chinese appetizers make great picnic food, especially the chilled meats and vegetable salads.

Chilled Agar-Agar
with Chicken

Serves 4-6

2	ounces agar-agar seaweed
1 ½	tablespoons sesame seeds
¼	pound chicken breast, cooked
3	tablespoons soy sauce
2	teaspoons Chinese sesame oil
1	teaspoon honey
½	teaspoon salt

1. Allow agar-agar to soak in cold water to cover for 15 minutes. Change the water 1 time during this period. Squeeze out the excess water and cut seaweed into 2-inch lengths.

2. Heat sesame seeds in a small heavy frying pan on a medium-low heat, stirring often. Remove when golden, not yet brown.

3. Shred chicken breast by pulling apart with your fingernails.

4. Combine agar-agar and chicken shreds.

5. Beat together the soy sauce, sesame oil, honey and salt. Stir well into the agar-agar mixture.

6. Chill for 30 minutes. Serve sprinkled with toasted sesame seeds.

Comments:

1. Chinese roast pork, red-cooked tongue, turkey or roast beef may be substituted for the chicken. Slice into thin strips.

2. Small dices of sweet red pepper may be used as a garnish for extra color.

Ancient Eggs

Serves 4-6

3 ancient eggs
  soy sauce, to taste

1. Scrape off coating of ancient eggs with a small paring knife, but do not break shell. Soak eggs in water for 30 minutes to soften black coating if especially hard. Rinse eggs. Carefully remove shells. Slice each egg into 6 sections.

2. Place eggs on an attractive platter, sprinkle lightly with soy sauce, or provide small dishes of soy sauce for dipping. For a less salty sauce, dilute soy sauce with tea to taste.

Comment:

A dipping sauce of 1 tablespoon minced ginger and 3 tablespoons vinegar, preferably mild rice wine or white wine vinegar, may be substituted for the soy sauce.

Chicken and Cucumber in Sesame Sauce

Serves 4-6

1 cup cooked chicken breast
2 cucumbers
1 scallion
3 tablespoons water (approximately)
3 tablespoons *tahini* (sesame paste)
  salt to taste

1. Shred chicken breast by hand into thin strips. Pull apart with your fingernails for a natural look, or cut with a sharp knife.

2. Peel cucumbers if skin has been sprayed or treated with oil. Cut in half and scrape out seeds with a spoon or cut out with a curved grapefruit knife. Slice flesh into thin strips.

3. Chop scallion.

4. Slowly stir enough water into *tahini* to thin it to the consistency of light cream or salad dressing.

5. Combine chicken and cucumber strips. Pour *tahini* dressing over chicken and mix well. Add salt to taste.

6. Garnish with chopped scallions and serve at once.

Comment:

Peanut butter may be substituted for sesame *tahini*.

Appetizers

Deep-Fried Chicken Livers

Serves 6

1	pound chicken livers
3	tablespoons soy sauce
2	tablespoons sherry
¼	cup cornstarch
	oil to deep fry
	salt and pepper to taste
	lemon wedges

1. Cut chicken livers in half and let soak in soy sauce and sherry for ½ hour. Drain.

2. Coat livers with cornstarch. Heat oil to 375° in an electric deep fryer or in a wok or saucepan using a cooking thermometer.

3. Fry livers in small batches, to avoid lowering the temperature of the oil below 350°. Cook for about 2 minutes, remove with a slotted spoon and drain well.

4. Serve at once with salt and freshly-ground pepper and lemon wedges.

Skewered Chicken Livers

Serves 6

1	pound chicken livers
2	slices fresh ginger root
1	clove garlic
3	tablespoons soy sauce
2	tablespoons sherry
½	tablespoon honey
¾	teaspoon salt

1. Cut chicken livers in half. Mince ginger root and garlic.

2. Combine all the ingredients and marinate for several hours, if possible. Cover and refrigerate if marinating more than 1 hour.

3. Reserving some of the marinade, place chicken livers on skewers and broil under a high heat until slightly brown, but still somewhat pink inside. Baste with marinade twice while broiling.

4. Serve hot or at room temperature, sprinkled lightly with more of the marinade.

Shrimp Egg Rolls

Serves 6

½	pound shelled, raw shrimps
¼	teaspoon salt
½	teaspoon cornstarch
1	teaspoon sherry
2	teaspoons soy sauce
½	teaspoon honey
2	scallions
1	tablespoon oil
1	tablespoon oil
1	cup celery cabbage, shredded
½	pound mung bean sprouts
¼	cup bamboo shoots, shredded
1	recipe *Whole Wheat Egg Roll Skins* (12 skins) (see index)
1	egg *Plum Sauce* (see index) dried mustard
2	cups oil for deep frying

1. Chop shrimps into ¼ to ½-inch dice. Mix with salt, cornstarch and sherry.

2. Blend soy sauce and honey.

3. Finely chop scallions.

4. Heat 1 tablespoon of oil in a wok or large, heavy skillet. Stir-fry shrimps until they turn pink. Take out shrimps and wipe pan clean.

5. In same pan, heat 1 table-spoon of oil. Stir-fry celery cabbage for 1 minute, then add bean sprouts. Stir-fry another minute and add bamboo shoots and scallions. Season with soy sauce-honey mixture, stirring well.

6. Replace shrimps, stir to blend flavors and turn into a colander or strainer to drain thoroughly and cool.

7. When shrimp mixture is well cooled, fill egg roll skins. With one corner of the skin pointing downward, place 2 heaping tablespoons of filling just below the center. Bring up bottom to cover filling and fold in left and right corners. Press lightly to remove air pockets, roll up and seal with a brush of beaten egg. Repeat with rest of egg roll skins.

8. Cover with a damp towel until ready to fry.

please turn page

Roast Pork

9. Prepare a dipping dish of Plum Sauce and one of mustard. Mix dried mustard with water to the consistency of heavy cream.

10. Heat oil for deep frying in a *wok* or electric fryer. If using a *wok* it is helpful to check the oil temperature with a cooking thermometer attached to the inside of the *wok*.

11. When oil reaches 375°, add 3 egg rolls. Fry until they are well-browned. Remove and drain them on paper towels. Fry the rest in the same manner.

12. Cut almost through each egg roll to make 3 parts, and serve immediately.

Comments:

1. Shredded chicken may be substituted for the shrimp.

2. Shredded spinach, onion, water chestnuts, or dried black mushrooms may be substituted for some of the vegetables.

2	pounds pork, from the loin, butt or leg
1	clove garlic
½	cup soy sauce
¼	cup sherry
1	tablespoon honey
2	tablespoons soy sauce
2	tablespoons honey

1. Remove all visible fat from pork. Cut pork into uniform strips 1 ½ inches to 2 inches wide and the same thickness.

2. Mince garlic.

3. In a small mixing bowl, thoroughly combine garlic, ½ cup of soy sauce, sherry and 1 tablespoon of honey.

4. Place pork in a shallow pan that will just hold the meat in one layer. Pour the garlic-soy mixture over the pork and marinate for 3 to 4 hours. Turn several times and baste meat with the marinade.

5. Preheat oven to 450°. Remove pork from marinade and lay on a rack in a large pan with an inch or two of water beneath the rack. Save the marinade.

6. Roast pork in preheated oven for 20 minutes, then reduce heat to 350° and continue cooking for another 30 minutes.

7. In a small bowl, mix 2 tablespoons of soy sauce and 2 tablespoons of honey. During the last 20 minutes of cooking, baste pork twice on each side with the mixture.

8. To serve roast pork hot, place reserved marinade in a small pot and heat to boiling. Slice pork, pour some of the hot marinade over it and serve immediately. Roast pork may also be served stir-fried with vegetables (see recipes).

9. To serve cold, slice pork and provide dipping dishes of home-made *Plum Sauce* (see index) and powdered mustard, mixed with enough water to produce the consistency of light cream.

Comments:

1. To vary the marinade, ½ teaspoon of five spice powder may be added to it.

2. Roast pork may be frozen for several months. Place in a plastic bag and close tightly.

3. Roast pork seen in Chinatown groceries or served in Chinese restaurants often appears red on the outside surface. A red coloring agent is added to the marinade to provide what the Chinese consider a "lucky" color. Since it in no way affects the taste, I have eliminated it to avoid a suspected carcinogen.

Appetizers

Kidney Salad

Serves 5-6

3   veal kidneys
1   quart cold water
1   teaspoon salt
1   tablespoon sesame seeds
2   cups water
2   tablespoons soy sauce
1   teaspoon Chinese sesame oil
     few grindings fresh pepper
1   green top of scallion or a few sprigs of Chinese parsley

1. Cut veal kidneys into quarters. Take off fat and veins. Wash kidneys and slice thinly.

2. Let kidneys soak in 1 quart of cold water with salt for 1 hour. Change the water one time. Drain.

3. Place sesame seeds in a small, heavy frying pan. Heat slowly while stirring occasionally. Toast to a golden color. Remove from pan.

4. Heat 2 cups of water in a medium-sized saucepan. Add kidneys and cook for ½ minute. Drain well.

5. Mix together soy sauce, Chinese sesame oil and pepper. Coat kidneys well with soy mixture.

6. Chop green part of scallion. Sprinkle over kidneys.

7. Serve at room temperature, garnished with toasted sesame seeds.

Comment:

Four pork kidneys may be substituted for veal kidneys.

Deep-Fried Bean Curd with Sesame Sauce

Serves 6-8

4 cakes bean curd
1 tablespoon *tahini* (sesame paste)
2 tablespoons oil
1 tablespoon soy sauce
few drops bottled hot sauce (optional)
oil to deep fry

1. Slice each bean curd into 9 pieces. Dry with paper toweling being careful not to break up the pieces.

2. Place *tahini* in a small bowl. Slowly stir in 2 tablespoons of oil. Add soy sauce and, if desired, hot sauce.

3. Heat remaining oil to 375° in an electric fryer, wok or sauce pan (use a candy thermometer). Fry just a few pieces of bean curd at one time so that the oil temperature does not drop below 350°.

4. When crisp and golden, remove bean curd to paper toweling to drain.

5. Serve hot, with dipping dishes of sesame sauce.

Comments:

1. *Tahini* may be replaced with peanut butter. Add 1 teaspoon of Chinese sesame oil to capture some of the sesame flavor.

2. Deep-fried bean curd may also be incorporated in stir-fried dishes. It is especially good in *Sliced Chicken with Fried Bean Curd and Snow Peas* or in *Vegetarian Dish of the Buddhists* (see index). Slice the deep-fried bean curd in four pieces, heat very briefly with the dish when ready to serve.

Appetizers

Barbecued Spareribs

Serves 5-6

1	whole rack of spareribs, 2½ to 3 pounds
2	cloves garlic
2	slices fresh ginger
½	cup soy sauce
1	cup stock
½	teaspoon five-spice powder
2	tablespoons sherry
1	tablespoon honey
	Plum Sauce (see index)
	powdered mustard

1. Shop around for young spareribs, with short bones; the meat is more tender and juicy. Cut off as much fat as possible and slice between each bone, but not quite through.

2. Mince garlic and ginger.

3. Mix together garlic and ginger with soy sauce, stock, five-spice powder, sherry and honey.

4. Place spareribs in a large, shallow pan in a single layer. Pour marinade over spareribs, and brush them completely, especially in the cuts between the bones.

5. Let marinate 3 to 4 hours, basting and turning several times.

6. Preheat oven to 375°. Remove spareribs from marinade and lay on a rack in a large pan with 1 to 2 inches of water beneath the rack. The spareribs should not touch the water. Save the marinade for basting.

7. Roast for about 50 minutes, turning once or twice. Baste spareribs several times with the marinade.

8. Meanwhile prepare dipping dishes of homemade plum sauce and powdered mustard, mixed with enough water to provide the consistency of light cream.

9. If spareribs have not browned sufficiently, broil for a few more minutes on each side.

10. Cut apart ribs with a very sharp knife and serve immediately with plum sauce and mustard.

Comments:

1. Barbecued spareribs may be prepared a day or two in advance. Roast until done, but do not brown under the broiler.

Stir-Fried Green Peppers in Sesame Oil

Serves 5-6

Wrap tightly when cool and re-frigerate. When ready to use, heat at 350° for 10 minutes, then broil for a couple of minutes on each side to brown fully. Proceed as above.

2. If serving spareribs as a main dish, a whole rack will serve 3 to 4 persons.

3. Spareribs seen in Chinatown groceries and served in Chinese restaurants often appear red on the outside surface. A red color-ing agent is added to the mari-nade to provide what the Chi-nese consider a "lucky" color. Since it in no way affects the taste, I have eliminated it to avoid a suspected carcinogen.

4. Canned *hoisin* sauce may be substituted for plum sauce as a dip.

3   large, green peppers
¼   cup Chinese sesame oil
3   tablespoons soy sauce
½   teaspoon honey

1. Remove seeds from green peppers. Cut in strips 1-inch wide and 2-inches long.

2. Heat sesame oil to a medium heat in a *wok* or large, heavy skillet. Stir-fry peppers until the skins begin to wrinkle. Pour off oil and discard.

3. Mix together soy sauce and honey. Pour over green peppers and stir-fry for 3 minutes. When cooled, chill for 30 minutes or serve at room temperature.

Comment:

Green peppers in sesame oil are excellent served with a curried meat or seafood dish.

Appetizers

Chilled Broccoli with Soy Sauce

Serves 4

1 pound broccoli stems and flowerets
3 tablespoons water
1 ½ tablespoons soy sauce
1-2 teaspoons Chinese sesame oil
1 teaspoon honey

No more than 2 hours before serving:

1. Separate broccoli stems and flowerets. Peel stems and cut diagonally into pieces ½-inch thick. Cut flowerets into 1-inch pieces.

2. Steam broccoli stems with water in a covered, heavy frying pan for 3 minutes. Add flowerets and steam 2 to 3 minutes longer until tender but crunchy and still bright green. Drain.

3. Mix remaining ingredients in a small dish. Place broccoli in a serving dish and pour in soy-honey mixture. Toss well.

4. Cover with foil or waxed paper, chill lightly and serve.

Comments:

1. In order to retain the natural sweetness of the broccoli, be sure to avoid preparing more than a couple of hours in advance.

2. To substitute asparagus for broccoli, prepare with a rolling cut, slicing the asparagus diagonally into 1 ½-inch lengths every quarter turn. Steam for 5 minutes.

Mung Bean Sprout Salad

Serves 6

1	pound mung bean sprouts
3	tablespoons water
1	cooked chicken breast
1	egg
2	tablespoons water
	pinch of salt
	cooking oil
2	tablespoons soy sauce
1	teaspoon honey
½	teaspoon Chinese sesame oil

1. Place sprouts in a large, heavy frying pan with 3 tablespoons of water. Cover and steam about 2 minutes until just wilted. Drain.

2. Shred chicken breast by hand using your fingernails for a natural look, or shred finely with a sharp knife.

3. Beat egg in a small bowl with 2 tablespoons of water and salt.

4. Heat a very small amount of oil in a medium-sized frying pan. Add enough egg mixture to cover the bottom of the pan. Pour off any excess. On a low heat, cook the egg until just firm. Remove egg pancake from pan and continue cooking the rest of the egg mixture in the same way, adding a little more oil for each pancake.

5. Roll up individual egg pancakes. Then cut across into narrow strips.

6. Mix together soy sauce, honey and sesame oil in a small dish.

7. Combine sprouts, shredded chicken breast and egg strips in a serving bowl, then pour soy mixture over all, stirring well. Chill lightly.

Comments:

1. Chinese roast pork may be substituted for the chicken breast. Shred finely.

2. Snow peas may be added as a sparkling green garnish. Steam 2 minutes covered in a small heavy frying pan with 2 table-spoons of water. Shred when cooled.

3. Soybean sprouts may be substituted for mung bean sprouts. Steam sprouts 10 to 12 minutes until softened slightly.

Appetizers

Braised Black Mushrooms

Serves 6

30	dried, black mushrooms
	warm water to cover
2	slices fresh ginger root
2	tablespoons oil
1	cup stock
1½	tablespoons soy sauce
2	teaspoons honey
	salt to taste
¼	teaspoon Chinese sesame oil

1. Soak dried mushrooms in warm water for 30 minutes. Squeeze out excess water. Cut large mushrooms in quarters, smaller ones in half, removing hard stems.

2. Mince ginger root.

3. Heat 2 tablespoons of oil in a wok or medium-sized heavy pan having a lid. Stir-fry ginger for a few seconds, then add soaked mushrooms. Stir-fry for 1 minute.

4. Pour in stock, soy sauce and honey. Heat to boiling, cover, reduce heat and simmer 45 minutes.

5. Salt sauce to taste.

6. Flavor with ¼ teaspoon of sesame oil.

Comment:

This recipe may be served hot or at room temperature.

Mushrooms Stuffed with Fish and Pork

Serves 6-8

18 medium-sized, dried black mushrooms
warm water to cover
¼ cup mushroom soaking liquid
¼ pound fish fillets
½ scallion
1 slice fresh ginger
¼ pound lean pork, ground
1 teaspoon soy sauce
¼ teaspoon salt
1 egg
2 teaspoons cornstarch
1 teaspoon soy sauce

1. Soak dried black mushrooms in warm water for 30 minutes. Squeeze out excess water. Save ¼ cup of the soaking liquid.

2. Grind fish or chop it finely with a cleaver or sharp, heavy knife.

3. Mince scallion and ginger finely.

4. Mix together chopped fish, scallion, ginger, ground pork, 1 teaspoon of soy sauce and salt.

5. Stuff mushrooms with fish-pork mixture and arrange them on a heat-proof platter.

6. Boil 1 or 2 inches of water in a large roasting pan, *wok,* or large, deep pot. Place stuffed mushrooms on a rack over boiling water. Cover and steam for 30 minutes.

7. Beat egg, and baste stuffing with it during the last few minutes of steaming time.

8. Remove mushrooms and keep warm. Pour remaining liquid into a small saucepan and bring to a boil.

9. Combine cornstarch, mushroom soaking liquid, and 1 teaspoon of soy sauce. Add to liquid in saucepan and stir until thick.

10. Pour over mushrooms and serve at once.

Comment:

If desired, the pork can be eliminated, using another ¼ pound of fish fillets instead and reducing steaming time to 10 to 20 minutes.

Appetizers

Soups

Chapter 15

We in the Occident are accustomed to serving soup as a separate course, a prelude to the main dining event. Ordinarily, the Chinese present all the food at once, including the soup, and the diner may sip it occasionally throughout the meal, rather than finishing it all at once.

A Western cook preparing a Chinese meal has the option of serving soup either way.

Chinese soups can be clear, refreshing broths, flavored with lightly-cooked meat slices or greens. They can be long-cooked, meaty stews, enriched with simmering bones or interesting variations of the familiar, thickened egg drop soup, or noodle soup.

The basis of most Chinese soups is a rich meat stock, usually prepared from chicken. Bony parts, such as necks and backs, release the best flavor and are most economical. Pork chop bones, from which the meat part has been removed for another dish, will greatly enrich a chicken stock.

In an emergency, canned College Inn chicken stock can be substituted for the homemade version. Since the canned stock is highly salted, dilute it with water to taste. Homemade stock is certainly preferable, however, for flavor and food value. All stock should be chilled for several hours or overnight so that the congealed fat can be lifted off and removed.

A last word of instruction: seasoning is always variable. Taste the soup before serving it and adjust to your own preference. Slight oversalting can be corrected with a touch of honey (start with ¼ teaspoon), stirred in thoroughly.

Egg Drop Soup

très bon
att: sel.

Serves 5-6

1 ½ tablespoons cornstarch
¼ cup cold water
2 eggs
6 cups chicken stock
½ teaspoon honey
salt to taste

1. Mix cornstarch and cold water.

2. Beat eggs.

3. In a medium-sized saucepan, heat chicken stock to boiling.

4. Add honey and mix well.

5. Stir cornstarch mixture thoroughly and pour into boiling stock. Stir until stock thickens.

6. Remove from the heat, pour in beaten eggs immediately, and stir well with a fork.

7. Add salt to taste.

Comments:

1. This soup can be prepared 1 to 2 hours ahead without loss of flavor. Reheat slowly when ready to serve, but do not boil.

2. One cup of shredded romaine or escarole lettuce may be stirred into the soup just before serving.

3. To prepare tomato egg drop soup, peel 2 fresh medium-sized tomatoes (drop into boiling water very briefly to loosen skins). Cut tomatoes in half and squeeze out the juice and seeds. Cut each half into 4 pieces. Simmer in chicken stock for 5 minutes before thickening with cornstarch.

Soups

Seaweed
Egg Drop Soup

Serves 5-6

3 sheets purple laver seaweed, or a small handful
of pressed laver
warm water to cover
2 eggs
1½ tablespoons cornstarch
¼ cup cold water
6 cups chicken stock
½ cup mung bean sprouts
½ teaspoon honey
½ tablespoon soy sauce
salt to taste

1. Rip purple laver seaweed into bite-sized pieces. Soak in warm water about 8 minutes. Rinse in clear water several times and squeeze out excess water.

2. Beat eggs in a small bowl.

3. Mix cornstarch in cold water.

4. In a medium-sized saucepan, bring chicken stock to a boil. Add purple seaweed and simmer 3 minutes.

5. Add mung bean sprouts, then season with honey and soy sauce.

6. Add salt to taste.

7. Cook broth 1 to 2 minutes. Stir cornstarch mixture well, then pour it into broth. Stir until soup thickens.

8. Remove from heat, add beaten eggs immediately, and stir well with a fork.

Comments:

1. This soup can be prepared several hours early and reheated until hot but not boiling.

2. Chinese dried red hair seaweed, occasionally found in Chinatown, can be substituted for purple laver. Soak for 10 minutes in warm water and rinse several times. Tear into bite-sized sprigs. Japanese Kobu seaweed may be substituted also. Soak in the same manner, then rip into bite-sized pieces.

Soups

Abalone Soup

Serves 6

15-20 snow peas
½ cup liquid from canned abalone
2 cups chicken stock
3½ cups water
½ teaspoon honey
½ cup shredded abalone (canned)
¼ cup shredded Smithfield ham (optional)
    salt to taste

1. Remove strings from snow peas and shred the peas.

2. In a medium-sized saucepan combine abalone liquid, stock and water and bring to a boil.

3. Add honey, abalone, Smithfield ham and snow peas. Bring slowly to a boil again. Add salt to taste and serve immediately.

Chicken Soup with Egg Ribbons

Serves 5-6

2 eggs
2 tablespoons water
    pinch salt
1 scallion
1 teaspoon oil, approximately
6 cups chicken stock

1. Beat the eggs in a small bowl with water and salt.

2. Chop scallion, including green top.

3. Heat a very small amount of oil in a medium-sized frying pan. Add enough egg mixture to cover the bottom of the pan. Pour off any excess. On low heat, cook the egg until just firm. Remove egg from pan and continue same procedure until the rest of the egg mixture is used.

4. To slice easily, roll up individual egg pancakes. Then cut across into narrow strips.

5. In a medium-sized saucepan, bring chicken stock to a boil.

6. Add egg strips and chopped scallion.

7. Heat briefly and serve immediately.

Tomato Egg Soup
with Chicken

Serves 7-8

2   quarts water
4   cups fresh tomatoes
¼   pound chicken or pork
2   slices fresh ginger (optional)
2   eggs
6   cups chicken stock
½   tablespoon soy sauce
1½ teaspoons honey
    salt to taste
    few grindings fresh pepper

1. In a large pot, bring water to a rolling boil, add fresh whole tomatoes and immediately turn off heat. After 3 minutes, remove tomatoes from the water and allow them to cool slightly. Peel and cut the tomatoes in half, then gently squeeze out the juice and seeds. Cut each half into 4 pieces.

2. Freeze chicken or pork long enough to stiffen it, which makes slicing easier. Cut meat into slivers.

3. Shred ginger slices.

4. Beat eggs.

5. In a large saucepan, boil chicken stock. Add slivered meat and ginger. Return to a boil, reduce heat and simmer gently for 1 minute while stirring.

6. Add tomatoes, stir and simmer 5 minutes.

7. Flavor with soy sauce and honey.

8. Season to taste with salt and freshly-ground pepper.

9. On a low heat, pour in beaten eggs and stir a few times. Remove from the heat immediately and serve.

Comment:

Count on tomatoes for rich quantities of Vitamins A, C, some of the B vitamins, and Vitamin E.

Soups

Lotus Stem Soup with Beef

Serves 5-6

¾	pound fresh lotus stem
1	pound lean short ribs of beef (have butcher saw into 1½-inch pieces)
6	dried Chinese red dates
1½	tablespoons sherry
1	tablespoon soy sauce
6	cups cold water
¾	teaspoon salt
1	scallion, chopped

1. Cut off dark skin of lotus stem. Slice lotus stem thinly.

2. Cut a deep slit through the meat at the center.

3. In a large saucepan, with cover, heat sliced lotus stem, beef ribs, dried red dates, sherry, soy sauce, and cold water to a boil.

4. Skim carefully to remove scum.

5. Cook on a low heat, covered, until ribs are very tender, 45 minutes to 1 hour.

6. Remove meat from soup and cool slightly. Discard bones and cut meat into ¾-inch cubes. Return to the soup.

7. Flavor with salt. Skim all fat from surface of soup and serve garnished with chopped scallions. Or chill overnight and scoop fat from surface before serving.

Comment:

When cooked, red dates may be mashed lightly with a fork and returned to the soup to release more of the sweet fruitiness. Remove dates before serving. Dried red dates may be purchased by mail order.

Red Beans in Beef Broth

Serves 6

2   pounds beef bones (choose lean soup bones with some meat on them, like beef shin or short ribs)
2   cloves garlic
2   scallions
6   cups water
½   cup red soybeans
1   teaspoon salt
2   teaspoons honey

1. Remove all visible fat from bones. Cut the meat off the bones and slice into 1½-inch chunks.

2. Peel garlic and cut in half.

3. Chop scallions.

4. Combine beef and bones with garlic and water in a medium-sized pot, bring to a boil and remove scum carefully. Reduce heat and simmer, covered, for 1 hour.

5. Add red soybeans to soup and continue simmering for 1½ to 2 hours until beans are tender. Do not overcook or the beans tend to fall apart.

6. Season with salt and honey. Skim fat from surface of soup or chill and remove hardened fat.

7. When ready to serve, discard bones and cut meat into bite-sized pieces.

8. Reheat soup and taste. If beef flavor is too strong, dilute with water, then reseason with salt, if necessary.

9. Serve sprinkled with chopped scallions.

Soups

Beef and Watercress Soup

Serves 5-6

½ pound flank steak or chip steak, lean
½ tablespoon soy sauce
1 teaspoon oil
½ teaspoon salt
1 bunch watercress
3 cups chicken stock
3 cups water
few drops sesame oil (optional)

1. Freeze beef until stiff and cut into fine dice.

2. Add soy sauce, 1 teaspoon of oil and the salt, mixing well with a fork. Let marinate for 30 minutes.

3. Cut off thick, lower stems of watercress and save to cook in soup at a later date. (see comment no. 3)

4. Heat chicken stock and water to boiling in a medium-sized pot. Add watercress and boil, uncovered, for 2 minutes.

5. Add finely-diced beef and a few drops of sesame oil, stirring well to break up the meat, which tends to clump together.

6. Taste and add more salt if desired. Serve immediately.

Comments:

1. Chicken breast may be substituted for the beef.

2. For variety, lightly poach 5 or 6 eggs and place 1 in each soup bowl.

3. Thick stems of watercress are crisply delicious cooked in soup.

Black Bean Soup
with Oxtail

Serves 9

¾ cup black soybeans
1 oxtail, about 2½ pounds (have butcher saw oxtail into 2-inch pieces)
9 dried Chinese red dates
4 slices fresh ginger root
10 cups cold water
1½ teaspoons salt

1. Soak black soybeans overnight. Drain.

2. Cut all visible fat from oxtail.

3. In large saucepan, with cover, heat black soybeans, oxtail, dried red dates, ginger slices and cold water to a boil. Skim carefully to remove scum, then cook on a low heat, covered, for 2 to 3 hours until beans are tender.

4. Season with salt.

5. Skim all fat from surface and serve. Or chill soup overnight and scoop fat from surface before serving.

Comments:

1. Unlike most bean soups, this broth remains perfectly clear and unthickened. Soybeans are unusually low in starch, which acts as a thickener.

2. When cooked, red dates may be mashed lightly with a fork and returned to the soup to release more of their sweet fruitiness. Remove dates before serving. Dried red dates may be purchased by mail order.

Soups

Chicken Stock

Serves 5-6

3-4 pounds chicken backs and necks or 3-4 pound chicken
2 carrots
1 onion
2 thin slices ginger (optional)
6 cups cold water
2 teaspoons salt
½ teaspoon honey

1. Remove all visible fat from chicken parts or chicken. (Do not remove skin.)

2. Scrub carrots.

3. Peel onion.

4. Place chicken parts, carrots, onion, ginger and cold water in a large pot with cover and bring to a boil. Remove scum that collects on the surface of the water.

5. Season with salt and honey.

6. Cover, turn heat to low and simmer 2 hours. Slow simmering will keep the broth clear. Taste and add more salt if necessary.

7. Strain soup and scoop all fat from the surface, or refrigerate overnight, then remove the congealed fat.

Comments:

1. Using backs and necks is an inexpensive way to make a good chicken stock, rich from the nutritive value of the bones. Parts from a stewing hen, if available, will produce a richer stock, but should be cooked up to 3 hours to extract the maximum flavor.

2. For an unusual licorice taste, add 1 clove of star anise to the simmering broth.

3. Pork bones may be cooked with the chicken as a flavor enricher.

Soups

Chicken and Bean Curd Stick Soup

Serves 5-6

¼ pound bean curd stick
  warm water to cover
3 dried black mushrooms
  warm water to cover
½ cup mushroom soaking liquid
½ chicken breast
6 cups chicken stock
½ teaspoon soy sauce
½ teaspoon honey
  salt to taste

1. Soak bean curd stick at least 1 hour in warm water. Keep submerged to soften fully. Slice it into thin noodles.

2. Soak black mushrooms 1 hour in warm water and sliver. Reserve ½ cup of soaking liquid.

3. Freeze chicken breast until stiff. Slice thin.

4. In a medium-sized saucepan, heat chicken stock to boiling with bean curd stick, black mushrooms, and mushroom soaking liquid.

5. Simmer, covered, for about 45 minutes, until bean curd noodles are tender, but still somewhat chewy.

6. Stir in chicken breast, soy sauce and honey.

7. Taste and add salt if necessary. Simmer for 3 minutes and serve.

Comment:

To prepare ahead, add chicken breast, stir, and immediately remove soup from the heat. Reheat briefly when ready to serve.

Soups

Bird's Nest Soup

Serves 6

3-4 ounces dried bird's nest
 water to cover
6 cups rich chicken stock
½ teaspoon salt
½ chicken breast
¼ cup stock
2 egg whites
1½ tablespoons cornstarch
¼ cup stock
3 tablespoons minced, smoked ham

1. In a medium-sized bowl, soak bird's nest overnight in cold water to cover.

2. Pick over bird's nest carefully, pulling out bird feathers or foreign matter with a tweezers. This job requires a great deal of time and patience.

3. In a large pot, heat chicken stock to boiling. Add well-cleaned bird's nest and salt. Cook on low heat, covered, for 15 minutes.

4. Remove skin and bones from chicken breast. Mince breast, place it in a small mixing bowl and stir in ¼ cup stock.

5. In a small dish, beat egg whites with a fork. Stir well into chicken mixture.

6. Combine cornstarch and ¼ cup stock.

7. Gently reheat bird's nest in stock. Stir cornstarch mixture, pour into soup and mix until thickened. Add minced chicken, stir a few times and remove from the heat.

8. Pour bird's nest soup into a tureen or soup bowls. Sprinkle with ham. Serve immediately.

Comments:

1. One or two finely-minced scallions may be substituted for the smoked ham.

2. To prepare in advance, cook the bird's nest soup, but reserve the smoked ham garnish. Refrigerate until ready to use. Reheat briefly and sprinkle with smoked ham.

Poached Fish in Broth

Serves 6

2½ pounds whole fish (sea bass, porgies, sea trout or carp)
3 slices fresh ginger
2 scallions
8 cups fish stock
1 teaspoon salt

1. Clean fish, but leave them whole.

2. Shred ginger.

3. Chop scallions.

4. Heat fish stock to boiling in a large saucepan with cover.

5. Add fish and ginger. Cook, covered, for 15 minutes on low heat.

6. Add chopped scallions and salt. Cook 5 minutes longer.

7. Serve soup and fish separately.

Comments:

1. Prepare fish stock by simmering fish bones in water for 30 minutes. Or substitute chicken stock.

2. A rich fish soup may be prepared with the bones of 2 medium-to-large fish instead of whole fish. Simmer fish bones with 6 cups of water, 1 teaspoon of salt and ½ teaspoon of honey for 45 minutes. Skim well when liquid comes to a boil. Discard bones and, if desired, thicken with 1½ tablespoons of cornstarch dissolved in ¼ cup of cold water. Garnish with chopped scallion.

Soups

Sliced Fish Soup
with
Cellophane Noodles

Serves 5-6

¼	pound flounder fillet
½	tablespoon cornstarch
½	tablespoon sherry
½	tablespoon soy sauce
2	ounces cellophane noodles (mung bean threads) warm water to cover
4-6	ounces celery cabbage or Chinese cabbage (bok choy)
3	cups fish or chicken stock
3	cups water
½	teaspoon honey
½	teaspoon salt

1. Freeze fish fillets until stiff. Slice thinly. Marinate fillets for 20 minutes in cornstarch, sherry and soy sauce, mixed well.

2. Soak cellophane noodles in warm water for 15 minutes.

3. Cut off tender, green tips of celery cabbage and thinly shred them. Cut coarser parts into 1-inch squares. Keep separate.

4. In a medium-sized saucepan, heat stock and water to boiling.

5. Add celery cabbage squares and noodles. Cook 5 minutes.

6. Mix fish mixture well and add to soup with honey and salt. Reduce heat and simmer 2 minutes.

7. Stir in shredded celery cabbage tops and serve within a few minutes.

Comments:

1. Fish fillets may be cut in 1-inch squares instead of sliced. Add marinated fish with celery cabbage and noodles. Simmer 7 minutes.

2. Pork balls may be added instead of fish fillets. See recipe for pork balls.

Shark's Fin Soup

Serves 6

½ pound dried shark's fin
3 quarts water
6 scallions, tied in a bunch
1 ¾-inch chunk fresh ginger root, peeled
1 small chicken breast (2 halves)
2 teaspoons cornstarch
6 cups rich chicken stock
½ teaspoon salt
2 tablespoons cornstarch
¼ cup stock
3 tablespoons minced, smoked ham

1. Place dried shark's fin in a colander or strainer and rinse well. Turn into a large bowl and fill with water. Soak shark's fin overnight. Pour contents of bowl into a colander, draining well. Rinse with warm water and drain.

2. In a large pot, heat shark's fin with 3 quarts of water, scallions, and ginger root. Bring water to a boil, turn down heat and simmer for 1 hour.

3. Skin and bone chicken breast. Place on a cookie sheet in the freezer until stiff. (This can be done in advance.) If fully frozen, thaw breast about 30 minutes. Slice it thinly, then shred finely. When shredded breast has thawed, mix it thoroughly with 2 teaspoons cornstarch.

4. Rinse shark's fin in colander again, discarding scallions and ginger root. Allow shark's fin to cool.

5. Examine shark's fin carefully, discarding any hard or dark particles. Rinse well in the colander.

6. In a medium-to-large pot, with a lid, heat the chicken stock to boiling. Add shark's fin and salt, bring to a boil again, turn down heat and simmer, covered, for 30 minutes.

7. Sprinkle in chicken shreds and stir thoroughly. Simmer for 2 more minutes.

please turn page

Soups

Shredded Pork Soup with Celery Cabbage

Serves 5-6

8. Combine 2 tablespoons cornstarch and ¼ cup stock, mixing well. Pour into soup and stir until thickened.

9. Pour the soup into a tureen or soup bowls. Sprinkle with ham and serve immediately.

Comments:

1. Shark's fin soup may be made a few hours in advance. Reserve minced ham when preparing. To serve, reheat briefly and garnish with ham.

2. One finely-minced scallion may be substituted for the minced, smoked ham.

2	pork chops
1	tablespoon soy sauce
½	teaspoon cornstarch
½	pound celery cabbage
6	cups water
½	teaspoon honey
½-1	teaspoon salt

1. Cut meat from pork bones and trim off all fat. Freeze meat until somewhat stiff, then shred it. Marinate shredded meat in mixture of soy sauce and cornstarch for 15 minutes or longer.

2. Shred celery cabbage.

3. In a medium-sized saucepan, with cover, bring water to a boil with the pork bones. Skim top to remove scum and simmer, covered, for 30 minutes or longer. Remove bones and discard.

4. Add shredded celery cabbage, honey, and salt to broth. Boil for 5 minutes.

5. Stir marinated meat, add to broth and cook for 2 more minutes.

Comment:

American round cabbage or zucchini may be substituted for celery cabbage.

Bean Curd and Greens Soup

Serves 6

1½ pieces fresh bean curd
½ pound Chinese green cabbage (*Gai Choy*)
6 cups chicken stock
¾ teaspoon honey
salt to taste

1. Cut bean curd into 1-inch dice.

2. Slice green cabbage into 1-inch squares.

3. In a medium-sized saucepan, heat chicken stock to boiling. Season with honey. Taste and add salt, if necessary.

4. Add bean curd and green cabbage and cook on medium heat for 8 minutes. Do not use a lid or you will dull the lovely green color of the cabbage. Serve immediately.

Comments:

1. The exquisite white-on-green colors in the soup are quite extraordinary, as is the clear fresh taste of the broth.

2. To prepare 1 to 2 hours ahead, cook bean curd and green cabbage for only 5 minutes; then remove from the heat.

3. Celery cabbage may be substituted for Chinese green cabbage if desired. Cook only 5 minutes in broth.

4. Canned bean curd may be used instead of fresh curd. Substitute ¼ to ½ pound of canned curd.

Soups

Buckwheat Noodle Soup

Serves 6-8

1 ½   quarts water
½   pound buckwheat noodles
1   teaspoon salt
3   scallions
¼   pound celery cabbage
6   cups stock
1   cup slivered Chinese roast
    pork
2   teaspoons soy sauce
½   teaspoon salt

1. In a large pot bring water to a boil and add buckwheat noodles and 1 teaspoon of salt. Boil until noodles are tender but still chewy, stirring occasionally.

2. Drain noodles and rinse with cold water. Drain again.

3. Mince scallions.

4. Slice celery cabbage across the rib into ¼-inch pieces.

5. In a large pot heat stock to boiling. Add celery cabbage and roast pork. Season with soy sauce and salt.

6. After 1 minute add noodles and scallions. As soon as noodles are reheated, serve soup in 6 or more individual soup bowls.

Comments:

1. Buckwheat supplements rice and wheat in China, especially in Northern parts. Buckwheat noodles can be purchased in Japanese groceries and can be ordered by mail from Katagiri (see address in chapter, Buying Chinese Ingredients).

2. Slivered raw or cooked chicken, pork or seafood may be substituted for the Chinese roast pork. If using raw meat, allow a few minutes extra cooking time in the stock.

3. A generous handful of snow peas may be used instead of the celery cabbage. Remove stems and slice in half, lengthwise.

4. The liquid from red-cooked meats is excellent as a base for noodle soup. To 2 cups of cooking juices add 4 cups of water.

Hot-and-Sour Soup

Serves 6

3 dried black mushrooms
1 cup warm water
½ cup mushroom soaking liquid
3 tablespoons cloud ear mushrooms
12 dried lily buds
1 cup warm water
¼ pound lean pork
2 fresh bean curd cakes
1 scallion
2 tablespoons cornstarch
¼ cup water
1 egg
6 cups chicken stock
2 tablespoons rice wine vinegar (or white wine vinegar)
1½ teaspoons soy sauce
½ teaspoon honey
    salt to taste
    few grindings fresh pepper (Szechwan pepper if available)
¼ teaspoon Chinese sesame oil

1. Soak black mushrooms in 1 cup warm water for 1 hour. Cut out hard stems and slice mushrooms into shreds. Save ½ cup of the soaking water.

2. Soak cloud ear mushrooms and lily buds together in 1 cup of warm water for 30 minutes. Rinse cloud ears well, cutting off any hard stems. Cut lily buds in half and cut off the hard ends.

3. Cut off any visible fat from pork. Freeze pork until stiff and cut it into shreds.

4. Sliver bean curd.

5. Chop scallion.

6. Mix cornstarch in ¼ cup of water.

7. Beat egg.

8. In a large pot, heat chicken stock and ½ cup of mushroom soaking water to boiling. Add shredded pork, black mushrooms, cloud ears, lily buds and bean curd. Simmer for 10 minutes.

9. Season with vinegar, soy sauce and honey.

10. Add salt to taste and grind in some fresh pepper.

11. Stir cornstarch mixture well and pour into soup. Stir until thickened.

please turn page

Soups

Squash Soup

Serves 5-6

12. Add beaten egg and stir several times. Remove from heat.

13. Flavor with sesame oil and chopped scallions when ready to serve.

Comments:

1. Prepare 1 or 2 hours in advance if desired and reheat slowly when serving.

2. One-quarter pound of canned bean curd can be substituted for the fresh bean curd.

3. Hot-and-sour soup is known for its peppery tang and complementing tartness. Increase the vinegar and pepper quantity to taste.

¾   pound young squash (yellow squash or zucchini)

6   cups chicken or beef broth
    salt to taste

1. If squash is not very young, peel off skin. Otherwise scrub squash well with a vegetable brush. Cut into triangular, bite-sized pieces by quartering lengthwise and slicing across.

2. Bring broth to a boil in a medium-sized pot, add squash and simmer for 3 to 5 minutes.

3. Add salt to taste.

Comment:

Chinese okra or hairy melon can be cooked in the same manner, giving the broth an excellent, fresh flavor. To prepare Chinese okra, peel off sharp ridges, cut in triangular pieces and follow above directions. Hairy melon must be peeled before it can be used in soup.

Winter Melon Soup

Serves 5-6

½   raw chicken breast
1   pound winter melon
2   tablespoons cornstarch
¼   cup cold water
6   cups chicken stock
1   teaspoon salt
¼   teaspoon honey
¼   cup shredded smoked
     ham (optional)

1. Freeze chicken breast until stiff. Cut into thin slices.

2. Remove seeds and spongy center from winter melon. Cut off rind and slice flesh into thin wafers, 1-inch by 1-inch.

3. In a small mixing bowl, mix cornstarch with cold water.

4. Combine stock, salt and honey in a pot and bring to a boil. Drop in chicken, ham and winter melon. Simmer until winter melon is transparent—about 5 minutes.

5. Stir cornstarch mixture thoroughly. Pour into simmering soup, stirring until thickened.

Comment:

To prepare 30 minutes ahead, simmer soup 2 minutes, then thicken. Reheat when ready to serve.

Soups

Wonton Soup

Serves 6

½   recipe for *Whole Wheat Wontons* (see index)
3   stalks Chinese cabbage *(bok choy)*
5   cups chicken stock
1   teaspoon soy sauce
     salt to taste

1. Parboil *wontons* for 3 minutes instead of cooking for 10 minutes as indicated in recipe for *Whole Wheat Wontons*. Drain well.

2. Cut Chinese cabbage in 1-inch lengths. Keep leafy ends separate.

3. In large saucepan, heat chicken stock to boiling, adding 1 teaspoon of soy sauce and salt to taste.

4. Add parboiled *wontons* and boil for 8 to 10 minutes.

5. Add Chinese cabbage stalks during the last 5 minutes of cooking. Stir in leaves just before serving. Simmer until leaves have wilted.

6. Serve in deep soup bowls, allowing 4 *wontons* per portion.

Comment:

Substitute shredded spinach, Swiss chard or watercress for the Chinese cabbage. Reserve thick stems of watercress to cook in soup at another time.

Bean Sprout Soup

Serves 5-6

2 eggs
1½ tablespoons cornstarch
¼ cup water
1 scallion
6 cups chicken stock
2 cups mung bean sprouts
½ teaspoon honey
salt to taste

1. Beat eggs.

2. Mix cornstarch and water.

3. Mince scallion.

4. In large saucepan, heat chicken stock to boiling and add bean sprouts. Reduce heat and simmer for 3 minutes.

5. Flavor with honey, and add salt to taste.

6. Stir cornstarch mixture well and pour it into hot soup. Stir until thickened.

7. Slowly pour in beaten eggs, stirring with a fork. Remove soup from heat immediately and serve garnished with scallions.

Seaweed and Chicken Soup

Serves 5-6

½ chicken breast
3 sheets purple laver sea-weed, or small handful of pressed laver
warm water to cover
2 scallions
6 cups chicken stock
½ tablespoon soy sauce
½ teaspoon honey
salt to taste

1. Freeze chicken breast until stiff. Cut it into slivers.

2. Rip purple laver into bite-sized pieces and soak them in warm water for 8 minutes. Rinse in clear water several times and squeeze out excess water.

3. Chop scallions, including green tops.

4. In a medium-sized saucepan, bring chicken stock to a boil. Add purple laver and chicken slivers. Simmer 5 minutes.

5. Season with soy sauce and honey.

6. Add salt to taste.

7. Sprinkle with chopped scallions.

Soups

Poultry

The Chinese have many different ways of cooking chicken. This bird is popular because it is the easiest animal to raise and to prepare. No special smoking or salting is needed, since the animal is small enough to be consumed entirely within a reasonable period of time.

Every part of the chicken is relished, often cooked separately. Many stir-fried dishes call for chicken breast, others for the dark meat of leg and thigh. The bones go into the stock pot. The gizzard, heart and liver are considered the treasures, enjoyed for their chewy texture and distinctive flavor.

When a chicken is cooked whole, the breast is fully cooked, and sometimes dry, before the dark meat is tender. Separating the parts before cooking, as the Chinese often do, solves that problem; each part is cooked only as long as necessary.

The Chinese roast birds in various ways, all intended to saturate the flesh with a highly-flavored sauce. Chicken can be marinated for several hours before roasting or it can be pre-simmered in the sauce. These methods produce a first-rate roasted chicken, with very crisp skin.

For the sake of convenience keep a supply of chicken breasts in the freezer. Buy a half-dozen or so chicken breasts, deboned, or debone them yourself, and lay them on a cookie sheet, on waxed paper in a single layer. Freeze the breasts for several hours, or until they are solid, then pack them in a plastic bag for storage in the freezer.

When you are ready to cook, remove as many breasts from the freezer as are needed and defrost them for half an hour. Then they can be diced, sliced or shredded as specified in the recipe. Allow to defrost, and proceed with the directions.

For parties and banquets, duck becomes the specialty, each region of China having invented its own unique version. Peking duck, whose involved preparation may require several days, is universally acclaimed the best. A special technique for drying the duck creates an extra-crisp skin, incredibly crunchy.

As the high point of a banquet, one is served thin pancakes, along with squares of glistening duck skin, frilly lengths of scallion and *hoisin* sauce—spicy, yet sweet. Each guest rolls some of each ingredient into the pancake and eats this as a sandwich, with his hands. This flavor and texture combination is considered the ultimate in Chinese cuisine. In Northern Chinese restaurants, the duck skin, scallion and sauce are inserted into a pouch in a steamed bun, instead of being rolled in a pancake.

My brother, Bob Rodale, dined at the Peking Roast Duck Restaurant in Peking recently, when visiting China with a group of fellow-journalists. He reports that each part of the duck appeared in some course during the banquet, including the gizzard, heart and neck.

In the Canton area of South China, duck is roasted with a marinating sauce filling its cavity. This is the cooked duck seen hanging in Chinatown groceries, and available for purchase by the piece.

For Chinese home-cooking, duck is marinated several hours or pre-simmered in a soy-based sauce before roasting.

Braised Chicken with Chestnuts

Serves 3-4

¾   pound fresh chestnuts
     boiling water
2   slices fresh ginger root
3   tablespoons soy sauce
2   tablespoons sherry
½   teaspoon salt
½   teaspoon honey
3   tablespoons oil
2   pounds chicken legs and
     thighs, disjointed
2   cups hot water
3   scallions
1½ tablespoons cornstarch
2   tablespoons water

1. Place chestnuts in a pot of boiling water. Cook for 20 minutes.

2. Meanwhile, mince ginger root.

3. Combine ginger, soy sauce, sherry, salt and honey, mixing well.

4. Heat oil in a heavy skillet which has a lid. Brown chicken pieces quickly, uncovered, and remove. Discard oil. Return chicken to the pan and pour soy sauce mixture over it. Stir well. Add hot water and scallions, cover, and cook on low heat for 30 minutes.

5. Remove chestnuts from boiling water. Peel off outer shells and membranes quickly while still hot. Cut in half.

6. Add chestnuts to chicken and continue to simmer for about 15 minutes, or until chicken is tender.

7. Mix cornstarch and water. Add to chicken and stir to thicken.

Comments:

1. To substitute dried chestnuts for fresh ones, parboil the chestnuts for 10 minutes in boiling water. Be sure to obtain chestnuts with the inner membranes removed.

2. Chicken may also be chopped in 2-inch pieces (Chinese fashion) before browning.

Poultry

Braised Chicken with Mushrooms and Lily Buds

Serves 4

6   dried black mushrooms
¼   cup cloud ear mushrooms
15   lily buds
2   slices fresh ginger root
1½   tablespoons soy sauce
2   tablespoons sherry
¼   teaspoon salt
       few grindings of fresh
       pepper
½   teaspoon honey
1   small roasting chicken, split
3   tablespoons oil
½   cup hot water
1   tablespoon cornstarch
2   tablespoons water

1. Soak dried black mushrooms in warm water for at least 1 hour. Cut out hard stem ends. Slice mushrooms in strips, or leave whole.

2. Soak cloud ear mushrooms and lily buds in warm water for 30 minutes and rinse well. Remove any hard parts of mushrooms.

3. Cut off hard tips of lily buds. Cut in half or make a knot in the middle of each strand.

4. Chop ginger root fine. Combine with soy sauce, sherry, salt, pepper, and honey. Brush all over chicken and marinate for 30 minutes.

5. Heat oil in a large, heavy skillet, which has a lid. Sauté chicken halves, uncovered, until browned on both sides. Remove chicken and pour away any remaining oil.

6. Replace chicken. Add soaked mushrooms, cloud ears and lily buds with ½ cup of hot water. Heat to boiling, cover, then simmer for about 45 minutes, until chicken is tender.

7. Cut chicken into western-style serving pieces, or chop into 1½-inch sections, Chinese style. Remove some of the large bones before chopping up the chicken.

8. Skim off any fat from sauce.

9. Mix cornstarch and water. Pour into sauce on a medium heat and stir until it thickens.

Poultry

Chicken Chop Suey

Serves 3-4

10. Place chicken pieces and other ingredients on a serving platter and pour sauce over all. Serve immediately.

Comment:

Braised chicken, cooked with crunchy goodies like cloud ears and lily buds, is a well-liked treat in our family. If desired, make it several days ahead and reheat to serve. Taste for final seasoning and add more salt if desired.

1	pound boneless chicken breasts
½	teaspoon salt
2	large onions
½	pound fresh mushrooms
1 ½	tablespoons cornstarch
2	tablespoons water
2	tablespoons soy sauce
1	teaspoon honey
2	tablespoons oil
3	cups celery, thinly sliced on the diagonal
1 ½	cups mung bean sprouts
½	teaspoon salt
1 ½	tablespoons oil
1 ½	cups stock
½	cup toasted almonds (optional)

1. Remove skin from chicken breasts. Freeze until somewhat firm and slice thin.

2. Mix in ½ teaspoon of salt.

3. Cut onions through lengthwise and slice them.

4. Slice mushrooms.

please turn page

Poultry

5. Combine cornstarch, water, soy sauce and honey. Set aside.

6. Heat 2 tablespoons of oil. Stir-fry celery, bean sprouts, onions and mushrooms at 1-minute intervals. Add ½ teaspoon of salt and remove vegetables from the pan.

7. Heat 1½ tablespoons of oil in the same pan until very hot. Stir-fry chicken until the slices turn white. Return vegetables to pan and reheat.

8. Pour stock into pan and bring to a boil. Stir soy sauce mixture and add to chicken. Mix until thickened.

9. Serve within a few minutes to preserve the crispness of the vegetables. Garnish with toasted almonds.

Comments:

1. Beef, shrimp, pork or veal may be substituted for the chicken.

2. Cooked, shredded chicken may be substituted for raw chicken.

3. This dish is usually converted to *chow mein* by serving it on a bed of fried, Chinese noodles. My husband discovered a delightful variation by replacing the noodles with popcorn, unbuttered and unsalted. Corn, freshly-popped at home, is crunchier than the commercially prepared product.

Cooked Chicken
with
Vegetables

Lisbon

Serves 3

½ pound boneless cooked chicken
1 tablespoon soy sauce
1 green pepper
1 large onion
2 carrots
1 clove garlic
1 tablespoon cornstarch
2 tablespoons water
1½ tablespoons oil
½ teaspoon salt
½ cup celery cabbage, sliced ½-inch thick across stalk
1 cup mung bean sprouts
¾ cup stock

1. Slice chicken thin. Marinate in soy sauce for 15 minutes.

2. Cut green pepper in half and remove seeds. Prepare green pepper in 1-inch squares.

3. Cut onion in half lengthwise, then slice about ¼-inch thick.

4. Cut carrots diagonally ⅛ to ¼-inch thick.

5. Mince garlic.

6. Mix cornstarch and water.

7. Heat oil and stir-fry garlic and salt for a few seconds in a *wok* or large skillet. Add celery cabbage and stir-fry for 2 minutes, then add green pepper and carrots. After 1 minute of stir-frying, add mung bean sprouts and continue to stir-fry. Add the onion and stir 1 minute longer.

8. Add sliced chicken, stir well and heat briefly. Pour in stock and heat to boiling.

9. Stir cornstarch mixture well, add to chicken and mix until thickened.

10. Serve immediately.

Comment:

Asparagus, broccoli, round cabbage, cauliflower, mushrooms, peas or spinach may be substituted for any of the above vegetables. Choose a combination in which the colors blend brightly but harmoniously.
Chinese vegetables such as Chinese cabbage, snow peas, water chestnuts and lotus root may also be used.

Poultry

Curried Chicken

Serves 4

1	small roasting chicken, about 3 pounds
2	onions
1	clove garlic
2	scallions
1½	tablespoons cornstarch
¼	cup water
2	tablespoons oil
½-1	tablespoon curry
1½	cups stock
½	tablespoon soy sauce
¼	teaspoon salt

1. Remove all visible fat from chicken. With a bone cleaver, chop chicken into 2-inch pieces, removing only the 2 thick thigh bones.

2. Peel and cut onions into large chunks.

3. Mince garlic and scallions.

4. In a small bowl, combine cornstarch and water.

5. In a large, heavy skillet, having a lid, heat oil until it is very hot. Add chicken and brown on all sides. Add onions and stir-fry for 1 to 2 minutes. Add curry and garlic, stirring for 1 minute.

6. Pour in stock and soy sauce, add salt and heat to boiling.

Cover and cook on low heat, about 45 minutes.

7. Skim off any fat from sauce. Mix cornstarch paste well and stir into chicken. When thickened, garnish with scallions and serve.

Comments:

1. This dish may be successfully prepared ahead. Cook chicken, adding all ingredients except cornstarch paste and scallions. Cool and refrigerate. When ready to use, scoop off surface fat, reheat chicken and thicken with cornstarch mixture. Garnish with scallions.

2. More curry may be added to chicken if desired.

3. During the last 5 to 10 minutes of cooking, 1 large green pepper with seeds removed may be cut in 1-inch squares and added. If cooking the chicken in advance, add the green pepper when reheating chicken to preserve the bright green color of the pepper.

4. As a change from rice, curried chicken is superb served with steamed buckwheat groats, or kasha, one of the traditional grains of Northern China.

Curried Chicken Breast

Serves 3

1	pound boneless chicken breasts
2	large onions
¾	cup stock
½	teaspoon salt
½	teaspoon honey
	freshly ground pepper to taste
1	tablespoon cornstarch
2	tablespoons water
1	tablespoon curry powder
1	tablespoon oil
	green top of 1 scallion, chopped

1. Remove skin from chicken breasts. Freeze meat until somewhat firm and slice thin.

2. Peel onions and cut in half vertically, through the root. Lay onions on cut surface and slice about ¼-inch thick.

3. Combine stock, salt, honey and freshly-ground pepper to taste. Blend well.

4. Mix cornstarch and water.

5. In a wok or large, heavy skillet having a lid, heat curry and sliced onions, uncovered, on a low heat without oil for 2 minutes, stirring well.

6. Add oil, bring to medium heat and put the sliced chicken breast in the pan. Stir-fry for 1 minute.

7. Pour in stock mixture, bring to a boil, cover and reduce heat to simmer for a few minutes until chicken is cooked.

8. Stir cornstarch mixture well, pour into chicken and mix until thickened.

9. Serve garnished with green scallion top.

Comments:

1. Dieters can eliminate the oil entirely. Stir-fry the chicken with curry powder and onions in a dry pan.

2. One pound of sliced flank steak can be substituted for the chicken.

Poultry

Diced Chicken
with
Green Peppers

Très bon

Serves 3

1	pound boneless chicken breasts
1	tablespoon soy sauce
1	tablespoon cornstarch
1	teaspoon oil
½	teaspoon salt
¼	teaspoon honey
	few grindings fresh pepper
2	large green peppers
1	clove garlic
1	large stalk celery
3	scallions
1½	tablespoons oil
2	tablespoons oil
½	teaspoon salt
½	cup stock
1-2	teaspoons cornstarch (optional)
2	tablespoons water

1. Remove skins from chicken breasts and cut breasts into ½-inch dice.

2. Mix together soy sauce, cornstarch, 1 teaspoon of oil, ½ teaspoon salt, honey and pepper. Combine with chicken and marinate for 30 minutes. Stir once or twice.

3. Discard green pepper seeds and cut pepper into ½-inch dice.

4. Chop garlic fine.

5. Cut celery stalk and scallions into ½-inch dice.

6. In a wok or large, heavy skillet, heat 1½ tablespoons of oil and add green peppers and celery. Stir-fry for 1 minute, then add scallions and continue to stir another minute. Remove vegetables from pan.

7. In the same pan, heat remaining 2 tablespoons of oil and stir-fry garlic for a few seconds. When oil is very hot add chicken and stir-fry until it turns white.

8. Add ½ teaspoon of salt to green peppers and return to the pan with chicken. Reheat quickly, then pour in stock. Heat to boiling and stir well.

9. If sauce is too thin, add a small amount of cornstarch (1 to 2 teaspoons) dissolved in 2 tablespoons of water. Stir thoroughly.

10. Serve immediately.

Diced Chicken
with
Vegetables and Almonds

Serves 3

Comments:

1. The ingredients may also be prepared sliced instead of diced cut. Slice chicken, green peppers and celery into thin pieces. You may also include 1/4 to 1/2 pound of sliced, fresh white mushrooms.

2. One and one-half cups of peeled zucchini, cut in 1/2-inch cubes, may be substituted for green peppers. Omit celery and stir-fry zucchini for 2 minutes. Six dried black mushrooms may be added after the chicken is stir-fried. First, soak the mushrooms 1 hour in warm water and cut into quarters.

1/2	pound boneless chicken
1	teaspoon soy sauce
1/4	teaspoon salt
1	tablespoon sherry
	few grindings fresh pepper
2	stalks celery
4	scallions
1/2	pound fresh mushrooms
2	teaspoons cornstarch
2	tablespoons water
1 1/2	tablespoons oil
1	cup peas
1/2	teaspoon salt
1	tablespoon oil
1/2	cup bamboo shoots, cut in 1/2-inch cubes
3/4	cup stock
1/2	cup toasted almonds

1. Remove skin from chicken and cut chicken into 1/2-inch dice. Marinate in soy sauce, 1/4 teaspoon of salt, sherry and pepper for 30 minutes.

2. Cut celery and scallions into 1/2-inch dice.

3. Slice mushrooms.

4. Combine cornstarch and water.

please turn page

133

Poultry

très bon

Diced Chicken
and Broccoli
in Cream Sauce

Serves 2-3

1	pound boneless chicken breast
1	tablespoon soy sauce
2	tablespoons sherry
¼	teaspoon honey
4	heaping teaspoons natural soybean flour
1	cup water
1	tablespoon cornstarch
2	tablespoons water
1	tablespoon oil
2	cups ½-inch cubes of broccoli (flowerets and tender part of stalks)
3	tablespoons water
2	tablespoons oil
½	teaspoon salt

1. Remove skins from chicken breasts and cut breasts into ½-inch dice.

2. Mix soy sauce, sherry and honey. Combine with chicken and marinate for 30 minutes. Stir once or twice.

5. Heat 1½ tablespoons of oil in a *wok* or large, heavy skillet having a lid. Add peas, celery, and mushrooms at 1 minute intervals while stir-frying, uncovered. Add ½ teaspoon of salt. Then remove vegetables from the pan.

6. In the same pan, heat 1 tablespoon of oil until very hot. Stir-fry chicken until cubes have turned white. Add cooked vegetables and bamboo shoots and reheat.

7. Pour in stock, heat to boiling, and simmer, covered, for 2 minutes. Stir cornstarch, add to chicken and mix until thickened.

8. Serve immediately, topped with toasted almonds.

Comments:

1. If desired, 1 or 1½ tablespoons of soy sauce may be added when pouring in the stock.

2. More celery, mushrooms or bamboo shoots may be added to increase the proportion of vegetables.

3. Measure soybean flour into a jar with 1 cup of water. Screw on lid tightly and shake well. Set "soybean milk" aside.

4. Mix cornstarch and 2 tablespoons of water.

5. Heat 1 tablespoon of oil in a wok or large, heavy skillet having a lid. Stir-fry broccoli, uncovered, for 2 minutes. Add 3 tablespoons of water, bring to a boil, cover, and reduce heat to simmer for 2 minutes, until barely tender, but still crisp. Remove broccoli from the pan.

6. In the same pan, heat 2 tablespoons of oil. When very hot, add chicken cubes and stir-fry until they turn white. Sprinkle on salt, add broccoli and stir-fry 1 minute.

7. Shake "soybean milk" well and pour into chicken. Heat to boiling. Stir cornstarch mixture well and add to chicken. Continue to stir until sauce is thickened.

8. Serve immediately.

Comments:

1. "Soybean milk" can be substituted for stock in other chicken recipes; it's especially attractive with green vegetables.

2. Serve also with skim milk or chicken stock substituting for "soybean milk." The white and green colors make a striking contrast.

Poultry

Diced Chicken
with Cashews

Serves 3

1	pound boneless chicken breasts
2	tablespoons sherry
¾	cup raw cashews
3	scallions
1½	tablespoons brown bean sauce
½	teaspoon honey
¼	cup water
2	teaspoons cornstarch
2	tablespoons water
1	teaspoon soy sauce
2	tablespoons oil

1. Preheat oven to 275°.

2. Remove skin from chicken breasts and cut breasts into ½-inch dice.

3. Marinate chicken in sherry for 15 minutes.

4. Roast cashews in a flat pan for 10 minutes, stirring once. Cut in half or leave whole.

5. Cut scallions into ½-inch pieces.

6. Mash brown bean sauce with a fork. Stir in honey and ¼ cup of water.

7. Combine cornstarch and 2 tablespoons of water with soy sauce.

8. Heat oil until very hot in a wok or large, heavy skillet. Stir-fry cubed chicken for 2 minutes.

9. Add brown bean mixture and mix for 1 minute.

10. Add scallions, then cornstarch mixture that has been stirred thoroughly. Mix until thickened.

11. Toss with roasted cashews and serve immediately.

Comment:

Unsalted roasted almonds or pinenuts may be substituted for the cashews. Roast raw almonds for 15 minutes at 275°, stirring once or twice. Pinenuts require 5 minutes toasting at 350°. Chicken may be slivered if you're using pinenuts. Slightly less cooking is then needed.

Poultry

Roast Chicken, Marinated

excellent

Serves 4

1 clove garlic
½ teaspoon salt
2/3 cup sherry
¼ cup soy sauce
4 tablespoons oil
½ teaspoon five-spice powder
1 3-4 pound chicken

1. Chop garlic fine. Combine all ingredients except chicken.

2. Place chicken in a deep bowl and pour soy sauce mixture over it. Marinate chicken a minimum of 2 hours (up to 4 hours for good penetration of flavors), turning several times. Save the marinade.

3. Preheat oven to 400°. Roast chicken for about 1½ hours on a rack in a roasting pan, over 1 to 2 inches of water (which pre-vents splattering the oven with fat.) Baste several times with marinade. Chicken should be well-browned and crusty. Turn down heat to 350° if browning too fast. Or roast chicken on a rotisserie until browned and crisp.

4. Carve chicken into Western-style serving pieces, or chop into 1½-inch sections, Chinese style. Remove some of the large bones before chopping up the bird.

5. Serve immediately.

Poultry

Roast Chicken, Pre-Simmered

Très Bon cuire un peu plus.

Serves 4

3 scallions
1 cup soy sauce
½ cup sherry
1 teaspoon honey
2 slices fresh ginger root
1 teaspoon salt
3 cups water
1 3-4 pound roasting chicken

1. Cut scallions into 1-inch lengths. Place in heavy, lidded pot with all the ingredients except chicken and heat to boiling.

2. Add chicken and when boiling again, reduce heat, cover, and simmer for 15 minutes. Turn once. Remove from the heat and keep chicken in liquid for 15 more minutes, covered.

3. Preheat oven to 450°.

4. Drain cooking liquid from chicken and dry chicken well. Save liquid to use later.

5. Roast chicken for 30 minutes on a rack in a roasting pan, over 1 to 2 inches of water, which prevents splattering the oven with fat. Chicken should be well-browned and crusty.

6. Carve chicken into Western-style serving pieces, or chop into 1½-inch sections, Chinese style. Remove some of the large bones before chopping up the bird.

7. Arrange chicken on a serving dish, and pour some heated cooking liquid over it.

Comments:

1. Three pounds of chicken leg and thigh joints may be substituted for the whole chicken. Simmer for 10 minutes with rest of the ingredients, then roast for 20 to 25 minutes. Broil for 5 minutes at the end if not sufficiently browned.

2. Add 2 cloves of star anise when simmering chicken, if desired.

Shredded Chicken,
Pork and String Beans

Serves 3

¾	pound boneless chicken breasts
1½	tablespoons sherry
¼	teaspoon salt
½	pound boneless lean pork
1	tablespoon sherry
1	tablespoon soy sauce
1	pound string beans
2	teaspoons cornstarch
2	tablespoons water
1	tablespoon oil
¼	cup water
½	teaspoon salt
1½	tablespoons oil
½	cup stock

1. Remove skin from chicken breasts, freeze breasts until stiff, and sliver. Marinate in 1½ tablespoons of sherry and ¼ teaspoon of salt for 15 minutes.

2. Freeze pork until stiff and sliver. Marinate in 1 tablespoon of sherry and soy sauce for 15 minutes.

3. Slice beans, lengthwise, in quarters, 2 inches long.

4. Mix cornstarch and 2 tablespoons of water.

5. Heat 1 tablespoon of oil in a *wok* or large, heavy skillet having a lid. Stir-fry slivered beans uncovered for 1 minute. Add ¼ cup of water and bring to a boil. Steam, covered, for about 5 minutes. Add ½ teaspoon of salt. Remove beans and juices from pan. Wipe out pan.

6. In the same pan, heat 1½ tablespoons of oil until very hot. Stir-fry pork for 1 minute. Add chicken and stir-fry until it has turned white.

7. Return steamed string beans with any juices to the meat and stir until reheated.

8. Pour in stock and heat to boiling. Stir cornstarch mixture, add to meat and mix until thickened.

9. Serve within a few minutes.

Poultry

Shredded Chicken with Mung Bean Sprouts

Serves 2-3

1	pound boneless chicken breasts
1	tablespoon cornstarch
1	egg white, lightly beaten
2	tablespoons soy sauce
1	tablespoon sherry
3	scallions
4	cups mung bean sprouts
1½	tablespoons oil
½	teaspoon salt
2	tablespoons oil

1. Remove skin from chicken breasts, freeze breasts until stiff, and sliver.

2. Combine cornstarch, egg white, soy sauce and sherry and pour mixture over chicken. Mix in well and marinate for 15 minutes.

3. Chop scallions.

4. Drain sprouts very well on paper toweling or in a strainer (shake a few times).

5. In a wok or large, heavy skillet, heat 1½ tablespoons of oil until hot and add mung bean sprouts. Stir-fry for 2 minutes, season with salt and remove from pan.

6. In the same pan, heat 2 tablespoons of oil until very hot. Stir-fry chicken until it turns white. Return bean sprouts to the pan and reheat for about 1 minute.

7. Stir in chopped scallions, cook for ½ minute and serve with Chinese pancakes or boiled rice.

Comment:

Asparagus may be substituted for mung bean sprouts. Snap off tough ends of 1-1½ pounds of asparagus. Slice tender stalks and tips diagonally into thin pieces.

moyer

Sliced Chicken with Fried Bean Curd and Snow Peas

Serves 3-4

1	pound boneless chicken breasts
2	tablespoons sherry
½	teaspoon salt
½	teaspoon honey
½	pound snow peas
4	scallions
8	water chestnuts
3-4	squares of bean curd
2	teaspoons cornstarch
2	tablespoons water
	oil for deep-frying
1½	tablespoons oil
2	tablespoons oil
½	cup stock

1. Remove skin from chicken breasts. Freeze breasts until stiff and slice thin. Combine sherry, salt and honey, then mix well into sliced chicken.

2. Remove stems from snow peas.

3. Cut scallions into ½-inch pieces.

4. Slice water chestnuts.

5. Cut bean curd into 1-inch cubes.

6. Mix cornstarch and water.

7. In a wok, saucepan or electric deep fryer, heat oil for deep-frying to 375°. Blot bean curd cubes with paper towels and fry a few cubes at a time until they are golden. Drain well on paper toweling.

8. In a wok or large, heavy skillet heat 1½ tablespoons of oil. Stir-fry snow peas for 1 minute. Add water chestnuts and scallions and stir-fry for ½ minute more. Remove mixture from the pan.

9. In the same pan, heat 2 tablespoons of oil until very hot. Stir-fry sliced chicken until it has turned white, using a wide spatula.

10. Pour in stock and heat to boiling. Return snow pea mixture to the pan with the fried bean curd.

11. Mix cornstarch paste and add to chicken, stirring until thickened.

12. Serve immediately.

Poultry

Sliced Chicken
with Mushrooms
(Moo Goo Gai Pan)

Serves 3

1	pound boneless chicken breasts
½	teaspoon salt
1	tablespoon sherry
1	teaspoon soy sauce
3	stalks Chinese cabbage *(bok choy)*
½	pound fresh white mushrooms
6	water chestnuts
¼	pound snow peas
2	cloves garlic
1	tablespoon cornstarch
2	tablespoons water
1	cup stock
½	teaspoon honey
1	tablespoon oil
½	teaspoon salt
2	tablespoons oil
	several tablespoons toasted almonds (optional)

1. Remove skin from chicken breasts. Freeze breasts until stiff and slice thin. Combine ½ teaspoon of salt, sherry and soy sauce. Mix with sliced chicken and marinate for 30 minutes.

2. Slice Chinese cabbage about ¼-inch wide, diagonally.

3. Slice mushrooms and water chestnuts.

4. Remove stems from snow peas. Cut in half lengthwise if large.

5. Mince garlic.

6. Mix together cornstarch and water. Combine stock and honey.

7. In a *wok* or large, heavy skillet, heat 1 tablespoon of oil and stir-fry garlic for a few seconds. Stir-fry Chinese cabbage for 2 minutes. Add snow peas and stir-fry for 1 minute. Add mushrooms, water chestnuts and ½ teaspoon of salt, stirring for 1 minute. Remove mixture from pan.

8. In the same pan, heat 2 tablespoons of oil until very hot. Stir-fry chicken for 2 minutes until it has turned white.

9. Return vegetables to the pan and reheat quickly. Pour in stock and heat to boiling.

Steamed Diced Chicken with Mushrooms and Lily Buds

Serves 2

10. Stir cornstarch mixture and add to chicken. Mix well until sauce is thickened.

11. Garnish with toasted almonds if desired, and serve immediately.

Comments:

1. Chinese cabbage is obtained in Chinese groceries and is not to be confused with celery cabbage. Celery stalks may be substituted for Chinese cabbage if necessary.

2. Instead of white mushrooms, substitute 8 dried, black mushrooms. Soak in warm water for at least 1 hour and cut in quarters.

4	dried black mushrooms
20	lily buds
1½	tablespoons cloud ear mushrooms
2	scallions
1	pound boneless chicken breasts
2	tablespoons soy sauce
¼	teaspoon salt
¼	teaspoon honey
2	teaspoons cornstarch
3	tablespoons mushroom soaking liquid or water
¼	cup diced bamboo shoots

1. Soak dried black mushrooms in warm water for at least 1 hour. Drain mushrooms saving 3 tablespoons of the soaking liquid. Cut mushrooms into ½-inch squares, discarding hard stems.

2. Soak lily buds in warm water for 30 minutes. Nip off hard ends. Quarter lily buds.

3. Soak cloud ears in warm water for 30 minutes and wash well. Discard any hard parts and coarsely chop cloud ears.

please turn page

Poultry

Serves 3-4

1	2½-3 pound frying chicken, fresh
1	slice fresh ginger root
¼	cup soy sauce
¼	cup stock
½	teaspoon Chinese sesame oil

4. Cut white part of scallions into ½-inch pieces. Chop green tops and reserve for a garnish.

5. Remove skin and dice chicken breast into ½-inch squares. Mix soy sauce, salt, honey, cornstarch and 3 tablespoons of mushroom soaking liquid. Toss with chicken dice. Then add vegetables.

6. Turn mixture into flat, heat proof dish and steam for 15 to 20 minutes (see index for instructions).

7. Serve garnished with some of the green scallion tops.

Comment:

Diced kohlrabi may be substituted for bamboo shoots.

1. Remove all fat from inside of chicken cavity. Place bird in a flat, heat proof dish and steam over medium heat for about 45 minutes. (See index for steaming instructions).

2. Mince ginger root.

3. Combine ginger, soy sauce, stock and Chinese sesame oil.

4. Carve steamed chicken into small serving pieces or chop into 1½-inch sections, Chinese style. Remove some of the large bones before chopping up the bird.

5. Serve with small bowls of the soy sauce mixture as a dipping sauce.

Walnut Chicken

Serves 2

Comments:

1. The bird may also be split in half before steaming.

2. To steam larger chickens, merely increase the cooking time —up to 2 hours for a 5 pound roaster. A convenient steamer may be devised from a large roasting pan.

3. Substitute 1 chopped scallion for the ginger root if desired.

4. As an alternative dipping sauce, mix together 3 table-spoons soy sauce, 3 tablespoons rice wine vinegar or cider vine-gar and 1 tablespoon honey, blending well.

1	pound boneless chicken breasts
1½	tablespoons cornstarch
1	tablespoon soy sauce
½	teaspoon salt
½	teaspoon honey
2	tablespoons sherry
2	cups shelled walnuts cold water
¾-1	cup diced bamboo shoots
2	slices fresh ginger root
1	scallion
2	tablespoons oil
2	tablespoons oil
½	cup stock

1. Remove skins from chicken breasts and cut meat into ¾ inch dice. Mix cornstarch, soy sauce, salt, honey and sherry. Combine with chicken and marinate for 30 minutes. Stir once or twice.

2. Blanch shelled walnuts by add-ing cold water to cover and bringing to a boil. Boil 3 minutes, drain right away and dry nuts thoroughly. Blanching removes the bitterness from walnuts.

3. Chop ginger fine.

please turn page

Serves 5-6

2-2½ quarts of water
1   4-5 pound roasting
       chicken, fresh
3   scallions
3   slices fresh ginger root
       (optional)
1   slice fresh ginger root
¼   cup stock
¼   cup soy sauce
½   teaspoon Chinese sesame
       oil

4. Mince scallion.

5. Heat 2 tablespoons of oil in a *wok* or large, heavy skillet which has a lid. Stir-fry walnuts, uncovered, until well-browned. Stir constantly to avoid burning the nuts. Drain on paper towels. Break nuts in half if desired.

6. In the same pan, heat 2 tablespoons of oil. Add minced ginger and stir for a few seconds. When pan is very hot, add chicken cubes and stir-fry until they turn white.

7. Put in bamboo shoots. Stir-fry a few times. Pour in stock, bringing to a boil. Reduce heat, cover pan and simmer for 2 minutes.

8. Add walnuts, heat briefly but thoroughly and serve immediately, garnished with scallions.

1. Heat water in a pot just large enough to hold the chicken.

2. Meanwhile, cut scallions in 2-inch lengths.

3. When water boils, add chicken, scallions, and 3 slices ginger root if desired. Bring back to a boil and reduce heat, cook on low, covered, for 15 minutes.

4. If chicken is not completely covered with water, turn it over. Simmer for 15 minutes. Remove from heat and keep chicken in the cooking broth for 30 minutes, covered.

Comment:

Toasted almonds may be substituted for sautéed walnuts. Heat raw, blanched almonds in a 275° oven until golden, stirring occasionally. Use whole or very coarsely-chopped nuts.

Poultry

Braised Chicken Gizzards with Vegetables

Serves 3

5. Take chicken from pot and drain well. Save the broth for stock. Cool bird and chill until 1 hour before serving.

6. Then carve in small serving pieces or chop into 1½-inch sections, Chinese style. Remove some of the large bones before chopping up the bird. Serve at room temperature. Place chicken on a serving platter skin side up.

7. Mince 1 slice of fresh ginger. Mix with stock, soy sauce, and sesame oil. Serve as a dip with the chicken.

Comment:

Substitute the following dipping sauces:
a. 3 tablespoons of oil with 4 tablespoons of soy sauce.
b. 6 tablespoons of soy sauce with 1 minced scallion.
c. 3 tablespoons soy sauce, 3 tablespoons rice wine vinegar or cider vinegar, and 1 tablespoon honey, blended well.

	small handful of cloud ear mushrooms (optional)
1	pound chicken gizzards
2	large onions
3	slices fresh ginger root
2	tablespoons oil
2	tablespoons sherry
6	tablespoons soy sauce
1	teaspoon salt
1	cup sliced bamboo shoots
1	tablespoon honey
2	cups water
1	tablespoon oil
2	cups 1-inch square pieces of head cabbage

1. Soak cloud ear mushrooms in warm water for ½ hour and wash well.

2. Cut fat from chicken gizzards and scrape the inside ridged surface. Rinse well.

3. Peel and dice one onion. Peel and slice other onion. Keep separate.

4. Mince ginger root.

5. Heat 2 tablespoons of oil in a *wok* or heavy pot. Stir-fry ginger for a few seconds, then add diced onion, stirring for 1 minute.

please turn page

147

Diced Chicken Gizzards with Almonds

Serves 3

1   pound chicken gizzards
1   onion
3   cups water
2   tablespoons soy sauce
½   cup unsalted, toasted almonds or raw blanched almonds
10   water chestnuts
2   squares of bean curd
2   scallions
1   tablespoon cornstarch
1   cup stock
½   cup diced bamboo shoots
      freshly ground pepper
      salt to taste

1. Cut fat away from chicken gizzards and scrape ridged inside surface. Rinse well.

2. Peel onion and cut in half.

3. Heat water to boiling with onion and add gizzards. Cover and reduce heat to simmer for 30 to 40 minutes until chicken is tender.

6. Add gizzards, stirring for 2 minutes on a high heat.

7. Reduce heat to medium and add sherry, soy sauce and salt. Stir for a few seconds.

8. Add bamboo shoots, honey and water. Bring to a boil, reduce to low heat and cook, covered, for 30 minutes.

9. In another pan, heat 1 tablespoon of oil and stir-fry cabbage for 2 minutes. Stir in cloud ears and sliced onions, stir-frying for 1 to 2 minutes.

10. Add cooked vegetables to chicken gizzards and serve within a few minutes.

Comments:

1. The cabbage, onions and cloud ears may be added to the gizzards during the last 5 minutes of cooking instead of stir-frying separately.

2. If desired, lightly thicken sauce with 1 to 1½ tablespoons cornstarch dissolved in 2 tablespoons of water.

4. Drain gizzards well, reserving cooking juices to mix with soup stock at another time.

5. When cool enough to handle, cut gizzards into ½-inch dice. Marinate with soy sauce for 30 minutes.

6. If using raw almonds, preheat oven to 275° and toast them for 15 minutes, stirring once or twice.

7. Cut water chestnuts and bean curd into dice.

8. Slice scallions into ½-inch pieces.

9. Heat cornstarch and stock together in a large saucepan, stirring until stock thickens. Add marinated gizzards, water chestnuts and bamboo shoots. Bring to a boil, cover, and reduce heat to simmer for 5 minutes.

10. Add bean curd squares and scallion, cooking for 2 minutes. Grind some fresh pepper into the gizzard mixture. Taste and if necessary, add some salt.

11. Serve garnished with toasted almonds.

Comment:

Turkey heart may be substituted for chicken gizzards, and is well liked by my children. Remove fat from hearts and cook as above until tender, about 30 to 40 minutes. Follow directions as for gizzards.

Poultry

Diced Chicken Gizzards
with
Bean Curd

Serves 3-4

1	pound chicken gizzards
3-4	cups water
6	cakes fresh bean curd
2	cups stock
3	tablespoons soy sauce
	salt to taste
	freshly-ground Szechwan pepper or black pepper to taste
1 ½	tablespoons cornstarch
3	tablespoons water

1. Rinse gizzards, and remove any visible fat. Scrape the ridged inside surface of the gizzards to clean them well.

2. Pour 3 to 4 cups water into a saucepan and heat to boiling. Add gizzards, and if not fully covered with water, add enough to cover. Bring to a boil, cover, reduce heat to medium-low and cook for 30 minutes.

3. Cool gizzards in cooking liquid. Remove gizzards, but save liquid to add to chicken stock for another use.

4. Cut gizzards and bean curd into ½-inch dice.

5. Clean the saucepan, and pour in stock and soy sauce. Season with salt and pepper to taste. Heat to boiling and add diced gizzards and bean curd. Heat briefly.

6. In a small bowl, mix cornstarch and 3 tablespoons of water and add to the gizzard and bean curd mixture. Mix over medium heat until sauce is thickened.

Comments:

1. This dish may be prepared 1 or 2 hours in advance and reheated.

2. The chicken gizzards may be cooked a day or two in advance and refrigerated in the cooking liquid until needed.

3. Canned bean curd may be substituted for fresh curd.

Sweet and Sour
Chicken Livers

Serves 1-2

½   pound chicken livers
1   green pepper
1   carrot
1   clove garlic
¼   cup vinegar
3-4 tablespoons honey
1   tablespoon cornstarch
1   tablespoon soy sauce
½   cup chicken stock
2   tablespoons oil
½   teaspoon salt
¼   cup chicken stock

1. Cut each chicken liver in half.

2. Cut green pepper in half and discard seeds. Dice into ½-inch pieces.

3. Slice carrot thinly on the diagonal.

4. Mince garlic.

5. In a medium-sized mixing bowl, combine vinegar, honey, cornstarch, soy sauce and ½ cup of the chicken stock.

6. In a wok or large, heavy skillet, having a lid, heat oil until it is very hot. Stir-fry garlic for a few seconds, then add chicken livers and salt. Stir-fry, uncovered, until livers lose most of their raw color. Remove from the pan with a slotted spoon.

7. Pour ¼ cup of the chicken stock into the same pan. Add peppers and carrots, bring to a boil and simmer, covered, for 5 minutes.

8. Return livers to the pan, add vinegar mixture and bring slowly to a boil, stirring constantly until sauce thickens.

9. Serve immediately.

Comment:

Substitute 2 slices of fresh pineapple, cut into small wedges, for the carrots.

Poultry

Stir-Fried Chicken Livers with Snow Peas

Serves 1-2

20	snow peas
½	pound chicken livers
1	teaspoon sherry
1	tablespoon soy sauce
1	teaspoon cornstarch
1	tablespoon soy sauce
2	teaspoons cornstarch
¼	cup water
1	tablespoon oil
1	slice fresh ginger
¼	teaspoon salt
1	tablespoon oil
¼	cup sliced bamboo shoots

1. Wash snow peas and remove strings on stem ends. Dry snow peas well with paper toweling.

2. Slice chicken livers ½-inch thick. Marinate with sherry, 1 tablespoon of soy sauce and 1 teaspoon of cornstarch for 5 minutes.

3. Mix 1 tablespoon of soy sauce, 2 teaspoons of cornstarch and water.

4. Heat 1 tablespoon of oil in a wok or large skillet. Stir-fry ginger slices for a few seconds. Add salt, then snow peas. Stir quickly until peas turn a bright green. Remove the peas from the pan and discard the ginger.

5. In the same pan, heat 1 tablespoon of oil until very hot. Stir-fry chicken livers until the surface of the livers no longer looks red.

6. Add bamboo shoots, then cornstarch mixture, well-stirred.

7. When mixture in pan has thickened, put in snow peas, heat quickly and serve at once.

Stir-Fried Chicken Livers with Vegetables

Serves 3-4

1	pound chicken livers
2	tablespoons soy sauce
1	tablespoon sherry
2	large onions
2	green peppers
4	stalks celery
2	slices of fresh ginger root
1	tablespoon cornstarch
1	cup stock or water
1½	tablespoons oil
½	teaspoon salt
1½	tablespoons oil
¼	cup unsalted roasted almonds, coarsely chopped

1. Slice chicken livers in ½-inch pieces. Marinate in soy sauce and sherry for 15 minutes.

2. Peel onions and cut in half vertically, through root. Lay onions on cut surface and slice them about ¼-inch thick.

3. Remove seeds from green peppers and cut peppers in slivers about 2 inches long.

4. Cut celery into strips 2 inches long.

5. Chop ginger fine.

6. Combine cornstarch and stock.

7. In a *wok* or large, heavy skillet, heat 1½ tablespoons of oil with salt and stir-fry celery strips for 1 minute.

8. Add green peppers and onions at 1 minute intervals and stir-fry on a high heat. Remove mixture from the pan.

9. In the same pan, heat remaining 1½ tablespoons of oil. Stir-fry ginger for a few seconds. When oil is very hot, add chicken livers, stir-frying until the outside of the livers is no longer red.

10. Return the cooked vegetables to the pan and reheat briefly. Add stock and heat to boiling.

11. Stir cornstarch mixture well, add to chicken livers and mix until thickened.

12. Serve garnished with chopped almonds.

Comment:

It is important, for maximum taste, not to overcook the livers. They should be still slightly pink inside, not well done.

Poultry

Roast Duck

Serves 3-4

1 lean duck, 4-5 pounds
1 clove garlic
½ teaspoon salt
½ teaspoon honey
2 tablespoons soy sauce
2 tablespoons sherry
1½ tablespoons honey
2 tablespoons hot water

1. Remove all visible fat from duck. Pull out all pin feathers. Cut out oil sac on the tail.

2. Mince garlic.

3. Mix garlic, salt, ½ teaspoon of honey, soy sauce and sherry. Brush over and inside duck and let stand for several hours.

4. Preheat oven to 400°. Place duck on a rack in a roasting pan and brown in oven for 20 to 30 minutes.

5. Reduce heat to 350° and roast duck 1 to 1½ hours until quite tender. Mix 1½ tablespoons of honey with hot water. Baste duck several times during the last 15 minutes of roasting.

6. Carve Western style into serving pieces or chop into 2-inch sections, as the Chinese do it.

7. Serve alone or with a dipping dish of *hoisin* sauce.

Comment:

The duck may be roasted 2 hours ahead. When ready to serve, cut into serving pieces and broil lightly to reheat. Baste with more honey dissolved in water.

Roast Duck, Pre-Simmered

Serves 3-4

1	lean duck, 5 pounds
3	slices fresh ginger root
4	scallions
½	teaspoon five-spice powder
6	tablespoons soy sauce
1	tablespoon honey
3	tablespoons sherry
1	cup water
1	tablespoon cornstarch
2	tablespoons water

1. Remove all visible fat from the duck. Pull out all pin feathers. Cut out oil sac on the tail.

2. Chop ginger fine.

3. Cut scallions into 1-inch lengths.

4. Combine ginger, five-spice powder, soy sauce, honey and sherry. Place duck in a heavy pot and brush the soy mixture outside and inside the duck.

5. Heat 1 cup water and add to duck along with the scallions. Bring to a boil, reduce heat and cook, covered, on low heat for 1½ hours. Turn several times.

6. Take duck out of cooking liquid, draining well, and allow to cool and dry on a rack for several hours. Place cooking liquid in a small sauce-pan.

7. Heat oven at 450°. Roast duck on a rack in a roasting pan over 1 to 2 inches of water. When nicely browned, turn over and brown other side.

8. Bring cooking liquid to a boil. Mix together cornstarch and 2 tablespoons of water, pour into liquid and stir until thickened.

9. Cut duck into serving pieces. Arrange on a platter and pour thickened juices over it.

Poultry

Seafood

Most Chinese prefer to prepare their fish *au naturel,* that is whole, with the head and tail still on. The flesh remains amazingly juicy when the bones are kept intact. Steaming, braising, or simmering in soup are the preferred cooking methods for whole fish. If the fish is small it may be deep-fried. It is essential that fish be fresh, not frozen, if it is to be prepared whole.

Fish steaks may be steamed, deep fried, braised or sautéed.

Fish fillets can be sliced and stir-fried, deep fried, sautéed in pieces, steamed or braised. Frozen fillets are acceptable if sliced and stir-fried or steamed with eggs, but only fair cooked any other way.

Salt-water fish, such as bass, flounder, sole, cod, haddock, halibut, bluefish, shad, sea trout and porgy can be prepared in most of the ways suggested.

Fresh-water fish, caught in the rivers or raised in ponds, is the kind most commonly used in China. Carp is the big favorite. In the United States, however, fresh-water stream fish are no longer considered safe, owing to water pollution. Only fish, like trout, found in fast-moving waters are thought to be uncontaminated by insecticides and industrial wastes. Shrimp and lobster figure prominently in certain classic Chinese dishes whose recipes are included here. Unfortunately, the pollution problem has also turned these creatures into a potential health hazard. Today, no shellfish can be presumed free of dangerous organisms. However, shellfish taken from the waters around sparsely populated, non-industrialized areas such as Greenland, Iceland and Alaska are less risky and readily available. If you decide to buy shellfish, ask for these. Recipes calling for crabs and bivalves, such as oysters, clams and scallops, have been omitted. They are creatures of waters close to polluted shores, and therefore present a serious health risk.

Steamed Whole Fish

cuire
nouns
longte

Serves 2

Finding a good fish market is the first essential in preparing a successful seafood dish. It is wise to learn what days the fresh fish arrive and shop accordingly. Buy fish fresh and use it the same day if possible. Some markets receive fish fillets preserved in brine. They are often oversalted so it's best to avoid them. If you do buy them, soak the fillets for 15 minutes in cold water and drain thoroughly. Omit salt in the cooking.

Most of us should eat more seafood than we do. Deep-sea fish are relatively free of the residues of growth-stimulating drugs and insecticides which turn up in many commercially-produced meats.

Hopefully, fish served Chinese style will please your family as it does mine. We find seafood is greatly enhanced by the flavor of soy sauce.

12 dried lily buds (optional)
    warm water to cover
1½ pounds fresh, whole fish
2   scallions
1   slice fresh ginger
2   tablespoons soy sauce
1   tablespoon oil
1   tablespoon sherry
¼   teaspoon salt
½   teaspoon honey

1. Soak dried lily buds for 30 minutes in warm water. Nip off hard stem ends. Cut lily buds in half.

2. Buy a fresh whole fish, leaving on head and tail. (Bass, sea trout or bluefish is excellent for steaming.) Scrape the skin of the fish with a knife to remove any remaining scales. Rinse fish and dry with paper toweling. Lay fish on a heat-proof platter.

3. Cut scallions into 1-inch pieces.

4. Mince ginger.

5. Combine soy sauce, oil, sherry, salt, honey, and ginger, mixing well.

6. Pour soy sauce mixture over fish.

7. Arrange lily buds neatly over fish in two rows, ladder fashion.

8. Sprinkle scallions over fish.

9. Boil 1 to 2 inches of water in a large roasting pan, *wok*, or deep pot. Place fish on a rack over boiling water. Cover and steam for about 20 minutes. Serve at once.

Comments:

1. The interesting flavor of fermented black beans is superb with steamed fish. Omit lily buds, and soak 1 tablespoon of beans in cold water for 30 minutes. Rinse them well to remove salt. Mince 1 clove of garlic, and mash with the black beans. Skip salt and add the black beans to the soy sauce mixture.

2. One or 1½ cakes of diced fresh bean curd may be arranged around the fish just before pouring on the soy sauce mixture.

3. Chewy noodles of dried bean curd may be added instead of the lily buds. Soak a folded sheet at least 1 hour in warm water. Keep well submerged to soften fully. Shred into noodles. Lay them around fish and pour on soy sauce mixture.

4. Steamed fish may also be flavored with 2 teaspoons canned brown bean sauce. Omit dried lily buds. Mash bean sauce well with a fork and mix in ¼ cup stock or water. Use only 2 teaspoons of soy sauce. Add bean sauce to soy sauce mixture. Ginger may be increased to ½ teaspoon, shredded.

Seafood

Braised Whole Fish

Serves 3-4

1	fresh, whole fish, 2-2½ pounds or 2 fish weighing the same
½	teaspoon salt
2	slices fresh ginger root
2	scallions
3	tablespoons soy sauce
½	teaspoon honey
2	tablespoons sherry
½	teaspoon salt
1	cup water
	cornstarch to dredge fish
3	tablespoons oil

1. Buy a whole fish, including the head and tail. Clean and scale the fish, wash and drain well.

2. Cut slashes into each side of the fish to help seasoning penetrate. Sprinkle on both sides with ½ teaspoon of salt.

3. Chop ginger root.

4. Cut scallions in ½-inch pieces. Add to soy sauce, honey, sherry, ½ teaspoon of salt and water, mixing well.

5. Dip fish into cornstarch on all sides and shake off excess.

6. In a *wok* or heavy skillet having a lid, heat the oil until it is very hot. Brown the fish on both sides, turning very carefully one time. Fry each fish separately if using 2 fish.

7. Pour in soy sauce mixture, and bring to a boil. Simmer, covered, for 20 minutes if cooking 1 large fish, and 10 to 15 minutes for 2 small fish. Turn the fish one time during cooking.

8. Serve hot on a platter with the sauce. Or cool, remove bones carefully and chill fish with sauce. Serve as an appetizer, very lightly chilled.

Comment:

Two squares of bean curd, diced into ½-inch dice may be added toward the end of the simmering.

Deep Fried Whole Fish in Sweet and Sour Sauce

Serves 2

1½ pounds fresh, whole fish (complete with head and tail)
    salt
1   scallion or a few sprigs fresh coriander
1   tablespoon cornstarch
¼   cup stock
½   cup stock
3-4 tablespoons honey
¼   cup rice wine vinegar or cider vinegar
1   tablespoon soy sauce
    cornstarch, enough to dredge fish
2-3 cups oil for deep frying

1. Cut several gashes on each side of fish, sprinkle lightly with salt and let stand for 30 minutes.

2. Chop scallion or coriander.

3. Combine 1 tablespoon of cornstarch with ¼ cup of stock.

4. In a small saucepan, heat to boiling ½ cup of stock, honey, vinegar and soy sauce.

5. Lower heat and stir in well-mixed cornstarch paste. When mixture thickens, turn heat off and set sauce aside.

6. Heat oil in a wok, (if possible) which, because of its slanting sides, is especially good for cooking whole fish. A frying (or candy) thermometer is helpful in maintaining the correct frying temperature.

7. Dredge fish in cornstarch.

8. When oil heats to 375°, carefully lower fish into wok. Fry until golden on both sides.

9. Reheat sweet and sour sauce. Pour over fried fish, sprinkle with scallion, and serve at once.

Comments:

1. The whole fried fish may also be served with a dip instead of the sweet and sour sauce. Combine 2 tablespoons of soy sauce, 2 tablespoons of vinegar and ½ tablespoon of honey, and pour into individual dipping dishes. Serve at room temperature.

2. One pound of fresh, white fish fillets may be substituted for whole fish. Cut the fish into 2-inch squares and marinate for 15 minutes in 4 teaspoons soy sauce and 2 teaspoons sherry. Dredge in cornstarch and deep-fry as in *Deep-Fried Fish Fillets with Almonds* (see index). Continue as directed above.

Seafood

Braised Fish Fillets
with
Mushroom Sauce

Serves 3

6	dried black mushrooms
	warm water to cover
1	pound fresh, white fish fillets
1-2	tablespoons cornstarch
1	slice fresh ginger root
2	scallions
1	tablespoon soy sauce
1	teaspoon honey
1	tablespoon sherry
½	teaspoon salt
2	tablespoons oil
½	cup shredded bamboo shoots
½	cup stock

1. Soak dried black mushrooms for 1 hour in warm water. Cut into slivers.

2. Cut fish fillets into 2-inch by 3-inch pieces. Dredge in cornstarch and shake off excess. Lay fillets on a piece of waxed paper.

3. Mince ginger root.

4. Cut white part of scallions in ½-inch pieces. Mince green tops and keep separate from the white stalks.

5. Combine soy sauce, honey, sherry and salt.

6. Put oil in a large, heavy skillet and heat until it is very hot. Brown fish fillets in the oil until they are crusty.

7. Remove fillets to a serving platter. In the same skillet stir-fry ginger and white part of scallions for 1 minute. Add mushrooms and bamboo shoots, stir-frying for another minute.

8. Pour in soy sauce mixture and stock. Heat to boiling. Return fish to the pan, bring to a boil again, and simmer, covered, for 10 minutes.

9. Serve garnished with green scallion tops.

Comment:

This dish may be prepared 30 minutes ahead with good results. Braise only 5 minutes and finish cooking when ready to serve.

Deep Fried Fish Fillets with Almonds

Serves 2-3

1	pound fresh, white fish fillets
2	teaspoons sherry
4	teaspoons soy sauce
1	egg
¼	cup cornstarch
4-5	tablespoons water
2/3	slivered almonds, coarsely-chopped
2	cups oil for deep frying
4	tablespoons soy sauce
2	tablespoons vinegar
½	teaspoon honey

1. Cut fish fillets into 2-inch square pieces. Marinate in sherry and 4 teaspoons of soy sauce for 15 minutes.

2. Beat egg lightly. Add cornstarch slowly, beating well. Thin with water.

3. Dip marinated fillets in cornstarch batter, then roll them in chopped almonds. Place in a single layer on a piece of waxed paper.

4. Heat frying oil in a *wok*, pot or electric fryer. If not using an electric pan with a built-in thermostat, attach a frying (or candy) thermometer to the inside of the utensil, with the tip submerged in oil.

5. When the oil heats to 375°, add several pieces of fish at a time and fry until golden in color. Do not let the oil temperature drop below 350° or go above 400°.

6. While fish is frying, make a dipping sauce by combining 4 tablespoons of soy sauce, vinegar and honey.

7. With paper toweling blot fried fish and serve it hot with side dishes of dipping sauce.

Comment:

Fish may be rolled in sesame seeds instead of chopped almonds if desired.

Seafood

Broiled Fish Fillets with Sesame Seeds

Serves 3

1	pound fresh fish fillets
3	tablespoons sesame seeds
3	scallions
¼	cup soy sauce
2	tablespoons oil
	few grindings fresh pepper

1. Cut fish fillets into 3-inch by 2-inch serving pieces.

2. Heat sesame seeds in a small frying pan on a medium-low flame, stirring often. Remove when golden, but not yet brown.

3. Mince scallions. Combine scallions, soy sauce, oil and pepper.

4. Dip the fish fillets in soy sauce mixture, then roll them in toasted sesame seeds.

5. Lay fillets on a broiling pan.

6. Broil fish 3 to 4 minutes, until flesh has turned white and will flake easily. Do not overcook, or fish will lose its savory, moist texture.

7. Serve immediately, with individual side dishes of the soy sauce mixture as a dip.

Sliced Fish Fillets with Chinese Vegetables

Serves 3-4

1	pound fresh fish fillets
2	slices fresh ginger
1	tablespoon cornstarch
1	tablespoon sherry
½	teaspoon salt
12	snow peas
¼	cup bamboo shoots
5	water chestnuts
1	clove garlic
2	tablespoons oil
1	tablespoon oil
¼	teaspoon salt
1	cup celery cabbage, shredded across the rib
½	cup stock
¼	teaspoon honey

1. Freeze fish fillets until stiff, but not completely hard. Cut them in slices ¼-inch thick.

2. Mince ginger.

3. Mix ginger, cornstarch, sherry, and ½ teaspoon of salt. Marinate fish in this mixture for 15 minutes.

4. Remove stem ends of snow peas.

5. Cut bamboo shoots and water chestnuts into thin slices.

6. Mince garlic.

7. In a *wok,* or large, heavy skillet having a lid, heat 2 tablespoons of oil until it is very hot. Add fish slices and carefully stir just enough to cook fish evenly. Take fish out and wipe pan clean.

8. Heat 1 tablespoon of oil in the same pan and stir-fry minced garlic for a few seconds with $\frac{1}{4}$ teaspoon of salt.

9. Stir-fry the celery cabbage for 1 minute, then add bamboo shoots and water chestnuts, stirring until heated. Add snow peas and stir-fry for 1 minute.

10. Mix stock and honey. Add to vegetables and bring to a boil. Cover, reduce heat, and simmer for 2 minutes.

11. Return fish to the pan, increase heat, and stir mixture carefully until it is hot. Serve immediately.

Comments:

1. Commercially frozen fish fillets are reasonably good substitutes for fresh fish in this dish.

2. One pound of mung bean sprouts may be substituted for the snow peas, bamboo shoots, water chestnuts and celery cabbage. Chop 4 scallions into 1-inch pieces. Dry sprouts well and stir-fry in 1 tablespoon of oil for 2 minutes. Mix in scallions and add 1 tablespoon of soy sauce. Add stock and honey and continue with directions.

Seafood

Diced Fish and Peppers in Black Bean Sauce

Serves 3-4

1 ½ tablespoons fermented black beans
1 pound haddock fillets
1/3 teaspoon salt
½ tablespoon cornstarch
2 teaspoons sherry
1 large clove garlic
1 slice fresh ginger
2 medium-sized green peppers
2 teaspoons cornstarch
2 tablespoons water
1 tablespoon oil
¼ cup oil
¼ teaspoon salt
½ cup stock

1. Soak fermented black beans for 30 minutes in cold water. Rinse well and drain.

2. Cut up fish fillets into 1-inch dice. Marinate with 1/3 teaspoon salt, ½ tablespoon of cornstarch and sherry for 15 minutes.

3. Mince garlic.

4. Shred ginger.

5. Cut green peppers into 1-inch squares, after discarding seeds.

6. Mix 2 teaspoons of cornstarch and water together.

7. Heat 1 tablespoon of oil in a wok or large, heavy skillet. Stir-fry garlic and fermented black beans on medium heat for 1 minute.

8. Turn up heat and add ginger and green peppers. Stir-fry about 2 minutes, until peppers have turned a rich, bright green. Remove from the pan.

9. In the same pan, heat ¼ cup of oil until very hot. Stir-fry diced fish for about 2 minutes until pieces turn white, turning carefully with a spatula. Discard oil remaining in the pan.

10. Return cooked green peppers and reheat. Add ¼ teaspoon of salt and pour in stock. Bring to a boil.

11. Stir cornstarch mixture and blend with fish and peppers, mixing well, until thickened. Serve at once.

Fish Fillets
Sautééd in Egg

Serves 3

1 pound fresh flounder or sole fillets
2 large eggs
¼ teaspoon salt
1½ tablespoons cornstarch
1 scallion
2-3 tablespoons oil
2 teaspoons sherry
1½ tablespoons water
¼ teaspoon salt

1. Cut fish fillets into 1½-inch squares.

2. Beat eggs in a bowl with ¼ teaspoon of salt. Slowly add cornstarch, beating well after each addition. A small wire whisk does this job admirably.

3. Mince scallion.

4. Add fish to egg mixture, gently stirring to coat fish thoroughly.

5. Heat oil in a large, heavy skillet until it is very hot. Remove fish from eggs with a slotted spoon and sauté fish, without stirring until lightly-browned.

6. Carefully turn fish with a spatula and cook for 1 minute.

7. While fish is cooking, add scallion, sherry, water and ¼ teaspoon of salt to the leftover egg mixture.

8. Pour egg mixture over fish, turn heat down to medium, and sauté, turning fish several times with a spatula, until the egg solidifies.

9. Serve immediately.

Seafood

Steamed Fish Fillets

Serves 3

1 pound fresh fish fillets (a white fish or well-boned shad)
1 scallion
1 tablespoon soy sauce
1 tablespoon oil
½ teaspoon honey
1 tablespoon sherry
¼ teaspoon salt

1. Cut fish into small serving pieces and lay them on a heat-proof platter.

2. Chop scallion.

3. Combine soy sauce, oil, honey, sherry and salt, and stir well.

4. Pour soy sauce mixture over fish fillets and sprinkle with chopped scallions.

5. Boil 1 to 2 inches of water in a large roasting pan, wok or deep pot. Place fish on a rack over boiling water. Cover and steam for about 7 minutes. Serve at once.

Comments:

1. Fermented black beans may be added to the fish fillets for a pungent flavor. Soak 1 table-spoon of fermented black beans in cold water for 30 minutes. Rinse them well to remove salt. Mince 1 clove of garlic, and mash it with the black beans. Skip salt and add black beans to the soy sauce mixture.

2. Bean curd may be steamed with the fish fillets. Slice 1 bean curd into 12 pieces. Chop 2 scal-lions. Increase soy sauce to 1 ½ tablespoons. Spread bean curd pieces over fish, then add soy sauce mixture and sprinkle with chopped scallions.

Fish and Shrimp Balls
with
Celery Cabbage

Serves 3

½	pound raw shrimps
½	pound fresh fish fillets
¾	pound celery cabbage
2	scallions
1	tablespoon soy sauce
1	teaspoon honey
1	tablespoon sherry
¼	teaspoon salt
1	tablespoon cornstarch
2	teaspoons oil
3	tablespoons oil
¼	teaspoon salt
½	cup water

1. Shell and devein shrimp.

2. Grind or finely chop both fish fillets and shrimp.

3. Cut celery cabbage into 1-inch pieces.

4. Mince scallions finely.

5. Blend soy sauce and honey.

6. Combine chopped fish and shrimp, scallions, soy sauce-honey mixture, ¼ teaspoon of salt, cornstarch and 2 teaspoons of oil. Mix well.

7. Shape fish blend into balls the size of small walnuts.

8. Heat 3 tablespoons of oil in a large, heavy frying pan, that has a cover. Sauté fish balls in hot oil until evenly-browned.

9. Remove fish balls from pan. Add celery cabbage and ¼ teaspoon of salt to remaining oil and stir-fry for 1 minute.

10. Return fish balls, add water to pan, cover, and bring to a boil. Simmer for 10 to 15 minutes.

Comment:

Young spinach may be substituted for celery cabbage. Remove heavy stems. Simmer fish balls in water for 5 minutes, after sautéing. Add spinach, cover, and simmer until spinach has wilted, about 3 minutes.

Seafood

Steamed Green Peppers Stuffed with Fish and Pork

Serves 3

½ pound fish fillets
1 scallion
½ pound lean pork, ground
1 teaspoon soy sauce
¼ teaspoon salt
  few grindings, freshly-ground pepper
4-5 medium-sized green peppers (choose peppers that will stand upright)
2 teaspoons sherry
2 teaspoons soy sauce
¼ teaspoon honey
2 teaspoons cornstarch
2 tablespoons water

1. Grind fish or chop it finely with a cleaver or sharp, heavy knife.

2. Mince scallion finely.

3. Mix together chopped fish, ground pork, minced scallion, 1 teaspoon of soy sauce, salt, and pepper.

4. Wash green peppers and cut out the stems. Remove seeds carefully without cutting into the sides of the peppers.

5. Fill green peppers with fish-pork mixture.

6. Boil water in a large roasting pan, wok or deep pot. Place peppers on a heat-proof platter. Put on a rack over boiling water. Cover and steam for 35 minutes.

7. Remove green peppers to a flat serving platter and cover with foil to keep warm.

8. Pour remaining juices into a small saucepan. If less than 1 cup is left, add water to bring up to 1 cup.

9. Add sherry, 2 teaspoons of soy sauce, and honey and bring to a boil.

10. Mix together cornstarch and water. Pour into pan and stir until mixture thickens.

11. Cut stuffed peppers in quarters, pour thickened sauce over them, and serve at once.

Seafood

Lobster Cantonese

Serves 4

Comments:

1. This dish may be prepared 1 to 2 hours in advance. Steam stuffed peppers and hold until ready to serve. Heat for 20 to 30 minutes, covered, in a 350° oven. Remove stuffed peppers as indicated above. Proceed as in Step 8.

2. Stuffed green peppers may be braised instead of steamed. Sauté peppers, cut side down in 2 tablespoons of oil until nicely browned. Pour 1 ½ cups stock or water into the pan. Bring to a boil, cover, and simmer 20 minutes. Proceed as in Step 7.

2	teaspoons fermented black beans (optional)
	cold water, to cover beans
2	live lobsters, 1 pound each
	boiling water, to cover
2	scallions
1	tablespoon soy sauce
½	teaspoon honey
1	cup stock
1	tablespoon cornstarch
2	tablespoons water
2	cloves garlic
2-3	tablespoons oil
¼	pound lean pork, ground or minced
½	teaspoon salt
2	eggs

1. Soak fermented black beans in cold water for 30 minutes. Drain.

2. Plunge live lobsters into boiling water to stun. As soon as they are motionless, remove them immediately from the water.

3. Chop lobsters into 2-inch pieces in the shell. Discard internal organs and cut off ends of legs.

please turn page

4. Chop scallions.

5. Combine soy sauce, honey and stock.

6. Mix cornstarch and 2 table-spoons of the water together.

7. Mince garlic.

8. Mash garlic and fermented black beans together.

9. In a *wok* or large, heavy fry-ing pan, heat oil on medium heat. Add garlic and fermented beans, stirring for 1/2 minute.

10. Raise heat to high, adding ground pork and salt. Stir-fry for about 2 minutes, until pork is no longer raw. With a fork, break up any lumps that form.

11. Remove pork with a slotted spoon.

12. Stir-fry lobster pieces in the remaining fat for about 3 min-utes, until shell turns red.

13. Return pork to the pan and reheat. Add soy-stock mixture and bring to a boil.

14. Stir cornstarch mixture and pour into pan. Mix until sauce is thickened.

15. Beat eggs. Stir into lobster mixture with scallions and re-move from the heat immediately. Serve at once.

Comments:

1. If fermented black beans are omitted, reduce honey to 1/4 teaspoon.

2. One large lobster, 1 1/2 to 2 pounds may be used instead of 2 smaller ones.

Diced Shrimp,
Kohlrabi and Mushrooms

Serves 3

8	dried black mushrooms
	water, to cover mushrooms
1	pound medium, raw shrimps
2	scallions
2	slices fresh ginger
1	tablespoon cornstarch
½	teaspoon salt
2	tablespoons sherry
3	kohlrabi, about 2½ inches in diameter
1	tablespoon oil
¼	teaspoon salt
1½	tablespoons oil
¼	cup water

1. Soak dried, black mushrooms in warm water for 1 hour. Drain, squeeze excess water from mushrooms and cut in ½-inch squares, discarding hard stem ends.

2. Shell shrimps and devein. (Cut out sandy black vein along the back.) Cut shrimps into ½-inch dice.

3. Cut scallions into ½-inch pieces.

4. Mince ginger.

5. Combine shrimps with scallions, cornstarch, ½ teaspoon of salt, the sherry and ginger. Marinate for about 30 minutes.

6. Peel kohlrabi and cut into ½-inch dice.

7. Heat 1 tablespoon of oil in a wok or large, heavy skillet. Stir-fry kohlrabi dice for 2 minutes. Add mushrooms and ¼ teaspoon of salt, cook for 1 minute and remove from pan. Wipe pan clean.

8. In same pan, heat 1½ tablespoons of oil until it is very hot. Add shrimps and stir-fry until they have turned pink.

9. Return the kohlrabi to the pan and reheat quickly.

10. Pour in ¼ cup of water and bring to a boil, stirring constantly.

11. Serve immediately.

Comment:

Diced bamboo shoots or celery may be substituted for the kohlrabi.

Seafood

Shrimp
with Lobster Sauce

Serves 3

2 teaspoons black beans, fermented
1 pound large, raw shrimps
1 tablespoon sherry
½ teaspoon salt
2 scallions
1 tablespoon sherry
1 tablespoon soy sauce
1 cup stock
½ teaspoon honey
1 tablespoon cornstarch
2 tablespoons water
1 clove garlic
1½ tablespoons oil
¼ pound lean pork, ground or minced
2 eggs
2 tablespoons oil

1. Soak fermented black beans in cold water to cover for 30 minutes. Rinse well.

2. Shell and devein shrimps. (Cut out sandy black vein along the back.) Butterfly shrimps by cutting partially through the back of the shrimp. Gently spread apart each "wing."

3. Mix 1 tablespoon of sherry and the salt with shrimp.

4. Cut scallions in ½-inch pieces.

5. Mix 1 tablespoon of sherry, and the soy sauce, stock and honey.

6. Combine cornstarch and 2 tablespoons of water.

7. Mince garlic.

8. Mash garlic and fermented beans together.

9. In a wok or large, heavy skillet having a lid, heat 1½ tablespoons of oil on medium heat. Stir-fry garlic and fermented black beans for ½ minute, uncovered.

10. Raise the heat to high and add ground pork. Stir-fry for about 2 minutes until pork is no longer raw. With a fork, break up any lumps that form.

11. Pour in soy-stock mixture and bring to a boil. Reduce heat, cover, and simmer for 3 minutes.

12. Stir cornstarch mixture and add to simmering pork. Mix until thickened.

13. Beat eggs and stir them into the pork mixture. Remove from heat immediately.

Stir-Fried Shrimp
with
Peppers and Tomatoes

Serves 3-4

14. In another large skillet, heat 2 tablespoons of oil until hot. Stir-fry shrimps until they turn pink, about 3 minutes. Add chopped scallions during the last minute of cooking.

15. Reheat pork mixture on a low flame and add stir-fried shrimps. Heat together for 2 minutes, stirring occasionally.

16. Serve immediately.

Comments:

1. Lobster sauce contains no lobster. It is merely the sauce served with lobster when it is prepared in the Cantonese manner.

2. The fermented black beans may be omitted. Taste finished sauce and add more salt if necessary.

1	pound medium or large raw shrimps
1	tablespoon sherry
½	teaspoon salt
3	green peppers
3	medium-sized tomatoes
2	cloves garlic
4	scallions
1	tablespoon cornstarch
2	tablespoons water
2	tablespoons oil
¾	cup stock
1½	tablespoons soy sauce

1. Shell and devein shrimps. (Cut out sandy vein along the back.) Butterfly shrimps by cutting partially through the backs of the shrimps. Gently spread apart each "wing."

2. Mix shrimps with sherry and salt.

3. Discard green pepper seeds and cut peppers into 1-inch squares.

4. Slice tomatoes into wedges, 6 to a tomato.

please turn page

Seafood

5. Mince garlic.

6. Cut scallions into ½-inch pieces.

7. Mix cornstarch and water together.

8. Heat oil until hot in a *wok* or large, heavy skillet having a lid. Add garlic and stir-fry for a few seconds. Add shrimps and stir-fry, uncovered, until they turn pink, 2 to 3 minutes.

9. Place in green peppers and stir-fry another 2 minutes.

10. Pour in stock and bring to a boil. Cover, reduce heat and simmer for 3 minutes.

11. Add tomatoes, scallions and soy sauce. Mix until heated.

12. Stir cornstarch mixture, then pour into shrimp dish. Mix gently until thickened. Serve immediately.

Comment:

One-half pound broccoli and 3 stalks of celery may be substituted for the peppers and tomatoes. Cut broccoli and celery in thin slices on the diagonal. Steam broccoli for 2 minutes in 3 tablespoons of water. Add broccoli with stock to shrimp as in Step #10. Simmer 2 minutes and add celery. Simmer 3 more minutes, then proceed as in Step #11.

Stir-Fried Shrimp with Snow Peas and Cloud Ears

Excellent.

Serves 3

¼	cup cloud ear mushrooms
1	pound medium shrimps
2	cloves garlic
2	slices fresh ginger
2	tablespoons soy sauce
¼	teaspoon honey
1	tablespoon sherry
½	pound snow peas
2	teaspoons cornstarch
2	tablespoons water
1	tablespoon oil
¼	teaspoon salt
1½	tablespoons oil
½	cup stock

1. Soak cloud ear mushrooms for 30 minutes in warm water. Rinse well and cut off any hard parts. Squeeze mushrooms dry.

2. Shell and devein shrimps. (Cut out sandy black vein along the back.)

3. Mince garlic and ginger.

4. Combine garlic, ginger, soy sauce, honey and sherry. Marinate shrimps in soy mixture for 30 minutes.

5. Remove stem ends from snow peas. Wash snow peas and dry them well.

6. Mix cornstarch and water together.

7. Heat 1 tablespoon of oil on medium heat in a *wok* or large, heavy skillet. Stir-fry snow peas for 1 minute. Add salt and cloud ear mushrooms, stirring for ½ minute. Remove mixture from the pan and wipe pan clean.

8. In same pan, heat 1½ tablespoons of oil until hot. Add shrimps and stir until they turn pink.

9. Return snow peas to the pan and pour in stock. Heat stock quickly, and when it is beginning to boil, add cornstarch mixture, well stirred.

10. Mix until stock has thickened. Add more salt if necessary. Serve immediately.

Comment:

Substitute 8 dried, black mushrooms instead of cloud ears if desired. Soak for 1 hour in warm water and cut in quarters if large, halves if smaller.

Seafood

Stir-Fried Shrimp
with Chinese Vegetables

Serves 2

½ pound small, raw shrimps
1 teaspoon soy sauce
1 tablespoon sherry
¼ pound snow peas
1 onion
1 pound mung bean sprouts
1 clove garlic
2 teaspoons cornstarch
2 tablespoons water
1½ tablespoons oil
½ teaspoon salt
1½ tablespoons oil
½ cup stock

1. Shell and devein shrimps. (Cut out sandy black vein along the back.)

2. Sprinkle shrimps with soy sauce and sherry.

3. Remove stems from snow peas.

4. Peel and slice onion.

5. Drain bean sprouts well and blot dry with paper toweling.

6. Mince garlic.

7. Combine cornstarch and water.

8. Heat 1½ tablespoons of oil until it is hot in a wok or large, heavy skillet. Stir-fry bean sprouts for 1 minute, then add onion. Stir-fry 1 minute more, then add snow peas and salt. Continue cooking on high heat while stirring for another minute. Remove vegetables from pan and wipe pan clean.

9. In the same pan, heat 1½ tablespoons of oil until hot. Stir in garlic and mix for a few seconds. Add shrimps, and stir-fry until they turn pink.

10. Return vegetables to the pan, reheat, then pour in stock. Bring quickly to a boil.

11. Reduce heat to medium, add cornstarch mixture, well stirred. Mix sauce until it thickens.

12. Taste, and add more salt if desired. Serve immediately.

Sliced Abalone
and Chicken

Serves 3

6	dried black mushrooms
	warm water
½	pound chicken breast
1	teaspoon soy sauce
¾	cup snow peas
2	slices fresh ginger
1	tablespoon cornstarch
2	tablespoons water
1½	tablespoons oil
½	teaspoon salt
¾	cup Chinese cabbage (*bok choy*) or celery cabbage, sliced 1 inch thick
½	cup sliced bamboo shoots
¼	cup sliced water chestnuts
1½	tablespoons oil
1	cup sliced abalone (canned)
¼	cup shredded Smithfield ham (optional)
¼	cup liquid from canned abalone
¾	cup water
	salt to taste

1. In a mixing bowl, soak dried black mushrooms in warm water to cover, for 1 hour. Remove hard stems and cut mushrooms in quarters.

2. Freeze chicken breast until it is firm enough to slice easily. Cut in thin pieces. Put chicken into medium-sized mixing bowl and mix in soy sauce.

3. Remove stem ends from snow peas.

4. Mince ginger.

5. In a small mixing bowl, combine cornstarch and water.

6. Heat 1½ tablespoons of oil in a *wok* or large, heavy frying pan. Add salt, then stir-fry Chinese cabbage for 2 minutes. Add bamboo shoots, mushrooms, and water chestnuts, stir-frying for 1 minute. Add snow peas last and stir for ½ minute. Remove vegetables from the pan and wipe it clean.

7. In the same pan, heat remaining 1½ tablespoons of oil until very hot. Stir-fry chicken until the meat turns white. Add abalone and smoked ham and stir-fry until hot.

please turn page

Seafood

Happy Family

8. Return vegetables to the pan and reheat. Pour in liquid from canned abalone and ¾ cup water. Bring to a slow boil.

9. Stir cornstarch mixture and add it to liquid, mixing until thickened.

10. Salt to taste and serve immediately.

Comment:

Two ounces of dried sea cucumber may be substituted for the abalone. See directions for preparation in recipe, *Happy Family* (see index). Use chicken stock instead of abalone liquid and water to make sauce.

2	ounces dried sea cucumber (beche de mer)
5	dried black mushrooms warm water
½	chicken breast, boiled
15	snow peas
2	teaspoons cornstarch
2	tablespoons water
1	cup stock
½	cup sliced bamboo shoots
9	*Pork Balls* (see index)
9	*Fish and Shrimp Balls* (see index)
¼	cup shredded smoked ham
1	teaspoon salt
½	teaspoon honey

1. In a medium-sized mixing bowl, soak dried sea cucumber in enough warm water to cover for fully 24 hours. Change the water several times. Cut open sea cucumber and scrape inside thoroughly.

2. Put sea cucumber in a small saucepan, cover with water, bring to a boil, and simmer, covered for 4 hours. Replenish water if necessary. Slice sea cucumber in ½-inch pieces.

3. In a medium-sized mixing bowl, soak dried black mushrooms in enough water to cover for 1 hour. Cut out hard stems and slice mushrooms in quarters.

4. Remove skin from chicken breast. Cut meat into slices.

5. Remove stem ends of snow peas.

6. In a small bowl, combine cornstarch and 2 tablespoons of water.

7. Heat stock in a wok or heavy, medium-sized saucepan.

8. Add bamboo shoots, pork balls, shrimp balls, smoked ham and black mushrooms. Bring to a boil and simmer for 3 minutes.

9. Add sea cucumber, salt and honey, mixing well. Put in chicken and snow peas, heating briefly.

10. Stir cornstarch mixture and pour it into simmering stock. Mix until thickened.

11. Serve immediately.

Seafood

Beef

Because meat has always been in short supply in China, beef is usually "stretched" by cooking it and serving it with sliced vegetables. The Chinese consume far less beef than we do, but they prepare it in ways that blend its rich flavor with other ingredients. The large hunks of red meat that are such favorites of people living our deluxe life style would seem bland and uninteresting to the Chinese.

Lean cuts of beef, like flank steak, sirloin, T-bone, tenderloin, chuck and round, can be quick-cooked by stir-frying. Flank steak is often preferred. Since its fibers all run one way, it is simple to cut across the grain for tender meat slices. Beef is frequently mixed with soy sauce, sherry and cornstarch to increase tenderness before stir-frying.

Long braising in soy sauce is a popular way of cooking shin meat, short ribs, oxtail and tongue.

Occasionally, beef, flavored with soy sauce, is steamed or broiled. Beneficial organ meats like liver, kidneys, and heart may also be stir-fried or in the case of kidneys, served cold with sesame seeds (very tasty). Veal kidneys have a more delicate flavor than beef kidneys.

To keep the larder stocked, buy flank steak in advance and freeze individual pieces. Cut each flank lengthwise, then crosswise to make four equal pieces. Place them on a cookie sheet lined with waxed paper in a single layer. Freeze the meat solid, then slip it into a plastic bag for long-term storage.

When they are needed, thaw beef pieces for half an hour. Slicing is far easier when the meat is partially frozen. Allow to defrost and proceed with the directions.

Liver and heart may also be frozen in advance for simpler slicing. Cut the heart vertically in quarters and remove all fat before freezing.

Beef provides rich quantities of the B vitamins.

Animal organ meats, headed by liver, are in a special class nutritionally. They are usually low in fat, compared with other parts of the animal, and extremely high in the B vitamins. They also contain impressive amounts of iron and phosphorus. Kidneys are particularly rich in vitamin A, while liver excels in vitamins A and D, and copper. Although organ meats contain fairly large quantities of cholesterol, it is balanced with lecithin, a substance which helps prevent cholesterol from damaging the arteries.

The Chinese value animal organ meats highly, recommending liver as a tonic for the aged.

Braised
Short Ribs of Beef

mayen

Serves 4

1 ½ tablespoons fermented black beans
2 pounds lean short ribs of beef (Have the butcher saw them in 2-inch lengths.)
2 cloves garlic
1 tablespoon soy sauce
1 ½ tablespoons sherry
1 ½ tablespoons oil
½ teaspoon salt
1 ½ cups water

1. Soak fermented black beans in water for 15 minutes.

2. Cut all visible fat from beef ribs and slice them in half lengthwise.

3. Rinse beans and drain.

4. Peel and chop garlic fine. In a small bowl, mash garlic and black beans together with a fork, then add soy sauce and sherry.

5. Heat oil and salt in a large, heavy pot having a cover. Stir-fry rib pieces until browned. Pour soy mixture over beef, stirring often for 2 to 3 minutes.

6. Add water, heat to boiling, reduce heat and cook on low heat, covered, for at least 1 hour or until tender.

7. Skim off fat or chill overnight and remove hardened fat.

Comments:

1. ¼ cup of sliced bamboo shoots may be added to the beef after the first ½ hour of simmering.

2. For a rich green color contrast, add ¼ cup pre-cooked snow peas. Steam, covered, for 1 to 2 minutes with 1 tablespoon water and add to beef just before serving.

Beef

Star Anise Beef

Serves 6

1½ pound beef shin
1   clove garlic
3   scallions
2   tablespoons oil
5   tablespoons soy sauce
2   tablespoons sherry
1   tablespoon honey
3   cloves star anise
1   cup watèr
     shin bones (optional)

1. Cut beef shin into bite-sized pieces, 1-inch square.

2. Peel and slice garlic.

3. Chop scallions into 1-inch pieces. Reserve some of the green tops for garnishing.

4. In a large, heavy skillet having a lid, heat oil and sauté cubed beef, uncovered, until well-browned, stirring often.

5. Mix in soy sauce, sherry and honey and cook for 2 minutes.

6. Add star anise, water, chopped scallions and shin bones, heat to boiling, cover, reduce heat and simmer for 1 to 1½ hours, until tender. Stir occasionally. During the last 15 minutes, remove lid and cook on medium heat, stirring often, to reduce the sauce.

7. Skim off fat and serve beef immediately, or chill overnight and lift fat from the surface.

8. Then remove bones but add marrow to liquid. Reheat slowly and serve, garnished with chopped scallion tops.

Comment:

To serve cold as an hors d'oeuvre, cook beef shin whole, but simmer 2 hours until just tender. Reduce sauce, as in above directions, during last 15 minutes. Chill, remove fat, and slice thin to serve.

Beef Balls with Spinach

Serves 4

1 ½ pounds ground beef
1 tablespoon soy sauce
2 eggs
¼ cup ice water
3 tablespoons cornstarch
1 tablespoon sherry
2 tablespoons oil
½ cup water
1 tablespoon soy sauce
1 pound young spinach
1 tablespoon oil
½ teaspoon salt

1. In a large bowl, add the following to the ground beef: 1 tablespoon soy sauce, eggs (slightly beaten), ice water, cornstarch and sherry. Mix well with a large kitchen fork. Shape into small balls.

2. In a large, heavy frying pan having a cover, heat 2 tablespoons of oil until very hot and sauté beef balls until lightly-browned, uncovered. Drain fat from pan. Add water and 1 tablespoon of soy sauce, reduce heat and simmer, covered, for 30 minutes.

3. Wash spinach well and drain. Remove any large stems.

4. Heat 1 tablespoon of oil in a wok or another large frying pan, having a cover. Add salt, then spinach. Stir-fry for 2 minutes, uncovered. Pour beef balls and cooking juice over spinach, cover and simmer 1 to 2 minutes. Serve immediately.

Comments:

1. Tender Swiss chard, collards, beet, mustard, or turnip greens may be cooked in the same manner. Increase the stir-fry time as needed until vegetable is tender.

2. Four ounces of dried bean curd and ½ pound of celery cabbage may be substituted for the spinach. Soak curd for at least 1 hour in warm water to cover. Keep well submerged to soften fully. Drain and shred. Slice celery cabbage into strips ½-inch wide. Cut 3 scallions into 1-inch pieces. Simmer dried curd and celery cabbage with beef balls for 5 minutes. Add scallions. Heat for 1 minute and serve. This dish may be prepared 1 to 2 hours in advance.

3. Lean ground pork may be substituted for beef. Simmer pork balls until fully cooked, about 40 minutes.

Beef

Minced Beef
with Bean Curd

Serves 2

2 teaspoons fermented black beans
lukewarm water to cover
5 cakes fresh bean curd
1 scallion or 1 teaspoon minced Chinese parsley
1 tablespoon oil
¼ pound lean ground beef
½ cup stock
1 teaspoon salt
½ tablespoon cornstarch
3 tablespoons water
1 teaspoon Chinese sesame oil
Szechwan or black pepper to taste

1. In a small bowl, soak fermented black beans in lukewarm water for 30 minutes. Pour off water, squeeze beans dry and mash them with a fork.

2. Dice bean curd into ½-inch cubes.

3. Mince scallion.

4. Heat oil in a wok or large heavy frying pan. Stir-fry ground beef until pink color is just gone, breaking up the lumps with a fork.

5. Add stock and salt, bring to a boil and add cubed bean curd. Cook slowly for several minutes to blend flavors.

6. In a small mixing bowl, mix cornstarch and 3 tablespoons of water. Pour into simmering beef dish and stir carefully until thickened.

7. Sprinkle with chopped scallions, Chinese sesame oil and pepper and mix lightly.

8. Serve immediately.

Comment:

This dish may be prepared several hours ahead and reheated. Add the scallion, sesame oil and pepper when serving.

Minced Beef
with Watercress

mayen - Bon

Serves 3

2	tablespoons soy sauce
2	tablespoons sherry
1	teaspoon honey
1	pound lean, ground beef
2	bunches watercress
4	scallions
1	tablespoon cornstarch
2	tablespoons water
2	tablespoons oil
1½	tablespoons oil
½	teaspoon salt
½	cup stock

1. In a large bowl, combine soy sauce, sherry and honey. Blend well.

2. Stir soy sauce mixture into ground beef with a fork. Marinate for ½ hour, stirring occasionally.

3. Cut off thick stems of the watercress and save them to use in a watercress soup at a later time. Wash watercress sprigs well. Drain thoroughly and pat dry gently with paper toweling.

4. Chop scallions.

5. In a small bowl, mix cornstarch and water.

6. In a wok or large, heavy frying pan, heat 2 tablespoons of oil until very hot. Add ground beef mixture and stir-fry until the redness is nearly gone. Use a large fork to break up the lumps as the beef is cooking. Remove beef from pan with a slotted spoon and discard the remaining fat. Wipe the pan dry.

7. In the same pan, heat 1½ tablespoons of oil. Stir-fry watercress until just wilted. Add salt and mix well.

8. Return beef to the pan with the scallions and stir-fry just to heat.

9. Pour in stock and heat to boiling. Stir cornstarch mixture thoroughly and add to beef. Continue to stir until the sauce thickens. Serve immediately.

Comments:

1. My children find this dish a great favorite. They enjoy healthful watercress when paired with all-popular hamburger meat.

2. Pork hamburger may be substituted for beef. Be sure to stir-fry meat until thoroughly cooked.

Shredded Beef with Wax Beans

Serves 3

1	pound flank steak
2	tablespoons soy sauce
2	tablespoons sherry
½	teaspoon honey
1	pound yellow wax beans (young, fresh, slender)
1	clove garlic
1	scallion
1	tablespoon cornstarch
3	tablespoons water
3	tablespoons water
1	tablespoon oil
½	teaspoon salt
1	cup stock or water

1. Freeze meat until partially stiff and slice thin against the grain. Pile up several slices and cut into shreds. Repeat this until all meat is shredded.

2. Mix together soy sauce, sherry and honey in a large bowl. Marinate shredded beef in soy sauce mixture for 15 minutes. Stir once or twice.

3. Cut off stem ends of wax beans and slice beans in half lengthwise. Cut in 2-inch lengths.

4. Mince garlic.

5. Chop scallion.

6. In a separate, small bowl, mix cornstarch with 3 tablespoons of water. Set aside.

7. Place beans in a heavy, medium-sized skillet having a lid, add 3 tablespoons of water, bring to a boil and steam, covered, on low heat 7 to 10 minutes, depending upon the age of the beans. They should be tender but still crunchy.

8. Heat 1 tablespoon of oil in a wok or large, heavy frying pan. Stir-fry garlic for a few seconds. When oil is very hot, add shredded beef and stir-fry until beef loses most of its redness.

9. Add steamed wax beans with any remaining liquid and salt, stirring a few times. Pour in stock and bring to a boil.

10. Mix cornstarch and water well and add to beef mixture. Stir until sauce thickens. Serve within a few minutes, garnished with chopped scallion.

Comment:

Green string beans or celery shreds may be substituted for wax beans. Omit the steaming for the celery; instead, stir-fry for 2 to 3 minutes in 1 tablespoon of oil before adding to the beef.

Beef

Stir-Fried Beef with Broccoli

Serves 3-4

1	pound flank steak
1	tablespoon cornstarch
2	tablespoons soy sauce
2	tablespoons sherry
½	teaspoon honey
2	pounds broccoli
5	tablespoons water
2	tablespoons oil
½	teaspoon salt
¾	cup stock

1. Freeze meat until partially stiff and slice thin, against the grain.

2. Mix cornstarch, soy sauce, sherry, and honey in a medium-sized bowl. Marinate sliced beef in soy sauce mixture for 15 to 30 minutes. Stir once or twice.

3. Cut off and discard tough lower ends of broccoli stalks. Pare skin from the rest of broccoli stalks. Do not throw away the main part of the stem, which is highly edible once the skin has been removed. Separate each small floweret and cut in half lengthwise. Slice the stem diagonally ¼-inch thick.

4. Bring water to a boil in a *wok* or a large, heavy skillet with a lid. Add broccoli, reboil, reduce heat and steam, covered, on a medium heat for about 5 minutes. Stir one time. Broccoli should be somewhat tender but still crunchy. Remove broccoli with liquid and wipe pan dry.

5. Heat oil until very hot in the same pan. Add beef and stir-fry until beef loses most of its redness.

6. Add broccoli, its cooking liquid and salt, stir-frying for 1 minute to reheat.

7. Pour in stock and stir well until sauce begins to thicken. Serve immediately.

Comments:

1. The proportion of beef to broccoli can easily be varied to taste. Broccoli may be increased to a 3 to 1 ratio by using 1½ pounds of broccoli to ½ pound of beef. Or, for a meatier dish, use 1 pound of broccoli to 1 pound of beef. Adjust the quantity of the beef marinade accordingly.

please turn page

Beef

Stir-Fried Beef
and
Green Peppers

Serves 3

1	pound flank or sirloin steak
2	tablespoons soy sauce
2	tablespoons sherry
½	teaspoon honey
4 3	green peppers
1	tablespoon cornstarch
2	tablespoons water
1-2	cloves garlic
1½	tablespoons oil
1½	tablespoons oil
½	teaspoon salt
¾	cup stock or water few drops Chinese sesame oil (optional)

2. Chinese broccoli may be substituted if available.

3. One large onion, sliced, may also be added. Stir-fry with ½ tablespoon of oil for 1 to 2 minutes before cooking beef and remove. Return to the pan when the broccoli is added.

4. To substitute asparagus for broccoli, pare thick spears, slice ¼-inch thick and steam as directed above.

5. Three cups of sliced lotus stems may be substituted for the broccoli. Peel lotus stems and slice thinly. Quarter each slice of lotus. Steam as directed for about 8 minutes. Cut 2 scallions into 1-inch lengths. Add scallions and lotus stems to the stir-fried beef.

1. Freeze meat until partially stiff and slice thin against the grain.

2. Mix together soy sauce, sherry and honey in a medium-sized bowl. Marinate sliced beef in soy sauce mixture for 15 to 30 minutes. Stir once or twice.

3. Remove seeds from green peppers. Cut peppers into 1-inch squares.

4. Mix cornstarch with water.

5. Peel and slice garlic.

Beef

6. Heat 1 ½ tablespoons of oil in a *wok* or large, heavy skillet. Stir-fry green peppers for about 2 minutes. Take out of skillet and set aside.

7. In the same pan, stir-fry garlic for a few seconds in the rest of the oil (1 ½ tablespoons); when oil is very hot, add sliced beef and stir-fry until beef loses most of its redness.

8. Salt peppers and put back into the pan with the beef. Stir-fry for 1 minute.

9. Pour in stock and Chinese sesame oil. Bring rapidly to a boil. Stir cornstarch mixture and pour into beef, mixing until thickened. Serve immediately.

Comment:

The following vegetables may be substituted for green peppers:

1. Red peppers—use alone or in combination with green peppers.

2. Three cups of mung bean sprouts, well drained.

3. Three cups of soybean sprouts, well drained. Stir-fry the sprouts in oil for 2 minutes, then add 3 tablespoons of water. Cover and steam on low heat for 12 minutes.

4. One-half pound of Chinese green cabbage, cut into 1-inch squares. Stir-fry for 3 minutes.

Beef

Stir-Fried Beef with Celery Cabbage

Bon

Serves 2

½ pound flank steak
1 pound celery cabbage
1 clove garlic
2 teaspoons cornstarch
2 tablespoons water
2 tablespoons oil
½ teaspoon salt
few grindings of fresh pepper
½ cup stock or water

1. Freeze meat until partially stiff and slice thin, against the grain.

2. Slice celery cabbage into ½-inch strips across the ribs.

3. Peel garlic.

4. Mix cornstarch and water.

5. Heat oil in a *wok* or large, heavy frying pan having a lid. Stir-fry whole garlic for 1 minute. Remove garlic and discard.

6. Add sliced beef and stir-fry, uncovered, until nearly cooked, when most of the raw color is gone. Add celery cabbage, stir-frying for 2 minutes.

7. Season with salt and pepper and pour in stock. Bring to a boil, reduce heat and simmer, covered, for 3 to 4 minutes.

8. Stir cornstarch mixture well and pour into beef. Mix until thickened. Serve immediately.

Comments:

1. For variety, add 6 dried black mushrooms. First soak them for at least 1 hour in warm water. Remove hard stems and cut mushrooms in quarters. Add the same time as the stock.

2. Substitute American round cabbage or Chinese cabbage (*bok choy*) for celery cabbage if desired. Cut round cabbage in ½-inch by 2-inch shreds. Chinese cabbage should be sliced diagonally in 1-inch pieces.

Stir-Fried Beef,
Snow Peas
and Black Mushrooms

Serves 3

8	dried black mushrooms
	warm water
1	pound flank or sirloin steak
2	tablespoons soy sauce
2	tablespoons sherry
½	teaspoon honey
½	pound snow peas
1	clove garlic
2	teaspoons cornstarch
2	tablespoons water
1½	tablespoons oil
½	teaspoon salt
½	cup stock

1. Soak dried black mushrooms for 1 hour in warm water to cover. Cut out hard stems and halve or quarter mushrooms if they are very large.

2. Freeze meat until partially stiff and slice thin against the grain.

3. Mix soy sauce, sherry and honey in a medium-sized bowl. Marinate sliced beef in soy sauce mixture for 15 to 30 minutes. Stir once or twice.

4. Remove stem ends from snow peas.

5. Mince garlic.

6. Combine cornstarch and water.

7. Heat oil in a wok, or large, heavy skillet. Stir-fry garlic for a few seconds. When oil is very hot, add beef and stir-fry until beef loses most of its redness.

8. Add snow peas, soaked mushrooms and salt, stir-frying 1 minute.

9. Pour in stock, bring to boiling and boil for 1 minute, while stirring.

10. Mix cornstarch well, pour into beef and stir until thickened. Serve immediately.

Comment:

Sliced beef may be stir-fried with 2 bunches of watercress. Omit snow peas and black mushrooms. Cut off tough stems of watercress. Wash and dry well on paper toweling. Stir-fry watercress in 1½ tablespoons of oil. Discard juices. Add to stir-fried beef. Continue with directions.

Beef

Stir-Fried Beef Heart

Serves 4-5

2	pounds beef or veal heart
4	slices fresh ginger root
2	tablespoons soy sauce
1	tablespoon cornstarch
1	teaspoon honey
1	teaspoon salt
2	tablespoons sherry
2	tablespoons water
3	scallions
2	tablespoons oil

1. Cut off all fat from the heart meat. Slice vertically into 4 parts. Cut across the grain (horizontally) into pieces about ⅛-inch thick, discarding the blood vessels and any internal fat. Rinse well.

2. Mince ginger slices. Mix ginger, soy sauce, cornstarch, honey, salt, sherry and water in a large bowl.

3. Marinate heart slices in soy mixture for 15 to 30 minutes.

4. Chop scallions into 1-inch lengths.

5. Remove heart from marinade. Discard marinade. Heat oil until very hot in a *wok* or large, heavy skillet. Add heart and stir-fry for 2 minutes.

6. Add scallions and continue to stir-fry for 1 to 2 minutes until heart is fully cooked. If the sauce is too thick, mix in a few teaspoons of water until the proper consistency is reached. Serve immediately.

Stir-Fried Kidneys

Serves 2-3

2 pounds veal, pork or lamb
   kidneys
2 scallions
1½ tablespoons soy sauce
1½ tablespoons sherry
2 teaspoons cornstarch
½ teaspoon salt
2 tablespoons oil

1. Rinse kidneys well. Freeze until partially stiff and cut off thin slices of kidney. Do not use the deep red middle of the kidneys nor the white fat. Only about 1/3 of the kidney is edible.

2. Place kidney slices in a large bowl of cold water and let soak for about 1 hour. Change the water at least twice.

3. Slice the scallions into 1-inch pieces.

4. Combine soy sauce, sherry, cornstarch and salt.

5. When ready to cook, drain kidneys well in a strainer and place in a small bowl. Stir soy sauce mixture and add it to kidneys.

6. Heat oil in a large, heavy skillet until very hot. Pour in kidney mixture and stir-fry for 1 minute. Add scallions and continue to stir-fry for 1 to 2 minutes until the pinkness of the kidneys is completely gone. Serve immediately.

Comment:

Prepare sweet and sour kidneys as follows: add ¼ cup rice wine vinegar or cider vinegar, ¼ cup honey and ¼ cup stock to soy sauce mixture. Use only 1 tablespoon of soy sauce.

Beef

Diced Liver
with Vegetables

Serves 3

¾ pound beef liver
1½ tablespoons soy sauce
1½ tablespoons sherry
½ tablespoon cornstarch
1 clove garlic
¾ pound celery stalks
½ pound carrots
1 tablespoon soy sauce
½ tablespoon cornstarch
2 tablespoons water
1½ tablespoons oil
1 cup shelled peas
½ tablespoon salt
½ cup stock
1½ tablespoons oil

1. Freeze beef liver until stiff enough to cut easily. Dice into ½-inch cubes.

2. In a medium-sized mixing bowl, combine 1½ tablespoons of soy sauce, sherry and ½ tablespoon of cornstarch. Add liver and marinate for 15 minutes.

3. Mince garlic.

4. Cut celery stalks and carrots into ½-inch dice.

5. In a small mixing bowl, combine 1 tablespoon of soy sauce, ½ tablespoon of cornstarch and water.

6. Heat 1½ tablespoons of oil in a wok or large, heavy frying pan having a lid. Add carrots and stir-fry for 1 minute uncovered. Add celery and peas at one minute intervals and stir-fry for 1 minute each.

7. Season with salt.

8. Pour in stock, heat to boiling, cover and simmer for about 3 minutes, until vegetables are tender but still crisp. Remove from pan and wipe pan clean.

9. Heat 1½ tablespoons of oil in the same pan. Stir-fry garlic for a few seconds, then add liver cubes. Stir-fry until their surface has changed color and the pieces no longer stick together.

10. Return vegetables to the pan, reheat and thicken mixture with cornstarch and water which has been well stirred before adding.

11. Serve immediately. Do not reheat this dish or liver will be dry and tough.

Shredded Liver
with Spinach

Serves 3

5 dried black mushrooms
warm water to cover
½ pound beef liver
1 clove garlic
3 scallions
1 pound young spinach
2 slices fresh ginger
2 tablespoons soy sauce
1 tablespoon sherry
1 tablespoon cornstarch
1 teaspoon honey
2 tablespoons oil

1. In a medium-sized mixing bowl, soak dried black mushrooms in enough warm water to cover for 1 hour. Remove hard stems and cut mushrooms in slivers.

2. Freeze liver until stiff but not completely solid. Cut in shreds.

3. Mince garlic.

4. Cut scallions in 1-inch lengths.

5. Remove stems from spinach and shred leaves coarsely.

6. Mince ginger and combine it with soy sauce, sherry, cornstarch and honey in a medium-sized mixing bowl. Add liver and mix well.

7. Heat oil in a *wok* or large, heavy frying pan. Stir-fry garlic and scallions for a few seconds and add shredded liver. Stir-fry until liver turns color, about 2 to 3 minutes.

8. Add mushrooms and stir-fry ½ minute.

9. Add spinach and stir until wilted.

10. Serve immediately.

Beef

Stir-Fried Lamb

Serves 3

1	pound tender lamb, from the leg
2	scallions
2	slices fresh ginger
2	tablespoons soy sauce
½	tablespoon sherry
½	teaspon salt
1½	tablespoons oil
	soy sauce to taste

1. Freeze lamb until stiff enough to slice easily. Cut in thin, 2-inch by 1-inch slices.

2. Cut scallions in 1-inch lengths.

3. Mince ginger.

4. In a medium-sized mixing bowl, marinate lamb with scallions, ginger, 2 tablespoons of soy sauce, sherry and salt for 15 minutes.

5. Heat oil until very hot, in a wok or large, heavy frying pan. Add lamb and marinade and stir-fry until lamb is just cooked, about 2 minutes.

6. Serve immediately, with soy sauce to taste.

Red-Cooked Oxtail

Serves 3-4

4	pounds oxtail—Have the butcher cut oxtails into approximately 1-inch pieces. The thin end can easily be cut through the cartilage, but the thick part must be sawed through.
5	cups water
6	tablespoons soy sauce
1½	tablespoons sherry
1	teaspoon salt
1	teaspoon honey
	few slices fresh ginger (optional)

1. Cut all visible fat from oxtail.

2. Heat water to boiling in a large, heavy pot with a cover. Add oxtails, return water to a boil and remove scum from surface. Now add soy sauce, sherry, salt, honey and ginger.

3. Simmer, covered, until very tender, about three hours.

4. Skim off fat or chill overnight and remove hardened fat.
Comments:
1. Freshly-cooked vegetables like carrots, green peppers or asparagus may be added just before serving.
2. Large cubes of winter radishes may be added during the last half hour of cooking.

Beef

200

Red-Cooked Beef Tongue

Serves 6

1	beef tongue, about 3 pounds
4	cups water
1	tablespoon sherry
3	slices ginger (optional)
¼	cup soy sauce
1	teaspoon salt
1	teaspoon honey

1. Place tongue and water in a large, heavy pot with cover. Heat to boiling and cook for 5 minutes, covered. Take the tongue out of the pot and remove the skin, either by peeling it off or cutting it off with a sharp knife. (Removal of the skin allows a better penetration of the seasoning flavors.) Trim off fat.

2. Replace tongue in the water, add sherry, ginger, soy sauce and salt. Heat to boiling. Reduce heat and simmer, covered, for 2 hours. Turn tongue after the first hour, being very careful to avoid splashing yourself.

3. Flavor with honey and simmer 1 more hour.

4. Skim off all the fat or chill overnight and remove the hardened fat.

5. To serve hot, slice and cut each slice in quarters. Serve with the hot juice the tongue was cooked in.

Comments:

1. Beef tongue, prepared by red-simmering, is highly versatile. Use in fried rice, as a substitute for roast pork in many dishes, or as a meat with assorted stir-fried vegetables. Add tongue merely to reheat. No further cooking is needed.

2. Serve cold sliced as part of an assorted cold platter of meats, or by itself as an appetizer.

Beef

Pork

Pork ranks as the favorite meat among the Chinese, far surpassing beef. Even in American-style Chinese restaurants, pork spareribs are undoubtedly the number one appetizer.

Fresh pork is sliced, diced or slivered and stir-fried with vegetables. Ground pork may be stir-fried, preferably drained of its fat, then combined with other ingredients. Well-flavored pork balls are popular served on a bed of greens or combined with seafood or in soup.

Strips of fresh pork may be marinated, then roasted and served with dipping sauces or cut up to be stir-fried with vegetables.

Pork kidney and liver, both of which have a lower fat content than other parts of the pig, may be prepared in interesting ways according to the Chinese manner, as can pigs' feet and tripe.

In stocking up on pork for stir-frying, it is especially convenient to buy chops. Cut out the boneless parts of the chop, trim off the fat and place the meat on a layer of waxed paper on a cookie sheet. Freeze the fillets solid and store them in a plastic bag in the freezer. Save the pork chop bones for the soup pot. Other cuts of lean, tender pork, sliced about ¾-inch thick, may be frozen in the same way. When needed, thaw pork pieces for half an hour. Cut as required, allow to defrost, and proceed with the recipe.

The Chinese most often cut pork in small pieces to prepare it. Then, just a few minutes of cooking will eliminate any possibility of trichinosis, a disease caused by a small parasite sometimes found in pork. This organism is killed by heating the meat to 137° F. or freezing it at 5° F. for 20 days.

Pork Balls

Très Bon

Serves 3

1 tablespoon soy sauce
1 ½ tablespoons cornstarch
½ teaspoon salt
1 teaspoon honey
1 tablespoon sherry
1 pound pork, ground with a little fat, or minced with a cleaver in the Chinese manner
3 tablespoons oil

1. Mix together soy sauce, cornstarch, salt, honey and sherry.

2. Combine minced pork with soy sauce mixture, blending well. Form into small balls the size of walnuts.

3. Heat oil in a large, heavy frying pan. Sauté pork balls until well-browned, turning occasionally. Remove pork balls from the pan.

4. The pork balls may now be cooked with spinach, dried bean curd or assorted vegetables (see index).

Comments:

1. Texture of the pork balls is softer if pork is minced with a cleaver, rather than ground. Chinese chefs often chop meat with 2 cleavers in unison, for greater efficiency.

2. Instead of sautéing, pork balls may be steamed over boiling water on a rack. Cover and cook them for 20 minutes, or until no longer rare inside.

3. To serve in soup, form into small balls, ¾ inch in diameter. Heat soup stock to boiling and drop in meat balls. Cook, covered, for 10 minutes. Skim off fat and serve garnished with finely-chopped scallions.

Pork

Pork Balls
and Vegetables

Serves 3-4

1	pound young cabbage
2	green peppers
½	tablespoon cornstarch
2	tablespoons water
½	cup pork or beef stock
1	teaspoon soy sauce
⅛	teaspoon five-spice powder
¼	teaspoon salt
1½	tablespoons oil
¼	teaspoon salt
1	pound *Pork Balls* (see index)

1. Cut cabbage into 1-inch squares.

2. Discard seeds of green peppers and cut peppers into 1-inch squares.

3. Mix cornstarch and water.

4. In a small saucepan, heat pork or beef stock to boiling.

5. Season with soy sauce, five-spice powder and ¼ teaspoon of salt.

6. Stir cornstarch mixture and add to stock, mixing well.

7. Heat oil in a wok or large, heavy skillet. Stir-fry cabbage for 2 minutes. Add green pepper and ¼ teaspoon of salt, stir-frying for another 2 minutes.

8. Mix pork balls with vegetables and stir-fry until hot.

9. Reheat stock mixture, then pour over pork balls and vegetables. Serve at once.

Pork

Lion's Head
or Pork Balls
with Celery Cabbage

Serves 3

8	water chestnuts
2	scallions
2	slices fresh ginger root (optional)
1	tablespoon sherry
1	teaspoon honey
1	pound ground pork
2	tablespoons cold water
½	teaspoon salt
½	tablespoon cornstarch
1½	pounds celery cabbage
2	tablespoons oil
¼	cup soy sauce
1	cup stock

1. Finely mince water chestnuts, scallions, and ginger.

2. Blend sherry and honey.

3. Place meat in a large mixing bowl and add chopped vegetables, sherry-honey mixture, cold water, salt and cornstarch.

4. Mix lightly, but well, with a large fork. Form into 4 large meatballs.

5. Cut celery cabbage across the rib into 2-inch pieces.

6. Heat oil in a large heavy skillet. Sauté meatballs until lightly-browned on all sides, turning carefully with a spatula.

7. Heat soy sauce and stock in a large, heavy pot with a lid. When meatballs are browned, place them in the soy-stock mixture, cover and simmer for 1½ hours.

8. Remove meatballs to a plate. Place sliced celery cabbage in remaining juices in pot. Arrange meatballs on top.

9. Cover, and cook on medium heat until celery cabbage is wilted and tender but still somewhat crisp, about 20 minutes.

10. To serve three, slice the fourth meatball in thirds.

Comments:

1. This dish is called Lion's Head because the massive meatballs and celery cabbage resemble the head of a lion with its mane.

2. Ground beef may be substituted for pork. Cooking time of meatballs may then be reduced, if desired, to 1 hour, instead of 1½ hours.

Diced Pork with Peas

Serves 2-3

½ pound lean pork
2 teaspoons soy sauce
2 teaspoons sherry
few grindings fresh pepper
2 teaspoons cornstarch
2 tablespoons water
1 tablespoon oil
3 cups shelled peas
½ teaspoon salt
3 tablespoons water
1½ tablespoons oil
½ cup stock or water

1. Freeze pork until stiff, then dice it into ¼-inch cubes.

2. Marinate with soy sauce, sherry and fresh pepper for 30 minutes.

3. Mix cornstarch and 2 tablespoons of water.

4. Heat 1 tablespoon of oil in a *wok* or large, heavy skillet having a lid. Stir-fry peas with salt for 1 minute, uncovered.

5. Pour in 3 tablespoons of water, bring to a boil and cook, covered, on a medium heat, for about 4 minutes. Young peas may not need a full 4 minutes of steaming time. Remove peas and wipe pan.

6. In same pan, heat 1½ tablespoons of oil until very hot. Add diced pork, stir-frying for 2 minutes.

7. Return peas to the pan, pour in stock and bring to a boil. Cover, reduce heat and simmer for 2 minutes.

8. Stir cornstarch mixture and pour into pork and peas. Continue stirring until thickened. Serve immediately.

Pork

Roast Pork, Broccoli and Celery Cabbage

Serves 2-3

½ pound roast pork (see index)
½ pound broccoli
½ pound celery cabbage
2 scallions
1 clove garlic
2 teaspoons cornstarch
1 tablespoon soy sauce
¼ teaspoon honey
1 tablespoon water
1½ tablespoons oil
½ teaspoon salt
½ cup stock

1. Cut roast pork in thin slices, after removing any visible fat.

2. Slice broccoli stems thinly on the diagonal. Cut each individual floweret in half.

3. Cut celery cabbage in 1-inch pieces, across the rib.

4. Cut scallions into ½-inch pieces.

5. Mince garlic.

6. Combine cornstarch, soy sauce, honey and water.

7. Heat oil in a wok or large, heavy skillet having a lid. Stir garlic rapidly in the pan for a few seconds, uncovered.

8. Add broccoli and stir-fry for 2 minutes. Put in celery cabbage and salt and stir 1 minute.

9. Add stock, bring to a boil, cover, reduce heat to medium and cook for 3 minutes.

10. Add roast pork and scallions and stir until meat is hot.

11. Stir cornstarch mixture, pour into pork and vegetables, and mix until thickened. Serve immediately.

Comment:

Roast pork and vegetables may be diced instead of sliced.

Roast Pork
with
Chinese Vegetables

Serves 2-3

½	pound roast pork (see index)
¼	pound snow peas
6	water chestnuts
¼	cup bamboo shoots
1	clove garlic
2	teaspoons cornstarch
1	tablespoon soy sauce
¼	teaspoon honey
1	tablespoon water
1½	tablespoons oil
2	cups mung bean sprouts
½	teaspoon salt
½	cup stock

1. Cut roast pork in thin slices, after removing any visible fat.

2. Remove stems from snow peas.

3. Slice water chestnuts and bamboo shoots.

4. Mince garlic.

5. Combine cornstarch, soy sauce, honey and water.

6. Heat oil in a wok or large, heavy skillet. Stir garlic rapidly in the oil for a few seconds. Add mung bean sprouts which have been well drained, and stir-fry for 2 minutes.

7. Add salt, water chestnuts, bamboo shoots, and snow peas, stirring for 1 minute.

8. Add roast pork, stir-frying until meat is hot.

9. Pour in stock and bring to a boil.

10. Mix cornstarch blend and add to roast pork and vegetables. Stir until thickened. Serve immediately.

Pork

Roast Pork
and
Bean Curd

Serves 2-3

½   pound roast pork
3   scallions
5   cakes fresh bean curd
½   cup stock
1   tablespoon cornstarch
2   tablespoons soy sauce
2   tablespoons sherry
½   teaspoon salt
1   tablespoon oil
1 ½   tablespoons oil

1. Cut roast pork into ½-inch dice, after removing any visible fat.

2. Cut scallions into 1-inch lengths.

3. Slice bean curd into ½-inch cubes.

4. Mix stock, cornstarch, soy sauce, sherry and salt in a small saucepan. Bring to a boil while stirring constantly. Remove from the heat when thickened.

5. Heat 1 tablespoon of oil in a *wok* or large, heavy skillet. Stir-fry roast pork to heat through. Take out of pan.

6. In same pan, heat 1 ½ tablespoons of oil and stir-fry bean curd and scallions on medium heat for 1 to 2 minutes. Stir carefully with a spatula to avoid breaking up the bean curd.

7. Replace roast pork and heat for ½ minute.

8. Reheat stock mixture in saucepan, and pour over pork and bean curd. When thoroughly heated, serve immediately.

Comment:

Fresh pork may be substituted for roast pork. Dice and stir-fry in 1 ½ tablespoons of oil for 2 to 3 minutes until no longer pink. Remove and proceed as above.

Pork

Shredded Pork with Dried Bean Curd

Serves 3

½ pound dried bean curd
  warm water to cover
6 dried black mushrooms
  warm water to cover
1 pound lean pork
2 scallions
1 tablespoon sherry
2 tablespoons soy sauce
1 teaspoon salt
1 teaspoon honey
2 teaspoons cornstarch
2 tablespoons water
2 tablespoons oil
½ cup stock or water

1. Soak dried bean curd in warm water for 1 hour. Keep dried curd well submerged so it will soften fully. Drain and cut into shreds.

2. Soak dried black mushrooms in warm water for 1 hour. Squeeze dry and shred, after removing hard stems.

3. Freeze pork until stiff, then cut it into shreds.

4. Mince scallions.

5. Mix together sherry, soy sauce, salt and honey.

6. Combine cornstarch and water.

7. In a wok or large, heavy skillet having a lid, heat oil until it is very hot. Stir-fry pork shreds for 2 minutes.

8. Add sherry-soy sauce mixture, tossing well. Add shreds of dried bean curd and mushrooms and blend into pork.

9. Pour in stock or water, bring to a boil, cover, reduce heat and simmer for 10 minutes.

10. Taste for seasoning and add more soy sauce if desired.

11. Stir cornstarch mixture well, and blend into pork mixture until thickened.

12. Mix in minced scallions and serve hot.

Comments:

1. To prepare 1 to 2 hours ahead simmer for 5 minutes and set aside. When ready to serve, reheat for a few minutes, thicken, and garnish with scallions.

2. Two tablespoons cloud ear mushrooms, soaked for 30 minutes in warm water, may be substituted for dried black mushrooms.

Pork

Shredded Pork
with
Mixed Vegetables

Serves 3-4

1   pound lean pork
1   pound young spinach
4   carrots
2   scallions
1   tablespoon cornstarch
¼   cup water
2   cups mung bean sprouts
¼   cup water
1   tablespoon oil
3   tablespoons oil
2   tablespoons soy sauce
½   teaspoon salt

1. Freeze pork until stiff, then cut it into shreds.

2. Remove tough stems of spinach and shred leaves coarsely.

3. Cut carrots into thin slices lengthwise. Cut slices into strips about 2 inches long. Or cut into long diagonal slices and shred.

4. Mince scallions.

5. Combine cornstarch and ¼ cup of water.

6. Drain bean sprouts well on paper toweling.

7. Heat ¼ cup of water in a heavy pot. Steam carrots, covered, for a few minutes until somewhat tender, but still crunchy.

8. In a wok or large, heavy skillet, heat 1 tablespoon of oil until very hot. Stir-fry bean sprouts for 2 minutes. Remove sprouts and wipe out the pan.

9. In same pan, heat 3 tablespoons of oil until very hot. Stir-fry scallions for ½ minute, then add shredded pork. Stir-fry until pork is well cooked.

10. Blend in soy sauce, then carrots with cooking liquid. Stir for 1 minute.

11. Add spinach and salt, stirring until leaves begin to wilt.

12. Return bean sprouts to the pan, and reheat.

13. Stir cornstarch mixture well, pour into pork and vegetables, and blend until thickened. Serve immediately.

Northern Egg Dish
or
Mo Shu Ro Pork

Serves 2

20	dried lily buds
	warm water to cover
4	dried black mushrooms
	warm water to cover
2	tablespoons cloud ear mushrooms
	warm water to cover
½	pound lean pork
2	scallions
1	cup mung bean sprouts
1	tablespoon oil
4	eggs
1	tablespoon oil
¼	teaspoon salt
1½	tablespoons oil
1½	tablespoons soy sauce
1	teaspoon honey

1. Soak dried lily buds in warm water to cover for 30 minutes. Nip off hard ends and cut lily buds in half.

2. Soak dried black mushrooms in warm water for 1 hour, squeeze out excess water and shred mushrooms. Discard hard stems.

3. Soak cloud ear mushrooms for 30 minutes in warm water and wash well. Cut out any hard parts and slice in shreds.

4. Freeze pork until stiff, then cut it into shreds.

5. Mince scallions.

6. Drain bean sprouts well on paper toweling.

7. In a medium-sized skillet, heat 1 tablespoon of oil until medium-hot. Scramble eggs until medium-soft, then remove them from the pan.

8. In a *wok* or large, heavy skillet, heat 1 tablespoon of oil until hot, add bean sprouts, and stir-fry for 2 minutes. Season with salt. Remove sprouts from the pan and wipe pan clean.

9. In the same pan, heat 1½ tablespoons of oil until very hot. Add shredded pork and scallions, stir-frying until pork is no longer rare (when it loses its pink color). Mix together soy sauce and honey, then blend into pork.

10. Add lily buds, cloud ears and black mushrooms, stirring for ½ minute.

please turn page

Pork

Sliced Pork
with
Vegetables

Serves 2-3

11. Return bean sprouts to the pan and reheat. Add scrambled eggs and mix well, cutting eggs into pieces with a large cooking spoon if necessary.

12. Serve hot with *Doilies (Chinese Pancakes)* (see index) or steamed rice.

Comments:

1. To make in advance, prepare with only white bottoms of scallions. Add chopped green scallion tops when reheating to serve.

2. Shredded bamboo shoots, ¼ cup, may be added.

3. Substitute 1 tablespoon of dark or heavy soy sauce, if available, for the light soy sauce usually used.

2	tablespoons cloud ear mushrooms (optional) warm water to cover
½	pound lean pork
1	tablespoon sherry
1	tablespoon soy sauce
½	teaspoon honey
½	pound broccoli
2	small onions
3	medium-sized stalks celery
2	teaspoons cornstarch
2	tablespoons water
3	tablespoons water
1	tablespoon oil
½	teaspoon salt
1½	tablespoons oil
½	cup stock
1	tablespoon soy sauce

1. Soak cloud ear mushrooms for 30 minutes in warm water, wash them well and squeeze dry.

2. Freeze pork until stiff, then cut it in thin slices 1-inch by 1½-inches.

3. Blend together sherry, 1 tablespoon of soy sauce and honey. Marinate mixture with pork slices for 15 minutes.

4. Slice broccoli stems in pieces diagonally, ¼ to ½-inch thick. Peel off tough outer skin if desired, to shorten cooking time and to tenderize. Cut flowerets into small pieces.

5. Peel onions and cut into thin slices, vertically, through the root end.

6. Cut celery diagonally into ¼-inch slices.

7. Combine cornstarch and 2 tablespoons of water.

8. Bring 3 tablespoons of water to a boil in a small, heavy pot with a lid. Add broccoli and steam, covered, until almost tender but still crunchy, about 3 minutes. Uncover, turn up heat, and quickly evaporate any remaining liquid while stirring.

9. Heat 1 tablespoon of oil in a wok or large, heavy skillet. Add celery and stir-fry for 2 minutes. Add broccoli and salt, stirring for ½ minute.

10. Add sliced onions and continue stir-frying for another minute. Remove from the pan and wipe pan clean.

11. In the same pan, heat 1½ tablespoons of oil until very hot. Stir-fry pork until slices are well done. Stir in cloud ear mushrooms.

12. Return vegetables to the pan and reheat.

13. Pour in stock and 1 tablespoon of soy sauce, bringing rapidly to a boil.

14. Stir cornstarch paste, add, and mix until sauce is thickened.

15. Serve at once.

Pork

Sliced Pork
with
Green Peppers

Serves 3

1	pound lean pork
2	teaspoons cornstarch
1	egg white
½	teaspoon salt
4	green peppers
1	large onion
2	teaspoons cornstarch
2	tablespoons water
1	tablespoon soy sauce
1½	tablespoons oil
½	teaspoon salt
2	tablespoons oil
1½	tablespoons sherry
¾	cup stock

1. Freeze pork until stiff, then slice thinly into pieces 1 inch by 1½ inches.

2. Marinate with 2 teaspoons of cornstarch, egg white and ½ teaspoon of salt.

3. Discard pepper seeds and cut peppers into strips 1½-inches long and ¼-inch wide.

4. Peel onion. Cut in half, horizontally, through the root, lay on cut side and slice about ¼ inch wide.

5. Combine 2 teaspoons of cornstarch, the water and soy sauce.

6. Heat 1½ tablespoons of oil in a *wok* or large, heavy skillet. Stir-fry green peppers for 1 minute. Add ½ teaspoon of salt, and onions, and stir-fry for another minute. Remove from the pan.

7. Heat 2 tablespoons of oil, in same pan, until very hot. Stir-fry pork until well cooked.

8. Add sherry, stir for 1 minute, then replace cooked vegetables.

9. When meat and vegetables are thoroughly heated, pour in stock and bring to a boil.

10. Stir cornstarch mixture well, add and blend until thickened.

11. Serve immediately.

Comment:

Pork and vegetables may be diced instead of sliced. Diced pork, however, may become dry and tough if cooked until well done as it should be as a precaution against trichinosis. Pork prepared sliced is more tender and juicy.

Pork

Spareribs
with
Black Bean Sauce

Serves 3

1½ tablespoons fermented black beans
2 scallions
3 cloves garlic
1½ pounds spareribs from young pig (ask butcher to cut spareribs into 1-inch pieces. Or, slice apart ribs and cut them into 1-inch sections with a bone cleaver)
1 tablespoon soy sauce
1½ tablespoons honey
½ tablespoon cornstarch

1. Soak fermented black beans in cold water to cover for 30 minutes. Rinse well and drain.

2. Cut white part of scallions into 1-inch lengths. Chop green tops.

3. Mince garlic.

4. With a fork, mash garlic and black beans together.

5. Blend soy sauce and honey.

6. Mix together all ingredients except chopped scallion tops and place on a heat-proof platter.

7. Steam on a rack over boiling water, covered, for 45 minutes.

8. Skim off fat and serve spareribs and juice garnished with chopped scallion tops.

Comment:

This dish may be prepared several days in advance and refrigerated until ready for use. It may also be frozen for several weeks. Defrost and reheat, covered, in a 300° oven. Taste and add more salt or honey, if necessary. Garnish with chopped scallion.

Pork

Red-Cooked
Pork Tripe

Serves 4

1½ pounds pork tripe
(thoroughly cleaned by
butcher)
cold water, to cover
1 large onion
2 scallions
1½ cups water
3 tablespoons soy sauce
2 tablespoons sherry
¾ teaspoon salt
1 teaspoon honey
3 slices fresh ginger

1. Soak tripe in enough cold water to cover for 2 hours. Throw away soaking water. Pre-soaking tones down any strong odors or off-tastes present in the tripe.

2. With a very sharp knife, cut tripe into pieces 2 inches long and ½-inch wide.

3. Peel onion and cut into thin slices.

4. Cut scallions into 1-inch pieces.

5. Bring 1½ cups of water to a boil in a heavy pot or wok. Add sliced tripe, onion, soy sauce, sherry, salt, honey and ginger. Reboil, cover, and simmer about 2 hours, until tripe is tender.

6. Add scallions, stir a few times, and serve.

Comments:

1. Red-cooked pork tripe may be prepared 1 or 2 days ahead. Add the scallions when reheating to serve.

2. When tripe is tender, sliced vegetables like green pepper, summer squash, celery cabbage, carrots or string beans may be added. Cook only until tender, but still crisp.

Red-Cooked Pigs' Feet

Serves 2-3

4	pigs' feet (Have butcher cut or saw pigs' feet in quarters.)
1	onion
1	scallion
2	tablespoons sherry
2	tablespoons soy sauce
1	teaspoon salt
2	slices fresh ginger
2	cups boiling water
2	teaspoons honey

1. Clean pigs' feet well and rinse them off.

2. Peel onion and cut in slices.

3. Mince scallion.

4. Put pigs' feet, onion, sherry, soy sauce, salt and ginger into a heavy pot with cover and stir well. Place over medium heat and continue stirring until liquid starts to boil.

5. Add boiling water, cover, reduce heat and cook on a low heat, for 2 hours.

6. Mix in honey and simmer until bones are falling apart, from 1 to 2 hours more.

7. Skim off fat, garnish with scallions and serve.

Comments:

1. Pigs' feet are somewhat difficult to manage with chopsticks. Provide hot, moist towels or paper napkins and eat with your hands if desired. This is not at all a neat dish, so perhaps it is best served for the family rather than for company. Don't miss enjoying its great chewy texture, dignified eating or not.

2. To serve jellied, add 1 cup of cold water and ½ teaspoon of salt when the pigs' feet are fully cooked. Stir well. Turn into a shallow baking or loaf pan and chill until fully set. Scrape off fat and cut into 2- to 3-inch squares.

Pork

Chapter 20

The Chinese excel in devising ingenious ways to use eggs in cooking. The ubiquitous chickens raised by so many Chinese lead to a ready supply of eggs. In America, fertilized eggs more nearly approach the flavor of eggs produced on the Chinese farm, where hens and roosters are not separated.

Egg dishes are not limited to breakfast and lunch, but often figure in dinner menus. One dish unique to the Chinese is steamed eggs, flavored with ground meat, fish, or other rich ingredients. Diluted with chicken stock, the eggs take on a soft, creamy texture.

Egg *foo yung* is another versatile favorite. The home-style version is pan-fried as pancakes—a crisp, fresh, thoroughly outstanding dish.

Eggs may be poached in soups, serving to enrich the flavor and nutrition of the broth, or they may be buried in cooked rice. The traditional methods of boiling, frying, and scrambling eggs are also frequently used.

One of the most nutritionally perfect foods available to man, eggs are a wonderful source of protein and are rich in all the essential vitamins and minerals, except for vitamin C. While high in cholesterol, eggs contain large amounts of lecithin, which helps to keep the artery walls free of cholesterol deposits.

Steamed Eggs

Bon *soul fin*

Serves 2-3

2	scallions
1 ½	cups chicken stock
5	eggs
½	teaspoon salt
	soy sauce, to taste

1. Chop scallions. Heat stock almost to boiling in small saucepan.

2. Meanwhile, break eggs into a mixing bowl. Add salt and chopped scallions, beating lightly.

3. Slowly pour stock into eggs, stirring gently to mix.

4. Then pour egg mixture into a shallow, heat-proof dish for steaming.

5. Boil 2 inches of water in a *wok* or large pan. Place dish on a rack above boiling water and cover. Reduce heat, steam on low heat until custard is just set, about 25 minutes.

6. Serve eggs in the steaming dish, dotted lightly with soy sauce.

Comments:

1. To vary, mix in ¾ cup slivered roast pork or red-simmered beef tongue before steaming.

2. One-half pound of fish fillets may be added to this recipe. First mince fish coarsely. Then mix with 1 teaspoon cornstarch, 1 teaspoon soy sauce and ½ tablespoon oil. Lay fish in a shallow, heat-proof dish. Pour egg mixture slowly over fish. Steam about 40 minutes.

Eggs

Steamed Eggs with Minced Beef

Serves 2-3

1   scallion
1   tablespoon oil
¼   pound minced beef
1   tablespoon soy sauce
4   eggs
½   teaspoon salt
1 ½   cups stock

1. Chop scallion. Set aside.

2. Heat oil in a medium-sized, heavy skillet. Stir-fry minced beef until no longer pink, breaking up any large lumps with a fork.

3. Remove beef from pan with a slotted spoon and place it in a bowl, discarding fat left in the pan. Stir soy sauce into beef.

4. Beat eggs lightly in a medium-sized mixing bowl, adding salt.

5. Heat stock until almost boiling in a small saucepan. Pour stock slowly into eggs while stirring gently.

6. Pour egg mixture slowly into a shallow, heat-proof dish. Sprinkle pre-cooked beef and chopped scallions over eggs.

7. Boil 2 inches of water in a large pan or wok. Place dish on a rack above boiling water and cover. Reduce heat and steam over low heat until custard is just set, 20 to 30 minutes.

8. Serve immediately in the steaming dish.

Comments:

1. To substitute minced pork, stir-fry, until meat is well cooked, but not dry.

2. One pound of fresh spinach may be substituted for the minced beef. Remove tough stems and cut spinach into thin shreds. Increase amount of salt to ¾ teaspoon. Add ½ tablespoon of oil and freshly ground pepper to taste to the egg mixture. Mix spinach into egg mixture and continue with directions. Steam 15 to 20 minutes. If you use frozen, chopped spinach, first defrost it thoroughly and squeeze out excess water.

Eggs

Chicken Egg *Foo Yung*

Serves 2-3

2	tablespoons water
1	cup mung bean sprouts, tightly packed
3	scallions
6	eggs
½	teaspoon salt
1	cup cooked chicken, shredded
¼	cup bamboo shoots, shredded
2	tablespoons oil
1	cup stock
1	tablespoon soy sauce
¼	teaspoon honey
1	tablespoon cornstarch
2	tablespoons water

1. In a small, heavy, lidded pan, bring 2 tablespoons of water to a boil. Steam bean sprouts, covered, for 2 minutes, until just wilting. Drain well.

2. Mince scallions.

3. Beat eggs in a mixing bowl with salt. Add scallions, chicken, bean sprouts, and bamboo shoots.

4. In a *wok* heat 2 tablespoons of oil. If you don't have a *wok*, use a small, heavy frying pan.

5. Fry about 3 tablespoons of egg mixture at a time: do not stir, but cook until the pancake is lightly browned on both sides. Replace some oil if necessary and continue to fry the pancakes one at a time.

6. Keep pancakes warm in a low oven.

7. While frying the pancakes, heat stock with soy sauce and honey in a small saucepan.

8. Mix cornstarch and 2 tablespoons of water together.

9. When stock is boiling, thicken it with cornstarch mixture.

10. Pile pancakes on an attractive platter and cover with hot sauce. Serve immediately.

Eggs

Stir-Fried Eggs
with Spinach

Serves 2-4

Comments:

1. Chinese restaurants customarily serve egg *foo yung* as deep-fried pancakes. For home cooking, the sautéed version given above is preferred, rating the very highest with my family. The same recipe can be prepared as scrambled eggs or in omelet form.

2. With experience, one can cook the small pancakes in 2 pans at once to save time.

3. Shredded celery, carrots, onions, and green peppers may be substituted for the suggested vegetables. Celery and carrots should be steamed for a few minutes in a covered, heavy pan with a few tablespoons of water, before adding to the beaten eggs. Onions and green peppers should be stir-fried in a small amount of oil, to soften slightly.

4. Any cooked, shredded meat or seafood, may be substituted for the chicken.

½	pound spinach
1	large onion
6	eggs
½	teaspoon salt
1½	tablespoons oil
	soy sauce to taste

1. Remove tough stems from spinach and shred leaves.

2. Peel onion and cut into small dice.

3. Beat eggs and add salt.

4. In a *wok* or large, heavy skillet, heat oil on medium heat and stir-fry onion for 1 minute. Add shredded spinach, stir-frying until just wilting.

5. Pour in eggs and stir with a fork or spoon until eggs solidify but are still soft.

6. Serve immediately, sprinkled lightly with soy sauce.

Eggs

Stir-Fried Eggs
with
Soybean Sprouts

Serves 3-4

3   tablespoons water
3   cups soybean sprouts
2   scallions
6   eggs
2   teaspoons soy sauce
1½ tablespoons oil

1. Heat water to boiling in a wok or heavy, lidded, frying pan. Add soybean sprouts (not mung bean sprouts), cover, and simmer 12 to 15 minutes.

2. Remove lid, turn up heat, and evaporate remaining liquid. Remove sprouts and wipe out pan.

3. Mince scallions.

4. Beat eggs in a medium-sized bowl and add soy sauce.

5. In the same frying pan, heat oil on a medium heat. Stir-fry scallions and soybean sprouts for 1 minute.

6. Pour in eggs, stirring with a fork or spoon until eggs solidify but are still soft.

7. Serve immediately.

Comments:

1. Stir-fried eggs may be prepared with any diced or shredded cooked meat or seafood.

2. Vegetables such as tomatoes, green peppers, onions, snow peas, mung bean sprouts, asparagus and broccoli may also be substituted. Tomatoes can be added to the eggs as they cook, merely to heat. Green peppers, onions, snow peas, and mung bean sprouts are stir-fried for 2 minutes before pouring in eggs. Hard vegetables like asparagus and broccoli must be precooked for a few minutes in 3 tablespoons water, covered, to tenderize first.

Eggs

Stir-Fried Eggs with Bean Curd

Serves 2-3

3   scallions
2   fresh bean curd cakes or ⅓ pound homemade bean curd
6   eggs
½   teaspoon salt
     fresh pepper to taste
1½ tablespoons oil

1. Mince scallions.

2. Dry bean curd well, then mash. If using home-made curd, place in strainer and let as much liquid drain out as possible.

3. Beat eggs, adding salt and freshly-ground pepper.

4. Heat oil in a heavy frying pan or *wok*. Stir-fry scallions for ½ minute, then add mashed bean curd. Stir with a spoon or spatula until well heated.

5. Pour in beaten eggs, reduce heat to medium, and stir until eggs solidify but are still soft.

6. Serve immediately.

Party Omelets Stuffed with Minced Fish

Serves 3

¼   pound fish fillets
1   scallion
½   tablespoon sherry
½   tablespoon soy sauce
¼   teaspoon honey
¼   teaspoon salt
1   tablespoon oil
4   eggs
¼   teaspoon salt
     oil for sautéing
1   tablespoon oil
½   pound peas, shelled
¼   teaspoon salt
½   cup stock or water

1. Finely chop fish fillets.

2. Mince scallion.

3. Blend together sherry, soy sauce and honey in a small cup.

4. Mix fish with scallion, sherry-soy sauce blend, and ¼ teaspoon of salt. Marinate for 10 minutes.

5. In a small, heavy skillet, heat 1 tablespoon of oil until it is hot. Stir-fry fish for 2 minutes until it is white.

6. Beat eggs well with ¼ teaspoon of salt in a small bowl.

please turn page

Eggs

7. Pour several tablespoons of oil into a small dish. Brush a *wok* or very small, 4-inch frying pan with a small amount of oil, and place over medium heat.

8. Add 1 tablespoon of beaten egg to the pan. Cook without stirring until almost set then place 1 teaspoon of cooked fish on the egg and fold over. Gently press edges to seal in filling.

9. Turn omelet over with a small spatula, cooking for ½ to 1 minute more. Remove from pan.

10. Repeat the process with the rest of the egg.

11. Heat 1 tablespoon of oil in a *wok* or heavy, lidded frying pan. Stir-fry peas for 1 minute, uncovered.

12. Add ¼ teaspoon of salt, pour in stock, and bring to a boil. Cover, reduce heat and steam for 3 to 5 minutes until peas are barely tender.

13. Lay tiny omelets on top of peas, cover and cook on a medium heat until completely hot, 2 to 3 minutes.

14. Serve immediately.

Comments:

1. The omelets may be prepared 1 day ahead, and reheated over the peas. Remove from the refrigerator 1 hour in advance to reach room temperature.

2. Ground beef or pork may be substituted for the fish. Mix meat with sherry. Stir-fry with scallion in 1 tablespoon of oil until well done and remove from the pan with a slotted spoon. Season meat with soy sauce, salt and honey.

3. One package (10 ounces) of frozen peas may be used instead of fresh peas. Defrost well and reduce cooking time by about 2 minutes.

Eggs

Ancient Egg Omelet

Serves 3

2	ancient eggs
2	fresh eggs
	dash salt
½	tablespoon oil
2	fresh eggs
	dash salt
½	tablespoon oil
2	fresh eggs
	dash salt
½	tablespoon oil
1	green scallion top, finely minced

1. If black coating on ancient eggs is hard, soak them in water for 30 minutes to soften. Scrape off coating with a small knife. Break shells carefully, and cut eggs into ½-inch dice.

2. Three individual omelets can be prepared from the ingredients in this recipe.

3. Beat 2 fresh eggs in a small bowl and add a dash of salt. Add ⅓ of the diced ancient eggs.

4. Heat ½ tablespoon of oil on medium heat in an omelet pan or medium-sized, heavy frying pan. When oil is hot, but not smoking, pour in eggs. Do not stir, but gently push congealed egg from the edges of the pan into the center. Tilt pan to let liquid egg flow to the outer edge of pan.

5. When egg is no longer liquid, but still quite soft, fold it in half with a spatula. Cook for ½ minute, then remove from the pan at once.

6. Prepare the next 2 omelets in the same manner. Serve garnished with finely-minced scallion tops.

Comment:

Omelets taste best when golden (not heavily-browned) on the outside and still soft on the inside. A high flame or long cooking will toughen eggs.

Grains

Chapter 21

Richly-flavored Chinese dishes need the balance of bland rice. Natural brown rice is best served with hearty meat dishes. Converted white rice, more delicate in flavor, is ideal with chicken or seafood.

Leftover boiled rice finds a natural place as "fried rice." Meat and vegetable tidbits from the refrigerator are fried with the rice and may be accompanied by a light soup. This satisfying menu is suitable for lunch or supper.

Fried rice seldom figures in dinner menus. Plain boiled rice is preferred. However, a special multi-ingredient fried rice may appear near the end of a banquet, for those not sated with the preceding delicacies.

Barley, a less common grain than rice, has been grown in northern China since 2000 B.C. It can be used as a substitute for rice in fried rice.

Chicken Fried Rice

Délicieux.

Serves 3-4

3 cups cooked long-grain brown rice
2 stalks celery
1 small green pepper
2 scallions
½ tablespoon oil
2 eggs
1½ tablespoons oil
1 cup mung bean sprouts
1 cup cooked, diced chicken
¼ teaspoon salt
2 tablespoons oil
soy sauce (optional)

1. Cook rice in advance and chill. Bring to room temperature when ready to use.

2. Dice celery and green pepper.

3. Chop scallions.

4. Heat ½ tablespoon of oil in a small frying pan. Beat eggs lightly and scramble in frying pan until just congealed but still very soft. Set aside.

5. Heat 1½ tablespoons of oil in a *wok* or large, heavy skillet. Stir-fry celery for 1 minute, then add mung bean sprouts well drained, and green pepper at 1 minute intervals, stir-frying 3 minutes in all. Add diced chicken to heat. Season with salt. Remove from pan.

6. In the same pan heat 2 tablespoons of oil and stir-fry cooked rice, gently breaking up any lumps with a fork.

7. When rice is fully hot, return vegetables and chicken to the pan to reheat. Stir in scrambled eggs, cutting them into small pieces with a large spoon.

8. Mix in chopped scallion. Sprinkle with soy sauce to taste, or add a bit more salt if omitting the soy sauce.

9. Serve within an hour (reheat on a medium heat, stirring frequently).

Three Tastes Fried Barley

Serves 3-4

Comments:

1. Diced cooked beef, pork, turkey, lamb, chicken gizzards, roast pork or shrimp may be substituted for the chicken.

2. Almost any vegetables may be used in fried rice. Vary with snow peas, shelled peas, mushrooms (fresh or dried), onions, carrots, string beans and cabbage. Diced, cooked vegetables can be added during step 7, while reheating.

1	cup whole hulled barley, cooked in advance
2	cups water
1	large carrot
2	scallions
1/2	tablespoon oil
2	eggs
1 1/2	tablespoons oil
1/2	cup peas, shelled
2	tablespoons water
1/4	cup bamboo shoots, diced
1/4	cup cooked beef, diced
1/4	cup cooked chicken, diced
1/4	cup cooked shrimp, diced
1/4	teaspoon salt
2	tablespoons oil
	soy sauce (optional)

1. Wash barley and soak in 2 cups of water for 1 hour. In a heavy pot, bring water and barley to a boil. Cover and simmer until tender, about 45 minutes. Cook barley early in the day and refrigerate. Bring barley to room temperature before using.

please turn page

Grains

2. Dice carrot.

3. Chop scallions.

4. Heat ½ tablespoon of oil in a small frying pan. Beat eggs lightly and scramble in oil until they are just congealed but still very soft. Set aside.

5. Heat 1 ½ tablespoons of oil in a wok or heavy medium-sized pot, having a lid. Stir-fry carrots for ½ minute, then add peas. Stir-fry for 1 minute. Add 2 tablespoons of water, bring to a boil and steam, covered, for 3 minutes.

6. Remove lid, add bamboo shoots, beef, chicken and shrimp, stirring on a medium heat for 1 minute. Season with salt.

7. If using a wok, remove from the pan and wipe clean. Otherwise, heat 2 tablespoons of oil in a large, heavy skillet and stir-fry cooked barley, gently breaking up any lumps with a fork.

8. When barley is fully hot, return vegetables and meats to the pan to reheat. Stir in scrambled eggs, cutting into small pieces with a large spoon.

9. Mix in chopped scallion. Sprinkle with soy sauce to taste, or add a bit more salt if omitting the soy sauce.

10. Serve within an hour (reheat on a medium heat, stirring frequently).

Comment:

See substitutions under *Chicken Fried Rice* (see index).

Boiled Brown Rice

Serves 3

1   cup brown rice
2   cups cold water

1. Combine brown rice and water in a heavy, lidded pot. Soak for 30 minutes to 1 hour if possible. Washing rice is unnecessary.

2. Bring to a boil and cook on medium heat, uncovered, for 5 minutes. Cover, reduce heat and simmer for 20 to 25 minutes, until tender.

3. Toss with a fork and serve in a deep bowl.

Comments:

1. Boiled rice will remain hot, covered in the pot, for 10 minutes.

2. To cook 2 cups of rice, use 3½ cups water.

Boiled Converted White Rice

Serves 3

1   cup converted rice (parboiled)
1½ cups cold water

1. Combine rice and water in a heavy, lidded pot. Washing rice is unnecessary.

2. Bring to a boil and cook on medium heat, uncovered, for 5 minutes. Cover, reduce heat and simmer for 15 minutes, until tender.

3. Toss with a fork and serve in a deep bowl.

Comments:

1. Boiled rice will remain hot, covered in the pot, for 10 to 15 minutes.

2. To cook 2 cups of rice, use 2½ cups of water.

Grains

Steamed Millet with Vegetables

Serves 4

1	cup millet
1	tablespoon oil
1	cup diced onions
1	cup diced carrots
½	teaspoon salt
2	cups boiling water
	soy sauce to taste

1. Heat a heavy, medium-sized frying pan, without fat. Add millet and stir constantly until it turns slightly brown. Remove pan from the heat.

2. Heat oil in a medium-sized heavy pot with cover. Stir-fry onions and carrots for 2 minutes.

3. Add toasted millet and salt. Pour in boiling water, cover, and simmer for 30 minutes, until water is absorbed.

4. Mix in soy sauce to taste (about 2 tablespoons) and serve.

Comment:

This dish may be prepared a few hours ahead and reheated.

Red Beans with Rice

Serves 4

¼	cup red soybeans
2	cups cold water
1	cup converted white rice

1. Wash red beans. Combine with cold water in a cooking pot. Let soak for 2 hours.

2. Bring water and beans to a boil, cover, and simmer for 1 hour, until tender.

3. Drain off cooking liquid and reserve. Add enough water to cooking liquid to bring it up to 2 cups.

4. Combine liquid, rice and beans in the pot, bring to a boil, cover, and simmer for 30 minutes. Do not uncover while cooking.

5. Serve with red-simmered meat such as beef, tongue, or chicken.

Congee with Fish

Serves 5

½ cup oval brown rice, short grain
6 cups water
1½-2 pounds chicken, turkey or pork bones
  salt to taste
½ pound fish fillets
1 slice fresh ginger
1 tablespoon soy sauce
¼ teaspoon honey
1 tablespoon sherry
½ tablespoon oil
½ teaspoon salt
2 scallions

1. Prepare rice porridge with the brown rice, water, bones and salt to taste as indicated in Congee with Chicken recipe (see index).

2. Freeze the fish fillets until stiff. Cut in thin slices.

3. Finely mince the ginger.

4. Blend soy sauce and honey.

5. Mix together the sliced fish, ginger, sherry, oil, soy sauce mixture, and ½ teaspoon of salt. Let stand for 30 minutes.

6. Mince the scallions.

7. Using 5 deep soup bowls, divide the marinated fish and scallions into even portions.

8. Heat the porridge to boiling, and pour over the fish.

9. Stir gently; the fish will be cooked by the time the liquid is cool enough to drink.

Comment:

One-half cup whole hulled barley may be substituted for rice. Barley is commonly grown and consumed in North China.

Grains

Congee (Rice Porridge) with Chicken

Serves 4-5

½ cup oval brown rice, short-grain
6 cups water
1½-2 pounds chicken, turkey or pork bones
¼ pound chicken breast
2 teaspoons soy sauce
¼ teaspoon salt
½ teaspoon honey
1 teaspoon sherry
1 teaspoon oil
2 scallions
salt to taste

1. Place rice in a blender. Use top speed to blend rice until grains are well broken up.

2. Combine pulverized rice, water and bones in a large, deep pot. Bring to a boil, reduce heat and simmer, covered, for about 2 hours. Stir several times during cooking. Add more water if gruel becomes too thick; it should be the consistency of thick cream.

3. Remove and discard bones. Blend porridge with a rotary beater to achieve a smooth texture.

4. Freeze chicken breast until it is stiff, then cut it into slivers.

5. Blend soy sauce, salt, honey, sherry and oil.

6. In a bowl, combine chicken breast with soy sauce mixture. Marinate for 30 minutes.

7. Mince scallions.

8. Add marinated chicken slivers to rice porridge and simmer for 5 to 8 minutes. Add salt to taste. Stir in minced scallions.

9. Serve hot in deep soup bowls.

Comments:

1. Eggs may be poached in the rice porridge instead of adding marinated chicken.

2. Three cups of chicken stock may be substituted for 3 cups of water if the bones are omitted.

3. To prepare ahead, cook rice soup and cool. Store in the refrigerator until ready to use (it will keep several days). Heat slowly in a large, deep pot, thinning with a little water or stock if necessary. Cook chicken in rice soup and serve.

Grains

Noodles and Pancakes

The Chinese, like the Italians, are fond of noodle dishes. In the Oriental version, noodles are often served with shredded meat and crisp vegetables (as in *Lo Mein*).

Although white flour is now the common base for Chinese egg noodles, for thousands of years before modern milling methods came into being, whole grains were the standard fare. The recipes that follow use that traditional natural whole wheat flour for a tasty, more healthful dish.

Homemade noodles and pancakes are easy to prepare and will keep for two weeks in the refrigerator. Any shredded Chinese dish may be used as a filler for pancakes, to be eaten with the hands.

An unusual, transparent noodle, known as the cellophane noodle, is made from mung beans. Like wheat noodles, they are frequently served with meat and vegetables.

Rice may be omitted from a meal that contains noodles or pancakes.

Shredded Beef
with Cellophane Noodles
and Soybean Sprouts

Serves 2

6	dried black mushrooms
	warm water
½	cup mushroom soak-ing liquid
½	pound flank steak
2	tablespoons soy sauce
2	tablespoons sherry
¼	pound cellophane noodles (mung bean threads)
12	snow peas (optional)
1	tablespoon oil
2	cups soybean sprouts
3	tablespoons water
½	cup shredded celery cabbage
2½-3½	cups stock
1	tablespoon oil

1. Soak dried black mushrooms for 1 hour in warm water to cover. Cut out hard stems and sliver mushrooms. Save ½ cup of soaking liquid.

2. Freeze meat until partially stiff, then slice thin against the grain and cut into shreds.

3. Mix soy sauce and sherry together in a medium-sized bowl. Marinate shredded beef in soy sauce mixture for 15 minutes. Stir once or twice.

4. Soak cellophane noodles for ½ hour in lukewarm water and drain in a colander.

5. Break off stem ends of snow peas and sliver.

6. Heat 1 tablespoon of oil in a wok or large, heavy frying pan having a cover. Stir-fry soybean sprouts for 1 minute. Add water, bring to a boil, reduce heat and simmer, covered, for 8 minutes. Add celery cabbage and continue cooking for 2 minutes.

7. Add soaked noodles, mushrooms, ½ cup of mushroom soaking liquid and 2½ cups of stock. Boil for 5 minutes. Add more stock if necessary.

Cellophane Noodles
with Pork

Serves 3

8	dried black mushrooms
	warm water
1	cup mushroom soaking liquid
½	pound cellophane noodles (mung bean threads)
	warm water
8	cups water
¼	pound snow peas
3	scallions
1	tablespoon oil
2	cups celery cabbage, shredded
2	cups mung bean sprouts
½	cup zucchini, shredded
¼	teaspoon salt
1½	tablespoons oil
1½-2	cups lean pork, shredded
1½	tablespoons soy sauce
¼	teaspoon honey
	few drops Chinese sesame oil (optional)

8. Heat 1 tablespoon of oil in a medium-sized, heavy frying pan. When very hot, add beef and stir-fry until beef loses most of its redness. Add to bean noodle mixture, along with slivered snow peas. Stir-fry for 1 minute. Serve immediately.

Comments:

1. To cook 1 hour ahead, reserve snow peas and add just before serving.

2. Scallions cut in 1-inch lengths can substitute for snow peas. Slivered zucchini can be used instead of celery cabbage.

1. Soak dried black mushrooms in warm water to cover for 1 hour. Drain, reserving 1 cup soaking liquid. Squeeze excess water from mushrooms and sliver them.

please turn page

2. Soak cellophane noodles in warm water for 30 minutes, and drain. In large pot, heat 8 cups of water to boiling, then add presoaked noodles. Bring to a boil again, remove from heat and drain noodles in a colander or strainer. Rinse with cold water, and let drain. Cut into 4-inch lengths.

3. Shred snow peas, after removing stem ends.

4. Mince scallions.

5. Heat 1 tablespoon of oil in a wok or large, heavy frying pan. Stir-fry celery cabbage for 1 minute, then add mung bean sprouts. Stir-fry for another minute, adding zucchini, salt, and mushrooms. After ½ minute, remove vegetables from the pan and wipe pan clean.

6. In same pan, heat 1½ tablespoons of oil. Stir-fry shredded pork for about 3 minutes until no longer raw.

7. Blend soy sauce and honey well in a small cup. Mix in with stir-fried pork. Return the vegetables to the pan. Reheat vegetables quickly.

8. Add shredded snow peas, pour in mushroom soaking liquid and bring to a boil.

9. Flavor with a few drops of Chinese sesame oil.

10. Add parboiled noodles and scallions. Stir until heated thoroughly. Serve immediately.

Comment:

Slivered chicken, roast pork or beef may be substituted for the pork. Add roast pork at the end merely to reheat.

Whole Wheat
Egg Roll Skins

Makes about 12 skins

2	cups whole wheat flour
½	teaspoon salt
1	egg
⅓-½	cup cold water
	cornstarch, to flour board

1. Sift together flour and salt.

2. Beat egg and mix it with flour.

3. Add enough water so that dough clings together in a ball. Knead dough until it is smooth and pliable, about 5 minutes, on a board floured with cornstarch.

4. Place dough in a small bowl. Cover with a damp towel and let it rest for 30 minutes.

5. Roll dough into a sausage shape and divide into 3 parts. On a board floured with cornstarch, roll 1 section into a 12-inch square. Be careful to avoid tearing the sheet. If dough will not stretch to 12 inches without tearing, reduce size of square slightly to roll out a whole sheet.

6. Cut the 12-inch square into four 6-inch squares (or somewhat smaller, if necessary). Rub lightly with cornstarch and stack.

7. Repeat with the other 2 pieces of dough.

8. The egg roll skins are now ready to be filled and deep fried.

9. See recipe for *Shrimp Egg Rolls*.

Comment:

If skins are prepared in advance, place in a plastic bag and refrigerate. They will keep for about 2 weeks. They can be frozen for several months.

Noodles
with Sesame Sauce

Serves 2

¼　cup *tahini* or Chinese
　　sesame paste
2　tablespoons soy sauce
　　chicken stock or water
　　salt to taste, optional
1　scallion
1　recipe *Whole Wheat
　　Noodles*
　　freshly ground pepper to
　　taste

1. In a small bowl, combine
tahini with soy sauce, mixing
well. Add a small amount of
stock or water to bring to the
consistency of light cream. Add
salt if necessary.

2. Boil whole wheat noodles as
directed in the recipe. Drain
well.

3. Mince scallion.

4. Place hot noodles in a serving
dish. Pour sesame sauce over the
noodles. Grind fresh pepper
over the mixture and toss well.

5. Garnish with minced scallion
and serve immediately.

Comment:

Dried mung bean threads (cellophane noodles) may be used instead of fresh whole wheat
noodles. Soak threads for ½
hour in lukewarm water and
drain. Heat 2 quarts of water to
boiling with 2 teaspoons salt.
Boil threads for 5 minutes and
drain well. Proceed as above.

Whole Wheat Noodles

2 cups whole wheat flour
1 teaspoon salt
1 egg
⅓ cup cold water, approximately
  cornstarch, to flour board
2 quarts boiling water
1½ teaspoons salt

1. Sift together flour and 1 teaspoon of salt.

2. Beat egg and mix with flour.

3. Add enough cold water so that dough just clings together in a ball. Knead dough until it is smooth and pliable, about 5 minutes, on a board floured with cornstarch.

4. Place dough in a small bowl. Cover with a damp towel and let it rest for 30 minutes.

5. Cut ball of dough in half. On a board floured with cornstarch, roll half of the dough into a circle 12 inches in diameter.

6. Loosely roll up circle of dough. Cut it into noodles ¹⁄₁₆ inch thick.

7. Repeat with second half of dough.

8. In a large pot, bring 2 quarts of water to a boil with 1½ teaspoons of salt.

9. Slowly add noodles, bring back to a boil and cook, uncovered, for about 5 minutes. Stir occasionally during this time. Remove noodles when they are tender, but still chewy.

10. Run cold water over noodles then drain them well. The noodles are now ready to use in soup or stir-fried as *Lo Mein*.

Comment:

If noodles are prepared in advance, mix with some cornstarch and refrigerate in a covered container. They will keep for about 2 weeks.

Chicken *Lo Mein*

Serves 2-3

5	dried black mushrooms
	warm water
½	pound boneless leg and
	thigh meat of chicken
3	scallions
1	tablespoon oil
1	cup shredded celery
	cabbage
1	cup mung bean sprouts
¼	teaspoon salt
½	cup shredded bamboo
	shoots
1½	tablespoons oil
1½	tablespoons soy sauce
½	teaspoon honey
½	cup stock
2	teaspoons cornstarch
2	tablespoons water
1	recipe *Whole Wheat Noodles*, parboiled (see index)

1. Soak dried black mushrooms in warm water to cover for 1 hour. Drain and squeeze out excess water. Cut mushrooms into slivers, discarding hard stem ends.

2. Freeze chicken until stiff. Cut in shreds.

3. Cut scallions in 1-inch pieces.

4. Heat 1 tablespoon of oil in a wok or large, heavy frying pan. Stir-fry celery cabbage for 1 minute, then add bean sprouts. Cook for another minute. Add salt, bamboo shoots, mushrooms and scallions, stir for ½ minute and remove from the frying pan. Wipe pan clean.

5. Heat 1½ tablespoons of oil in same pan. Stir-fry shredded chicken for 2 minutes, until no longer raw.

6. Mix together soy sauce and honey. Blend well into chicken. Add cooked vegetables to the pan, and reheat quickly.

7. Pour in stock and bring to a boil.

8. Mix cornstarch and water together. Add to boiling sauce and stir until thickened.

9. Gently mix in parboiled noodles, stirring until heated.

10. Taste and sprinkle in more soy sauce if desired. Serve immediately.

Comments:

1. Parboiled noodles may also be stir-fried gently in 2 tablespoons of oil, then meat and vegetables are added.

2. Breast of chicken, fresh pork, roast pork or beef may be substituted for chicken. Fresh pork needs a few more minutes cooking; stir-fry pork for 2 minutes, then cook vegetables in the same pan in the time sequence described above. Use 1 cup shredded roast pork. Add to vegetables merely to reheat.

3. Vary the vegetables with shredded onions, Swiss chard, spinach, snow peas or celery.

Doilies
(Chinese Pancakes)

Serves 4 (3 pancakes per person)

2 cups sifted whole wheat flour
1 cup boiling water
cornstarch, to flour board
1 tablespoon Chinese sesame oil (or peanut oil)

1. Place sifted flour in a small bowl. Slowly add boiling water and, with a wooden spoon, mix until dough forms a ball.

2. Knead dough on a board floured with cornstarch until dough is smooth and pliable, about 5 minutes. Let dough rest in a bowl covered with a damp towel for 30 minutes.

3. On a board floured with cornstarch, shape dough into a sausage roll 12 inches long. Cut into 1-inch pieces. Flatten 1 piece into a circle ¼ inch thick. Brush lightly with oil and top with a second circle ¼ inch thick. Continue with rest of dough until there are 6 pairs of dough circles.

4. Roll each double circle evenly to form a larger circle 5 inches in diameter.

5. Heat an ungreased, medium-sized frying pan on low heat. Cook each pancake pair individually, until each side is lightly-browned. This should take about 2 minutes.

6. As each pair is finished, gently pull the 2 pancakes apart. Make a pile of pancakes and cover it with a damp towel.

7. When ready to serve, heat pancakes by steaming them, covered, on a rack over boiling water for 10 minutes.

8. Serve with *Northern Egg Dish, Shredded Chicken* or any other shredded dish (see index). Fold doilies in quarters on the serving plate. Each diner unfolds a pancake, places some meat dish on it and rolls the pancake up to be eaten by hand. Turn up one end to avoid dripping.

Whole Wheat Wontons

Makes about 48 wontons

2   cups whole wheat flour
1   teaspoon salt
1   egg
⅓   cup cold water, approxi-
    mately
    cornstarch, to flour board

Comments:

1. To use pancakes the day after cooking them, refrigerate them in foil or a plastic bag, then steam when ready to serve.

2. Doilies can be frozen for a few weeks. Steam to heat without thawing.

3. These pancakes are also the traditional wrapping for crisp Peking Duck Skin, a banquet specialty. The recipe is not included in this book since it is too complicated for most home cooks.

1. Sift together flour and salt.

2. Beat egg and mix with flour.

3. Add enough water so that dough just clings together in a ball. Knead dough until it is smooth and pliable, about 5 minutes, on a board floured with cornstarch.

4. Place dough in a small bowl. Cover with a damp towel and let it rest for 30 minutes.

5. Divide dough into 3 parts. On a board floured with cornstarch, roll 1 section into a circle about 10 inches in diameter.

6. Cut in strips 2 to 2½ inches wide. It is helpful to use a ruler as a guide for the knife. Cut strips into 2 to 2½-inch squares. Lightly flour squares with cornstarch and put them into a stack.

7. Repeat same process with the 2 other pieces of dough.

please turn page

Filling for Wontons

2	scallions
1	pound lean pork, finely-ground
½	teaspoon salt
1	tablespoon soy sauce
1	tablespoon sherry freshly-ground pepper
2	quarts water
2	teaspoons salt

1. Mince scallions.

2. Mix together scallions, ground pork, ½ teaspoon of salt, 1 tablespoon of soy sauce, sherry, and freshly-ground pepper as desired. Stir well with a large kitchen fork until ingredients are blended.

3. Spoon out ½ teaspoon or more of pork filling just below the center of a square of wonton dough, or skin. Lightly wet edges of dough and fold over in half to seal. Gently bring both lower corners together, moisten with water and seal.

4. Cover filled wonton with a towel.

5. Bring 2 quarts of water to a boil with 2 teaspoons of salt.

6. Add wontons gradually and bring back to a boil. Cook for 10 minutes and drain well.

Comments:

1. If wonton skins are prepared in advance without filling, place the skins in a plastic bag and refrigerate. They will keep for about 2 weeks. They can be frozen for several months. Filled wontons may be frozen for several weeks. Freeze in a single layer on a cookie sheet. Then store in a plastic bag. When using, boil without first defrosting.

2. Filled wontons may be used in *Wonton Soup* (see index) or sautéed.

3. To sauté filled wontons, heat about 2 tablespoons of oil in a large, heavy frying pan. Add as many wontons as will fit in a single layer. Sauté both sides until golden brown, turning carefully. Place cooked wontons in a 300° oven to keep warm. Add more oil to frying pan and sauté the rest of the wontons. Use 2 frying pans at once to save time, if desired. Combine ⅓ cup each of soy sauce and rice-wine vinegar or red wine vinegar. Pour into individual dishes as a dip. Or substitute ¾ to 1 cup of *Plum Sauce* (see index).

Vegetables

The Chinese cuisine is one of the few in the world that honors vegetables for their own beautiful sake. Fresh, bright-colored vegetables cooked to perfection are part of every Chinese dinner.

The stir-fry method is particularly suitable for vegetable cookery. A vegetable may be sliced and fried alone or combined with several other harmonious vegetables. Pulpy types, like eggplant, are braised or steamed. Lightly-cooked vegetables, bathed in a soy sauce dressing, are served cold as appetizers.

The most versatile Chinese vegetable is the soybean, a major source of protein from which a number of ingenious food products have been developed. Soybeans are ground in water, strained, then congealed into a delicate and rather perishable custard-like substance called bean curd (dow foo). The curd can be dried into thin, noodle-like sheets, called dried bean curd or bean stick (foo jook), which keeps for several months.

Neat, firm cakes of curd are produced in Chinese shops where vises are used to exert tremendous pressure on a mixture of ground soybeans and water. Without these presses the final product is a soft, unformed custard, unsuitable for slicing. However, homemade curd can be used in dishes such as scrambled eggs with bean curd and pudding dessert, dribbled with honey, that call for mashed bean curd.

By fermenting soybeans with wheat and salt, the Chinese produce soy sauce, their master flavoring.

Dried soybeans that are moistened and kept moist, sprout into 2- to 3-inch roots that have a marvelously crunchy texture and a rich, nut-like taste.

Taken to its acme by vegetarian Buddhist monks, the soybean in its many forms has been used in artful imitations of meat dishes that look and taste like chicken or pork.

Almost any vegetable can be cooked in the Chinese style. In addition to our usual ones, some off-beat types are especially interesting to try. A Chinese friend once identified a common weed in my garden as a favorite ingredient in soups and stir-fried dishes. It was purslane, that pest to all gardeners, which is now no longer a pest to me.

The white flesh of watermelon rind is remarkably crisp, and can be substituted for water chestnuts. First, cut out the pink, sweet flesh then carefully peel away the hard, green outer rind before thinly slicing the white rind.

The crunchiness of Jerusalem artichokes and rutabagas is useful in the same manner. Artichokes tend to disintegrate, so cook them as briefly as possible.

Vegetables taste best when they are fresh, young and tender. Don't buy them far in advance of use, although you might be tempted to do so to save time shopping. Flavor suffers and vitamins are diminished.

On the whole, one can't cook in the Chinese manner with frozen vegetables. The crispness, so prized in stir-frying, is destroyed by freezing. One of the few exceptions to this is shelled peas.

Some Examples of Vitamins in Vegetables

Vitamin A—Asparagus, broccoli, carrots, celery cabbage, parsley, spinach, sweet potatoes, turnip greens, watercress

Vitamin B_1—Soybeans, peas

Vitamin B_2—Soybeans, turnip greens

Pantothenic Acid—Broccoli, soybeans, mushrooms

Vitamin B_6—Peas, turnips

Vitamin B_{12}—Soybeans

Vitamin C—Broccoli, peppers

Vitamin E— Carrots, peas, sweet potatoes

Stir-Fried Bean Curd with Celery Cabbage

Bon

Serves 3-4

3   cakes fresh bean curd
½   pound celery cabbage
2   teaspoons cornstarch
2   tablespoons water
½   cup stock
1   tablespoon soy sauce
1½ tablespoons oil
½   teaspoon salt

1. Cut each cake of bean curd in 3 equal parts. Then slice each part in fourths.

2. Slice celery cabbage into 1-inch pieces across the rib.

3. Combine cornstarch and water.

4. Mix together stock and soy sauce.

5. Heat oil in a *wok* or large, heavy skillet having a lid. Stir-fry celery cabbage sprinkled with salt for 2 minutes.

6. Add sliced bean curd and stir carefully with a spatula for 1 minute.

7. Pour in stock-soy mixture, bring to a boil, cover, reduce heat, and simmer for 5 minutes.

8. Stir cornstarch mixture and add to celery cabbage and bean curd. Mix until sauce is thickened.

Comments:

1. Canned bean curd may be substituted satisfactorily for fresh curd.

2. *Bok choy*, or Chinese cabbage may be substituted for celery cabbage. It is sold in oriental groceries.

Vegetables

Bean Curd Sautéed with Eggs

moyer

Serves 5-6

3 eggs
1½ tablespoons cornstarch
3 tablespoons water
1 teaspoon salt
4 cakes fresh bean curd
3 tablespoons oil
  salt and pepper, to taste

1. Beat the eggs well in a bowl.

2. Mix cornstarch and water. Pour into eggs and add 1 teaspoon of salt.

3. Cut each bean curd into 1½-inch squares. Then cut each piece into slices ¼-inch thick.

4. Add bean curd to egg mixture.

5. Heat oil until hot in a large, heavy frying pan. Remove sliced bean curd from egg dip with a slotted spoon and place the curd in frying pan.

6. Sauté bean curd until light brown, then turn with a spatula and brown on the other side.

7. Stir remaining egg, pour in, and cook until set. Divide into serving portions and serve at once.

8. Sprinkle with salt and freshly-ground pepper if desired.

Comment:

I frequently prepare thinner, crisp pancakes by cooking this quantity in 2 frying pans at the same time. Our family has adopted it as a favorite breakfast dish.

Stir-Fried Bean Curd with Black Mushrooms

Serves 4

12	dried black mushrooms warm water to cover
1	pound fresh bean curd (about 5 pieces)
2	scallions
½	teaspoon salt
¼	teaspoon honey
½	cup mushroom soaking liquid
3	tablespoons oil
2	tablespoons soy sauce

1. Soak dried black mushrooms in warm water for 1 hour. Save ½ cup of soaking liquid. Remove hard stems and cut mushrooms in slices.

2. Cut each bean curd in half. Then slice each half in 4 pieces. Dry on paper toweling.

3. Cut scallions into 1-inch pieces.

4. Mix salt and honey with the mushroom soaking liquid.

5. Heat oil in a large, heavy skillet having a lid. Add bean curd and cook for 2 minutes, uncovered, turning gently with a spatula.

6. Add scallions and mushrooms. Sprinkle with soy sauce, mixing carefully. Pour in salt, honey mixture, heat to boiling, reduce heat and simmer, covered, for 3 to 5 minutes.

Comments:

1. Canned bean curd is a quite good substitute for fresh curd in this recipe.

2. One-half pound of fresh mushrooms may be substituted for dried black mushrooms. Cut mushrooms into ¼-inch slices and start with Step 2. Increase to 4 scallions. In Step 4, use stock instead of mushroom soaking liquid. Stir-fry mushrooms for 2 minutes, *then* add scallions and bean curd. Cook for 2 minutes, stirring carefully with a spatula. Continue as directed in Step 6. Two teaspoons cornstarch may be added to the stock, if desired.

please turn page

Vegetables

Stir-Fried Bean Curd with Squash

Serves 4

3. To serve bean curd as a cold appetizer, simmer whole curd in water for 3 minutes. Drain well, being careful not to break cakes. When cool, slice each cake in half, then cut each half in 3 pieces. Combine amounts of salt, honey, oil and soy sauce used in this recipe and pour over bean curd. Sprinkle with chopped scallion and freshly-ground pepper and serve. Or, eliminate salt and honey, increasing soy sauce to taste.

1	pound fresh bean curd (about 5 pieces)
¼ - ½	pound young yellow squash
4	scallions
3	tablespoons oil
¼	teaspoon salt
2	tablespoons soy sauce
¼	teaspoon salt

1. Cut each cake of bean curd in 3 equal parts. Then slice each part in 4 pieces.

2. Scrub yellow squash. Cut in thin slices.

3. Cut scallions into 1-inch pieces.

4. Heat oil until hot in a *wok* or large, heavy skillet. Add ¼ teaspoon of salt and scallions, stir-frying for a few seconds. Add yellow squash and stir-fry for 1 minute. Add bean curd, and stir gently with a spatula for 2 minutes.

5. Sprinkle with soy sauce and ¼ teaspoon of salt, turning carefully to blend in seasonings.

6. Serve immediately.

Homemade Bean Curd with Soybeans

Comments:

1. Kohlrabi or Chinese pleated melon may be substituted for yellow squash. Peel and cut kohlrabi into thin slices 1½ by 1-inch. Pleated melon must be peeled of its sharp edges, then sliced thinly. When cooked, it turns a lovely translucent green.

2. "Bean curd with scallions" may be prepared by eliminating the squash and increasing the scallions to eight. In Step 4, stir-fry scallions for 1 minute. Add sliced bean curd and stir gently with a spatula on high heat for 2 minutes. Omit Step 5. Mix soy sauce with 1 teaspoon of salt, stirring well to dissolve. Sprinkle over bean curd. Cook for another minute, mixing carefully. Add more salt to taste, if desired.

1	pound dried soybeans
3	quarts water
1	cup cider vinegar or 5 teaspoons gypsum
1	teaspoon salt

1. Soak soybeans 4 to 5 hours or overnight in a large bowl, fully covered with water. Discard soaking water.

2. Add 3 quarts of fresh water. Grind mixture very fine in a blender to make a soybean "milk."

3. Heat soybean milk until warm. Strain through several layers of cheesecloth. Squeeze residue very dry.

4. Bring soybean milk to a boil in a large pot, reduce heat and simmer for 20 minutes, stirring occasionally. Place an asbestos pad under the pot to avoid scorching the soybean milk.

5. Let cool for 10 minutes (until temperature drops to 180°). Add vinegar or gypsum slowly and stir gently to mix.

please turn page

Homemade Bean Curd with Soybean Powder

6. Leave undisturbed for 15 minutes. Then strain through cheesecloth. Discard liquid. Place bean curd in a cheesecloth bag. Rinse in a large pot of cold water to remove remaining vinegar or gypsum.

7. Place cheesecloth bag in a colander or sieve and allow to drain for at least 1 hour. Press out all liquid possible.

8. Remove curd from bag and mix with salt. Refrigerate and serve in recipes calling for mashed curd, or as a pudding dessert with honey.

Comments:

1. Gypsum is calcium sulfate, available in drug stores.

2. An asbestos pad can be purchased in shops specializing in cooking utensils.

3. Soybean pulp may be added to ground beef up to a 1 to 2 ratio. Prepare beef as usual.

3   cups soybean powder
2   quarts water
1   cup cider vinegar or 5 teaspoons gypsum
     cold water
1   teaspoon salt

1. Mix soybean powder in a large bowl with 2 cups of the water to make a paste. Add remaining water (1 ½ quarts) and beat until smooth. Let stand for 2 hours.

2. Bring soybean solution to a boil in a large pot, reduce heat and simmer for 20 minutes, stirring occasionally. Place an asbestos pad (available in shops selling cooking utensils) under the pot to avoid scorching the soybean milk.

3. Let cool for 10 minutes (until temperature drops to 180°). Add vinegar or gypsum slowly and stir gently to mix.

4. Leave undisturbed for 15 minutes. Then strain through cheesecloth. Discard liquid. Place bean curd in a cheesecloth bag. Rinse in a large pot of cold water to remove remaining vinegar or gypsum.

Bean Sprouts,
Peppers and Tomatoes

Serves 4-6

1   pound mung bean sprouts
2   medium-sized tomatoes
     boiling water
1   green pepper
2   tablespoons soy sauce
¼   teaspoon honey
2   tablespoons oil
½   teaspoon salt

5. Place cheesecloth bag in a colander or sieve and allow to drain for at least 1 hour. Press out all liquid possible.

6. Remove curd from bag and mix with salt. Refrigerate and serve in recipes calling for mashed curd, or as a pudding dessert with honey.

Comments:

1. Soybean powder is available at health food stores and many supermarkets.

2. Japanese markets sell an instant *tofu* (bean curd) mix, which produces virtually the same type of curd.

3. Gypsum is calcium sulfate, available in drug stores.

1. Drain bean sprouts and dry well on paper toweling.

2. Drop tomatoes into pot of boiling water. Turn off heat. After 3 minutes, remove tomatoes, cool slightly and peel. Cut into ½-inch cubes.

3. Discard seeds of green pepper and cut pepper into thin slivers.

4. Thoroughly blend soy sauce and honey in a cup.

5. Heat oil until hot in a wok or large, heavy frying pan. Add salt, then bean sprouts. Stir-fry for 1 minute.

6. Add green peppers and stir-fry for 2 minutes. Pour in soy sauce-honey mixture. Mix well.

7. Add tomato cubes, and stir until heated through.

8. Serve immediately.

Vegetables

Stir-Fried Broccoli

Serves 4

1	pound broccoli
1	clove garlic
2	tablespoons oil
½	teaspoon salt
1	tablespoon soy sauce
¼	teaspoon honey
½	cup stock or water

1. Pare skin off heavy stalks of broccoli. Cut broccoli stalks diagonally into ½-inch slices. Cut flowering ends into 1-inch cubes.

2. Mince garlic.

3. Heat oil in a *wok* or large, heavy frying pan having a lid. Stir-fry garlic and salt for a few seconds. Add broccoli and stir-fry for 2 minutes, uncovered.

4. Blend together soy sauce and honey. Sprinkle mixture on broccoli, stirring until well mixed. Pour in stock and bring to a boil.

5. Cover, reduce heat and cook on medium for about 3 minutes, until broccoli is tender, but still crisp.

6. Serve immediately. Do not overcook or broccoli will lose its clear green color.

Comments:

1. If desired, thicken with 2 teaspoons of cornstarch mixed with 3 tablespoons of water.

2. One pound tender part of asparagus may be substituted for broccoli. Slice asparagus diagonally into ½-inch pieces. Very thick asparagus stalks may be pared to remove tough skins.

Vegetables

Bean Sprouts with Mixed Vegetables

Serves 4

1	large carrot
2	tablespoons water
2	stalks celery
½	pound mung bean sprouts
1	large onion
1½	tablespoons oil
¼	teaspoon salt
1	tablespoon soy sauce

1. Cut carrot into thin strips. Heat water in a small, heavy pot. Add carrot strips and steam, covered, for a few minutes, until somewhat softened.

2. Cut celery into thin slivers.

3. Dry bean sprouts well on paper toweling.

4. Peel onion and cut in half vertically, through the root. Lay on the cut side and slice thinly.

5. Heat oil until hot in a *wok* or large, heavy skillet. Add salt and celery strips, stir-frying for 1 minute. Add bean sprouts, onions and carrots at 1-minute intervals and stir-fry.

6. Sprinkle soy sauce on mixture and mix well for 1 minute. Serve immediately.

Steamed Eggplant with Sesame Sauce

Serves 4

1	large eggplant
2	tablespoons *tahini* (sesame paste)
2	tablespoons water
2	teaspoons Chinese sesame oil
1	teaspoon salt

1. Rinse off eggplant. Cut through the skin in several places to help the steam penetrate.

2. Prepare a steaming pot with a rack over boiling water. Place eggplant on a heat-resistant platter, then steam on the rack, covered, for 20 minutes.

3. Mix sesame paste and water.

4. Let eggplant cool just enough to handle, then remove the skin. With a sharp, large knife, slice the eggplant quickly into bite-sized pieces.

5. Arrange on a serving dish. Mix with Chinese sesame oil and salt.

6. Sprinkle half the diluted sesame paste over the eggplant. Serve immediately. Pass a small dish of the remaining sesame paste for those who prefer a stronger flavor.

265

Vegetables

Round Cabbage
with
Green Peppers

Serves 5-6

1	pound round cabbage
2	medium-sized green peppers
½	cup stock or water
1	tablespoon soy sauce
½	teaspoon honey
1 ½	tablespoons oil
½	teaspoon salt

1. Cut cabbage into 1-inch squares.

2. Cut green peppers into 1-inch squares, after discarding seeds.

3. Combine stock, soy sauce and honey.

4. Heat oil in a *wok* or large, heavy skillet having a lid. Add salt, then cabbage and stir-fry for 2 minutes uncovered. Add green peppers and stir-fry for 1 minute.

5. Stir stock mixture and pour into cabbage. Heat to boiling, cover, and cook on medium heat for about 3 minutes, until just tender but still crunchy. Old cabbage may require longer cooking.

6. Serve immediately.

Comments:

1. The vegetables may be slivered instead. Reduce cooking time slightly.

2. Black mushrooms may be substituted for green peppers, using ¼ cup mushroom soaking liquid instead of stock. Soak mushrooms in warm water for at least 1 hour. Squeeze dry. Cut large mushrooms in quarters, smaller ones in half. To prepare 1 hour in advance, reduce cooking time and finish when ready to serve.

Celery Cabbage with Dried Chestnuts

Serves 5-6

25   dried chestnuts
      boiling water to cover
1   pound celery cabbage
¾   cup stock or water
½   teaspoon salt
½   teaspoon honey
½   tablespoon cornstarch
2   tablespoons water
1½   tablespoons oil

1. Drop dried chestnuts into a pot of boiling water. Parboil for 1½ to 2 hours, until almost tender. Drain.

2. Cut celery cabbage into 1½-inch pieces across the rib.

3. Combine stock, salt and honey.

4. Mix together cornstarch and 2 tablespoons of water.

5. Heat oil in a wok or large, heavy skillet having a lid. Stir-fry celery cabbage for 1 minute, uncovered.

6. Add parboiled whole chestnuts and stir well. Stir stock mixture and pour into celery cabbage. Bring to a boil, cover, reduce heat, and simmer for 10 minutes.

7. Stir cornstarch mixture and pour into celery cabbage. Mix until sauce is thickened.

Comment:

This dish may be prepared 1 hour in advance and reheated when ready to serve.

Vegetables

Sweet and Sour Cabbage

Serves 4-5

1 pound round cabbage
1 clove garlic
2 tablespoons vinegar, preferably rice wine or white
   wine
2 tablespoons honey
1 tablespoon soy sauce
1 teaspoon cornstarch
1 tablespoon water
1½ tablespoons oil
½ teaspoon salt

1. Cut cabbage into 1-inch squares.

2. Mince garlic.

3. Combine vinegar, honey, and soy sauce.

4. Mix together cornstarch and water.

5. Heat oil in a *wok* or large, heavy skillet. Stir-fry garlic and salt for a few seconds. Add cabbage and stir-fry for 2 minutes.

6. Mix vinegar-honey liquid and pour into cabbage. Stir-fry cabbage for 2 more minutes, or until tender, but still crisp.

7. Stir cornstarch mixture and pour into cabbage. Mix until sauce is thickened.

8. Serve immediately.

Comments:

1. To prepare 1 hour in advance, reduce cooking time and finish when ready to serve.

2. Sweet and sour cabbage may be served lightly chilled. Refrigerate, then take out 30 minutes before serving.

Celery Cabbage
Creamed in Soy Milk

Serves 4

1	pound celery cabbage
4	heaping teaspoons soybean powder
1	cup water
1½	tablespoons cornstarch
½	teaspoon honey
2	tablespoons oil
½	teaspoon salt
½	cup stock

1. Cut celery cabbage into 1-inch pieces across the rib.

2. Place soybean powder and water in a pint jar. Tighten lid and shake well. Add cornstarch and honey to soybean "milk."

3. Heat oil in a *wok* or large, heavy skillet having a lid. Add salt and celery cabbage, stirring for 2 minutes, uncovered.

4. Pour in stock, heat to boiling, cover, reduce heat and cook on medium for about 6 minutes.

5. Stir cornstarch-soybean mixture well. Add to celery cabbage and stir 1 to 2 minutes, until sauce is thickened.

Comments:

1. This dish may be prepared 1 hour in advance and reheated when ready to serve.

2. Soybean milk serves as a delicate but flavorful sauce for celery cabbage and other vegetables. Substitute skim milk if desired. Reduce heat to low when adding to celery cabbage and stir until thickened.

Vegetables

Lima Beans
with
Bamboo Shoots

Serves 4

2	cups frozen baby lima beans
2	tablespoons cloud ear mushrooms
	warm water to cover
4	scallions
1½	tablespoons oil
¼	cup stock or water
½	cup thinly-sliced bamboo shoots
1	tablespoon soy sauce

1. Thaw baby limas completely. Slip off skins, which are much tougher than the inside flesh.

2. Soak cloud ear mushrooms for 30 minutes in warm water. Rinse well. Cut out any hard parts.

3. Mince scallions.

4. Heat oil in a *wok* or large, heavy skillet having a lid. Stir-fry de-skinned limas for 1 minute. Add stock or water, bring to a boil, cover, reduce heat and simmer until tender, 5 to 8 minutes.

5. Add cloud ear mushrooms, bamboo shoots, chopped scallions and soy sauce. Stir well and serve immediately.

Comment:

To prepare 1 hour in advance, reserve the scallions and add when reheating the dish.

Red and Green Peppers   Chinese Radishes

Serves 4

2   tablespoons cloud ear
    mushrooms (optional)
2   large green peppers
1   sweet red pepper
¼   cup stock
½   teaspoon honey
1   tablespoon soy sauce
1½ tablespoons oil
½   teaspoon salt

1. Soak cloud ear mushrooms for 30 minutes in warm water. Rinse well. Cut out any hard parts.

2. Cut peppers in strips after discarding seeds.

3. Combine stock, honey and soy sauce.

4. Heat oil in a *wok* or large, heavy skillet having a lid. Add salt and peppers, stir-frying for 1 minute, uncovered.

5. Add cloud ear mushrooms. Pour stock mixture in pan. Heat to boiling, cover, and simmer for 2 to 3 minutes.

6. Serve immediately.

Serves 4

1   pound Chinese radishes
2   scallions
1½ tablespoons oil
1   tablespoon soy sauce

1. Peel radishes. Grate them coarsely and drain on paper toweling. Do not grate in advance, or considerable liquid seeps out of the vegetable.

2. Mince scallions.

3. Heat oil until very hot in a *wok* or large, heavy skillet. Stir-fry radishes for about 2 minutes, until just tender, but still crisp.

4. Mix in soy sauce and scallions.

5. Serve immediately.

Vegetables

Diced Winter Radishes and Carrots

Serves 5-6

1 pound winter radishes
3 carrots
2 scallions
1½ tablespoons soy sauce
½ teaspoon honey
¼ cup stock or water
1½ tablespoons oil

1. Peel winter radishes and cut in ½-inch dice.

2. Dice carrots the same size.

3. Cut scallions in ½-inch pieces.

4. In a small mixing bowl, combine soy sauce, honey and stock, stirring well.

5. Heat oil in wok or large, heavy frying pan having a lid. Stir-fry radishes for 1 minute, uncovered, then add carrots, stir-frying for another minute.

6. Pour in soy sauce mixture and bring to a boil. Cover and simmer for about 5 minutes, until vegetables are just tender but still crisp.

7. Remove lid, add scallions, and cook on a high heat for 2 minutes to evaporate some of the remaining juices.

Comment:

To cook 1 hour ahead, add soy sauce mixture and simmer 3 minutes. Finish cooking when ready to serve.

Soybean Sprouts with Celery

Serves 4-5

1	pound soybean sprouts
¼	cup water
3	stalks celery
2	scallions
½	cup stock or water
1	tablespoon soy sauce
½	teaspoon honey
½	tablespoon cornstarch
2	tablespoons water
1 ½	tablespoons oil
½	teaspoon salt

1. Place soybean sprouts and ¼ cup of water in a heavy pot. Bring water to a boil, cover, and steam until just tender, about 12 minutes.

2. Shred celery finely.

3. Cut scallions into 1-inch pieces.

4. Combine stock, soy sauce and honey.

5. Mix together cornstarch and 2 tablespoons of water.

6. Heat oil in a wok or large, heavy skillet. Stir-fry celery strips for 2 minutes. Add soybean sprouts and stir-fry for 1 to 2 minutes.

7. Stir in scallions. Stir stock-soy combination and pour into sprouts. Bring to a boil and stir for ½ minute.

8. Stir cornstarch mixture. Pour into sprouts and mix until sauce is thickened.

9. Serve immediately.

Vegetables

Spinach
with
Black Mushrooms

Serves 5

12 dried black mushrooms
2   cups warm water
1   pound fresh, young
    spinach
1   clove garlic (optional)
1   tablespoon sherry
2   tablespoons soy sauce
½   teaspoon honey
½   teaspoon salt
1   tablespoon cornstarch
2   tablespoons water
1½ tablespoons oil
1   cup mushroom soaking
    water

1. Soak dried black mushrooms in 2 cups of warm water for at least 1 hour. Squeeze out excess water. Remove hard stems. Save 1 cup of the soaking water. Leave mushrooms whole unless they are very large; then cut in half.

2. Rinse spinach well and cut off any tough stems. Don't shake off all moisture.

3. Mince garlic.

4. Mix together sherry, soy sauce, honey and salt.

5. Combine cornstarch and water.

6. Heat oil in a *wok* or medium-sized heavy skillet having a lid. Stir-fry black mushrooms for 2 minutes. Mix in sherry-soy blend and stir for 1 minute.

7. Add mushroom soaking water, heat to boiling, cover, reduce heat and simmer for about 10 minutes, until mushrooms are very tender.

8. Stir cornstarch mixture. Pour into mushrooms and mix until sauce is thickened.

9. Place spinach in a large, heavy pot, covered. Steam on a medium heat until spinach has just wilted. Check occasionally, stirring, and add a tablespoon or two of water if all moisture is gone. When spinach is limp, turn heat on high to evaporate any remaining water. Stir constantly.

Spinach
with
Ground Sesame

Bon trop salé.

Serves 4

10. Arrange spinach on a serving dish. Pour hot mushrooms and sauce over spinach and serve immediately.

Comments:

1. Spinach with black mushrooms is an excellent accompaniment for delicate meats like veal, fresh beef tongue, or fish fillets, cooked western style.

2. Frozen spinach may be substituted for fresh spinach. Thaw a 10-ounce package completely and place on a high heat until the moisture has evaporated. Stir frequently.

1 tablespoon sesame seeds
1 pound fresh young spinach
1 clove garlic
1 scallion, white stem only
1 tablespoon Chinese sesame oil
2 tablespoons soy sauce
1 teaspoon honey

1. Place sesame seeds in a small, heavy frying pan. On a moderate flame, heat until lightly-browned. Stir frequently.

2. Grind roasted seeds, coarsely, with a mortar and pestle or in a blender. Extra ground sesame seeds may be prepared at the same time for other recipes, such as *Carrots with Ground Sesame* (see index).

3. Rinse spinach well, cutting off any tough stems. Shake off all water possible.

4. Mince garlic, then mince white stem of scallion.

please turn page

Vegetables

Spinach
in
Soy Sauce

Serves 4

1 pound fresh, young spinach
2 slices fresh ginger (optional)
1 ½ tablespoons oil
3 tablespoons soy sauce
½ teaspoon honey

5. Heat Chinese sesame oil in large *wok* or frying pan. Stir-fry spinach until it has just wilted.

6. Mix in garlic and scallion. Blend together soy sauce and honey, then pour over spinach. Stir well.

7. Sprinkle with ground sesame seeds, mix them in and serve immediately.

Comments:

1. Frozen spinach may be substituted for fresh spinach. Thaw a 10-ounce package completely and squeeze dry.

2. If Chinese sesame oil is unavailable, peanut oil may be substituted.

1. Rinse spinach well and remove root ends and any large stems. Shake off as much water as possible. Cut spinach in 2-inch pieces.

2. Mince ginger.

3. Heat oil until hot in a *wok* or large, heavy skillet. Stir-fry ginger for a few seconds. Add enough spinach to fill pan, stir-fry until it begins to wilt, and continue adding more until all the spinach is used.

Vegetarian Dish
of the Buddhists

Serves 4-6

4. Stir-fry on high heat to evaporate any remaining water on the spinach. Blend together soy sauce and honey. Pour over spinach and stir for ½ minute.

5. Serve immediately.

Comments:

1. The secret of this dish is to start with *young* spinach, mild and delicate, without the bitter, oxalic acid taste that develops in mature spinach. The home gardener who grows spinach has the great advantage of being able to pick when the flavor is at its peak.

2. Frozen spinach may be substituted for fresh spinach. Thaw a 10-ounce package completely and squeeze dry.

6	dried black mushrooms
	warm water to cover
16	dried lily buds
2	tablespoons cloud ear mushrooms
	warm water to cover
2	ounces dried bean curd
2	ounces cellophane noodles (mung bean threads)
3	cakes fresh bean curd
	boiling water
	frying oil
¼	cup hair seaweed
	boiling water
¼	pound snow peas
1	onion
3	tablespoons oil
1	cup celery cabbage, cut across rib into 2-inch pieces
½	cup shredded bamboo shoots
20	canned ginkgo nuts
2	tablespoons soy sauce
½	teaspoon salt
¼	teaspoon honey
1½	cups water
2	teaspoons Chinese sesame oil

1. Soak dried black mushrooms in warm water for 30 minutes. Squeeze dry. Remove hard stems. Cut large mushrooms in half.

please turn page

277

Vegetables

2. Soak lily buds and cloud ear mushrooms for 30 minutes in warm water. Cut off hard ends of lily buds and cut buds in half. Cut out any hard parts of cloud ear mushrooms. Pull "ears" apart.

3. Break up dried bean curd into a few pieces. Boil for 20 minutes and drain. Cut in strips 1 inch wide and 2 inches long.

4. Cover cellophane noodles with boiling water and soak for 20 minutes. Cut into 4-inch lengths.

5. Cut fresh bean curd into 1-inch cubes and deep fry (for recipe for *Deep-Fried Bean Curd with Sesame Sauce,* see index).

6. Cook hair seaweed in boiling water for 3 minutes. Drain and wash thoroughly in cold water. Squeeze out excess water.

7. Remove stem ends from snow peas. Cut in slivers.

8. Peel onion and cut vertically through the root end. Lay down on cut surface and shred.

9. Heat 3 tablespoons of oil in a large, heavy pot. Stir-fry celery cabbage for 1 minute. Add onion and stir-fry for 1 minute.

10. Add fried bean curd, bamboo shoots, ginkgo nuts and drained, soaked ingredients. Stir until heated.

11. Add soy sauce, salt, honey and water. Heat to boiling, cover, reduce heat and simmer for 10 to 12 minutes.

12. Add snow peas and stir until they turn a bright green. Taste for seasoning and add more soy sauce or salt if desired.

13. Flavor with Chinese sesame oil just before serving.

Comments:

1. This exotic meal-in-one will keep up to a week, refrigerated. It may be reheated several times without harming its delicate flavor. Preferably add snow peas just before serving

2. Although the Buddhist dish traditionally requires 10 to 12 major ingredients, it can be prepared with fewer. For the most authentic taste, however, use as many ingredients as you can possibly obtain.

3. One teaspoon or more of bean curd cheese may be added when simmering the ingredients.

String Beans with Fresh Mushrooms

Serves 4-5

1 pound young string beans
½ pound fresh mushrooms
2 scallions
¼ cup stock or water
½ teaspoon honey
1 tablespoon soy sauce
1 tablespoon oil
1 ½ tablespoons oil
½ teaspoon salt

1. Cut ends off beans and slice into 1 ½-inch pieces.

2. Wash mushrooms well and dry on paper toweling. Slice ¼ inch thick.

3. Cut scallions into ½-inch pieces.

4. Combine stock, honey and soy sauce.

5. Heat 1 tablespoon of oil until hot in a *wok* or large, heavy skillet having a lid. Stir-fry mushrooms for 1 minute. Add scallions and stir-fry 1 minute. Remove mixture from the pan.

6. In the same pan, heat 1 ½ tablespoons of oil. Stir-fry string beans for 2 minutes. Mix in salt and stir well.

7. Pour in stock mixture and heat to boiling. Cover, reduce heat and simmer about 5 minutes until tender but still crunchy.

8. Return mushrooms to the pan and heat thoroughly.

Comments:

1. This dish may be prepared 30 minutes in advance and re-heated.

2. Cloud ear mushrooms may be substituted for fresh mushrooms. Soak for 30 minutes in warm water, rinse well and cut out any hard parts. Add at the same time as the stock mixture.

Vegetables

Slivered String Beans with Water Chestnuts

Serves 4

1	pound young string beans
1	clove garlic
10-12	water chestnuts
¼	cup stock
½	teaspoon honey
1½	tablespoons oil
½	teaspoon salt
1	tablespoon soy sauce

1. Cut ends off string beans. "French" each bean by slicing lengthwise in half.

2. Mince garlic.

3. Lay water chestnuts flat on wooden board. Slice vertically into thin slices.

4. Combine stock and honey.

5. Heat oil in a *wok* or large, heavy skillet having a lid. Stir-fry garlic and salt for a few seconds, then add "frenched" beans. Stir-fry for 3 minutes. Mix in soy sauce.

6. Pour in stock and honey, and add water chestnuts. Heat to boiling, cover, reduce heat and simmer for 3 to 4 minutes, until beans are just tender, but still crisp.

7. Serve immediately.

Comments:

1. If desired, thicken sauce by cooking with 1 teaspoon of cornstarch dissolved in 1 tablespoon of water. Stir constantly.

2. Whole beans, cut in 1½-inch lengths, may be substituted for "frenched" beans. Increase simmering time about 2 minutes, until beans are just tender.

Cauliflower
and Black Mushrooms

Serves 4

6   dried black mushrooms
       warm water to cover
1   pound cauliflower
3   scallions
2   teaspoons cornstarch
2   tablespoons water
1½   tablespoons oil
¼   cup stock or water
2   tablespoons soy sauce
½   cup mushroom soaking
       water

1. Soak dried black mushrooms in warm water for at least 1 hour. Squeeze out excess water, saving ½ cup of the soaking water. Cut in quarters.

2. Slice cauliflower thinly in pieces about 1½ by 1 inch in size.

3. Cut scallions in 1-inch pieces.

4. Mix together cornstarch and water.

5. Heat oil in a *wok* or large, heavy skillet having a lid. Stir-fry cauliflower for 2 minutes, uncovered. Add stock or water, bring to a boil, cover, and steam on medium heat for about 5 minutes, until almost tender.

6. Remove lid and add mushrooms and scallions, stirring for ½ minute. Pour in soy sauce and mushroom soaking water and bring to a boil.

7. Stir cornstarch mixture, pour into cauliflower, and mix until thickened.

Vegetables

Desserts

Chapter 24

Sweets are rarely served at the end of a typical Chinese dinner. Perhaps it is because the main dishes are so varied and savory that the Chinese seem to have little desire for a rich dessert.

This does not mean that the Chinese do not enjoy a sweet occasionally. Cakes or pastries often accompany tea as a snack. One of the most popular sweets, *Steamed Sponge Cake* (see index), is easily prepared, using whole wheat flour.

During a banquet, a warm, sweet soup or multi-ingredient rice pudding may be included to stimulate the palate. Watermelon slices and bananas were served at a Chinese state-banquet recently given for an important newsman from the United States.

If dessert is to be served, fresh fruit is usually most suitable. Pears, apples, pineapples, navel oranges, and bananas are refreshing. To prepare oranges, peel them, cutting off all the white membrane under the skin and slice cross-wise ¼-inch thick to serve. To use bananas, peel and slice with the rolling cut (see "The Shape of Things: Cutting Foods for Chinese Cooking").

In season, vary desserts with fresh peaches, apricots, kumquats, papaya, persimmons, tangerines or watermelon.

For a special Chinese flavor, serve canned loquats or lychees (also dried). During June and July, fresh lychees are sold in Chinatown, or may be ordered in advance by mail. (See "A Guide To Chinese Cooking Ingredients")

Almond Float

Serves 6

2 packages unflavored gelatin
1½ cups water
¼ pound raw blanched almonds (skinless)
2 cups water
5 tablespoons honey
2½ teaspoons almond extract
2 cups water
4½ tablespoons honey
1 teaspoon almond extract
1 cup assorted fresh fruit (pears, grapes, strawberries, bananas, watermelon, navel oranges, etc.)

1. In a small saucepan, soak unflavored gelatin in 1½ cups of water.

2. Put blanched almonds and 2 cups of water in a blender. Pulverize until almonds are very fine.

3. Strain almond mixture into a medium-sized mixing bowl, through several layers of cheesecloth. Squeeze out all possible liquid. Save almond pulp for use in baking or in a meatloaf.

4. Heat gelatin and water until boiling and gelatin is thoroughly dissolved.

5. Pour in almond liquid and 5 tablespoons of the honey, cooking until honey is dissolved. Allow to cool, then add almond extract.

6. Pour into rectangular 6-inch by 10-inch pan, and refrigerate overnight.

7. In a medium-sized saucepan, heat 2 cups of water with 4½ tablespoons of honey. Bring to a boil and dissolve honey completely. Cool and stir in almond extract. Chill for several hours.

8. Choose two or more types of fruits, different but harmonious in color. Slice or dice fruit.

9. Cut almond gelatin into diamond-shaped pieces.

10. Divide gelatin among 6 individual deep soup bowls. Add sweetened water and fresh fruit.

Comment:

Canned lychees or loquats may be added to the fresh fruits for a more Chinese flavor.

Almond Soup with Honey

Serves 6

1	pound raw blanched almonds (skinless)
2	cups water
2	cups water
½	cup honey
⅛	teaspoon salt
4	teaspoons almond extract slivered almonds

1. Combine half of the blanched almonds and 2 cups of water in a blender. Pulverize until almonds are very fine. Repeat with other half of almonds and 2 more cups of water.

2. In a large saucepan, heat almond puree to boiling. Reduce heat and simmer, covered, for 10 minutes. Allow to cool.

3. Strain into a large mixing bowl through several layers of cheesecloth. Squeeze out all possible liquid. Save almond pulp for another use.

4. Add enough water to make 6 cups of liquid. Pour back into the saucepan, add honey and salt and heat to dissolve.

5. Add almond extract. Taste and add more honey, if desired.

6. Serve immediately in deep soup bowls, garnished with slivered almonds.

Desserts

Steamed Sponge Cake

Serves 8

butter for greasing pan
5   eggs, separated
¾   cup raw sugar
1   teaspoon vanilla
    pinch of salt
1   cup sifted whole wheat flour

1. Butter an 8-inch square cake pan.

2. In a medium-sized mixing bowl, beat egg yolks well with a fork. Add sugar slowly and beat until well blended. Flavor with vanilla and salt.

3. In a large mixing bowl beat egg whites until stiff. (To test, hold egg beater upside down, and egg white will keep its shaped.)

4. Mix egg yolks into egg whites and stir gently but well. Sift flour over egg mixture and fold in lightly.

5. Pour batter into buttered cake pan. Run a knife through the batter several times to burst any large air pockets.

6. Place pan on a rack in a large wok or pot over boiling water. Cover and steam for about 25 minutes.

7. Turn pan upside down on a plate to remove cake. When the cake has cooled enough to handle, turn right side up. Cut cake into 2-inch squares, and serve, preferably hot.

Comment:

In this book, honey has been used consistently as the sweetening agent for its nutritive value, contrasted to the empty calories of sugar. In this recipe, however, I am specifying sugar for improved texture.

Ginger Tea

Serves 2-3

2 cups water
¼ cup sliced fresh ginger root
2-3 tablespoons honey

1. In a saucepan combine water and ginger. Bring to a boil and cook covered for 15 minutes.

2. Remove ginger. Stir in 2 tablespoons of honey. Taste, and add another tablespoon of honey, if desired.

3. Serve hot.

Comment:

The Chinese prescribe ginger tea for an upset stomach.

Peanut Soup with Honey

Serves 6

1½ cups raw blanched peanuts (skinless)
4½ cups water
⅛ teaspoon salt
3 tablespoons honey

1. Put peanuts and water in a heavy saucepan. Heat to boiling, and simmer, covered, for 2½ to 3 hours, stirring occasionally.

2. Add salt and honey. Let stand for several hours to allow seasonings to penetrate.

3. Heat and serve moderately hot.

Desserts

Plum Sauce

1	cup skinned, pitted plums
1	cup skinned, pitted apricots
½	cup apple sauce
½	cup chopped pimiento
1	cup honey
½	cup vinegar

1. Skin plums and apricots by dropping them in boiling water. Turn off heat and let stand for 3 minutes. The skins and pits are then easily removed.

2. In a heavy, medium-sized saucepan having a lid, combine all the ingredients. Heat to boiling, cover and simmer for 1 hour, stirring occasionally.

3. If the plum sauce has not thickened, remove cover and cook on a medium heat, stirring, until lightly thickened.

4. Pour into jars while still hot and tightly screw on caps. Put aside for 1 month in a cool dark place.

5. Serve in a dipping dish to accompany Chinese roast pork, barbecued spareribs, and egg rolls.

Desserts

Chapter 25

A Guide
to Chinese
Cooking Ingredients

Cooking with Chinese ingredients need not be confusing or difficult. They are much too delicious to ignore; so spend a few moments with the list in this chapter to learn what they are, how they are used, and why they are so special.

All the foods described can be ordered by mail from the Chinese sources listed here, unless otherwise specified. Some can also be purchased locally in supermarkets, health food stores, or gourmet shops. Most companies will send catalog sheets, listing many dried or canned (as a last resort) ingredients, which will last for months.

Kwong On Lung Importers
680 North Spring Street
Los Angeles, California 90012

Gim Fat Co., Inc.
953 Grant Avenue
San Francisco, California 94108

Wing Sing Chong Co., Inc.
921-931 Clay Street
San Francisco, California 94108

Kam Shing Company
2246 Wentworth Avenue
Chicago, Illinois 60616

Star Market
3349 North Clark Street
Chicago, Illinois 60657

Wing Wing
79 Harrison Avenue
Boston, Massachusetts 02111

The Infinity Company
173 Duane Street
New York, New York 10013

Katagiri & Co., Inc.
224 E. 59th Street
New York, New York 10022

Mon Fong Wo Company
36 Pell Street
New York, New York 10013

Oriental Country Store
12 Mott Street
New York, New York 10013

Oriental Import and Export Co.,
2009 Polk Street
Houston, Texas 77003

Should you want the pleasure of cooking with fresh Chinese vegetables, plan a trip to the nearest Chinatown with a well-thought-out marketing list. During this shopping expedition you will find a new world of foods, remarkable to the eye and to the palate. The Chinese have preserved "the old country" in their groceries as no other nationality has. They combine green grocer, butcher, fish market, china shop, hardware store, apothecary and delicacy shop under a single roof for very convenient shopping. Here are a few I know of in various parts of the U.S.:

Tuck Cheong and Co.
617 H Street, NW
Washington, D.C. 20001

Sam Wah Yick Kee Co.
2146 Rockwell Avenue
Cleveland, Ohio 44114

Wing On
1005 Race Street
Philadelphia, Pennsylvania
19107

Wing Fat Co.
35 Mott Street
New York, New York 10013

Wah Young Company
717 South King Street
Seattle, Washington 98104

Perhaps a description of a typical Chinese grocery will be helpful:

At the entrance is a large window displaying colorful fresh produce: snow peas, several kinds of Chinese cabbages, kohlrabi, lotus stems, fresh ginger root and other root vegetables. On the floor within the entrance you find a number of large barrels containing peanuts, fresh water chestnuts, *fava* beans and a variety of loose dried or fresh items. Ancient eggs are imported from Formosa and lately from mainland China, and presented in huge urns decorated with dragons. A cluster of barrels set to one side houses perishables like creamy fresh bean curd, mung bean sprouts, soybean sprouts, and soaked sea cucumber.

The refrigerator case displays an array of meats quite different from the usual supermarket selection. T-bone steak or prime ribs of beef are rarely found here. Instead, you see the Chinese favorites—oxtail, heart, liver, pig's feet, tongue, chicken feet and gizzards, pork bones, and very lean flank steak—an outstanding selection of nutrition-rich meats, which will be prepared to perfection by the Chinese.

Next to the fresh meat department is a small delicatessen showing freshly-roasted pork, often a complete side, barbecued spareribs, roast pork heads and ears, and roast duck and chicken prepared with the heads on. The heads remain to keep the marinating juices in the body cavity while roasting.

The fish department carries such varieties as butterfish, red snapper, squid, sea bass and shrimp, all very fresh.

Rows of jars line the nearby counters. They are filled with dried spices; raw almonds, walnuts and cashews; barley; nut and sesame candies, and mysterious ingredients (no doubt partly medicinal) mostly unknown to Westerners.

Canned and bottled items are found on shelves along the walls. Shark's fin and other expensive delicacies often rest behind a glass case on high.

Massive smoked hams hang above the refrigerator cases, along with twisted clouds of fish maw (the air bladder), slim sausages and packages of agar-agar seaweed.

Along a side wall hangs a rather complete collection of china and utensils, including cleavers, *woks* and steaming equipment.

If you want a lot of help in making your selections at a Chinese grocery, plan your trip for a weekday. On the weekends these stores are much too crowded to allow for individual attention, as Chinese families customarily visit with friends and relatives as they shop.

It has been discovered that many ingredients in Chinese foods are highly nutritious and medically valuable. Now that our physicians are seriously investigating Chinese folk medicine, perhaps more of these ingredients will find new uses in the Western world.

Abalone (Bow Yee) This large mollusk from the waters of Mexico, Japan, and South Africa, is imported canned. A favorite Cantonese banquet fish with a distinctive, clam-like flavor, abalone is best used in soups or stir-fry dishes, or as a cold *hors d'oeuvre*. Heat it briefly, or the abalone will toughen. The Mexican and South African varieties are preferable, as they are less likely to be living in polluted shore waters than those from Japan. Abalone is expensive, but delicious, and rich in vitamin B.

Agar-Agar (Tai Choy Go) A transparent dried seaweed, in long strips, agar-agar is rich in iodine, iron and other trace elements. It is served cold as an appetizer with a soy-flavored sauce. Agar-agar is prepared by soaking it in cold water for one hour, changing the water twice, draining it well and squeezing out excess liquid. Then it is cut in two-inch pieces.

Agar Agar Seaweed

Almonds (Nam Hong) Used as a crunchy garnish, almonds should be toasted in the oven in a flat pan until golden, but not brown. Heat raw, blanched almonds for about 15 minutes at 250°, stirring twice.

Almonds are rich in phosphorus, magnesium, and the B vitamins. They contain some unsaturated fatty acids, as do all nuts.

Insecticide residues are not a problem since the nut meat is protected by its heavy shell.

Bamboo Shoots (Jook Soon) The growing tip of the bamboo plant is known as the bamboo shoot, crisp and delicately nut-like in flavor. Canned, spring-harvested shoots, usually available in supermarkets, are slightly fibrous; the canned winter-cut shoots sold in Chinese stores are more tender and succulent.

This vegetable is a staple in Chinese cooking and appears in many recipes for soups, stir-frying and steaming. It is best to buy the small cans of bamboo shoots, since only small quantities are used at a time. Store any left-over shoots in water and refrigerate them. Change the water every day or two. They will keep this way for more than a week.

Bean Curd (Dow Foo) Bean curd is a creamy, firm custard made from soybeans and pressed into squares. Its flavor is very bland, but it becomes an excellent partner for sauces and rich-flavored ingredients. Curd is delicious in soups, stir-fried with meats and vegetables, steamed with fish, or served cold as an appetizer. One of the best-tasting Chinese dishes is bean curd with eggs, which is very simple to prepare.

A drier, firmer curd, called pressed curd, can be purchased in Chinatown; it can be slivered for stir-frying without falling apart. Canned bean curd is somewhat less creamy than the fresh, which is too perishable for mail order, but it is suitable in many dishes. It is available in gourmet shops and health food stores, as well as by mail order from Chinese stores. Whether the bean curd is fresh or out of the can, keep it submerged in water and refrigerated; change the water every day and it will last for up to two weeks.

Bean Curd

Bean curd is a first-rate source of protein. It has sustained the Chinese as a popular meat substitute for centuries. Physicians who have studied the Oriental diet suggest that bean curd might have a role in maintaining the very low rate of heart disease among the Chinese.

Bean curd, dried (Foo Jook) Dried bean curd comes in shiny sheets or strips, also known as bean curd stick. When soaked, it becomes very pliable, and has a rich soybean flavor.

Before use, it must be soaked at least one hour in warm water. Keep it well submerged to soften thoroughly. Dried bean curd is commonly served with fish, pork or vegetables, and as noodles in soup.

A thicker, somewhat sweet type of dried bean curd, called "second bamboo" (Tiem Jook), is prepared with vegetarian dishes, fish and as the outside wrapper for a type of egg roll. Prior to use, it must be soaked for two hours in warm water.

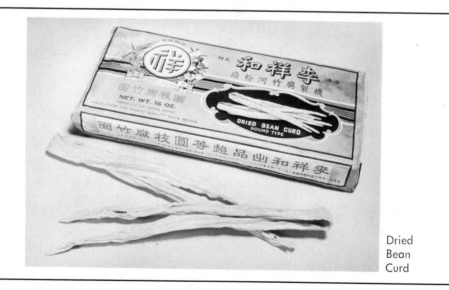

Dried Bean Curd

Bean Curd Cheese (Fooh Yu) This highly flavored soybean product is bean curd cut in cubes and fermented in wine to a cheese-like taste and consistency. It is used to season fish, meats and vegetable dishes.

Once opened, it may be kept at room temperature indefinitely.

See "bean curd" for its nutrient value. Also known as Chinese white cheese.

Bean Paste, Yellow (Wong Dow Sa) This is a salty, fermented sauce prepared from ground yellow soybeans and used in cooking.

Available canned, by mail, from Chinatown, yellow bean paste may also be interchanged with Japanese miso, a similarly-flavored soybean product. Miso can be bought at many health food stores.

See "soybean sprouts" for nutrient value. Also known as yellow sauce.

Bean Sauce, Brown (Min See Jeung) Brown bean sauce is a well-fermented soybean product made from mashed yellow beans, flour and salt. The Chinese find it flavorful cooked with bean curd, fish and meats.

See "soybean sprouts" for nutrient value.

Bean Sprouts (Ngah Choy) The sprouts grown from small peas called mung beans are called bean sprouts. They are a staple of Chinese cooking, especially in stir-frying with meats and fish. They are easy to sprout at home (see sprouting instructions). Canned sprouts can be bought at most supermarkets, although they lack the crispness of the fresh sprouts. Personally, I don't consider them a good substitute.

Mung Bean Sprouts

Dried mung beans for sprouting can be bought in specialty food stores and health food shops, as well as by mail order from Chinese stores. In Chinatown you can buy freshly-sprouted mung beans by the pound, very inexpensively. Bean sprouts will keep up to a week if they are covered with water. Change the water daily and refrigerate.

Bean sprouts are a good source of vitamins B and C. These valuable nutrients increase as the beans sprout.

Soybeans can also be sprouted in the same manner.

Beans, Black *(Kei tou)* Related to the commonly-used yellow soybeans, small black soybeans are preferred in long-cooking soups.

They make a fine partner for succulent oxtail, for example. These beans, like all soybeans, are not starchy.

Before cooking, soak the beans for several hours in cold water. Discard soaking water.

Black Soybeans
(enlarged)

You can often find black soybeans in health food stores. Try growing them in your home garden (see "Growing Your Own Chinese Vegetables").

The nutrient value of black beans is essentially as outstanding as that of yellow soybeans (see "soybean sprouts").

Beans, Black Fermented (Dow See) These black soybeans, fermented, dried and salted, provide an aromatic flavoring used especially with finned fish and shellfish. They are often added to meat dishes as a pungent accessory; use sparingly.

Fermented Black Beans

Soak fermented beans for 30 minutes in cold water and rinse well to remove excess salt.

Occasionally gourmet shops will carry fermented black beans in their Chinese department.

See "soybean sprouts" for data on nutrient values.

Beans, Red (*Hoong Dow*) Useful in long-cooking soups, red soybeans are small enough to need no soaking if simmered up to two hours. They are popular also as a sweet bean paste in pastries.

Grow them in your home garden (see "Growing Your Own Chinese Vegetables").

Bird's Nest (*Yin Wo*) A great Chinese delicacy, bird's nest is actually produced by swallows, from the fish and gelidium seaweed they eat. Prepared bird's nest is a semi-transparent gelatinous product, dried and shredded, rich in protein and vitamins. Bird's nest is frequently served in soup for Cantonese banquets.

To prepare, first soak the bird's nest in lukewarm water overnight. Remove bird feathers. Then boil it in chicken stock about 20 minutes. This is arduous to prepare and very expensive, but interesting in texture.

Dried Bird's Nest

Broccoli, Chinese (Gai Lon) The Chinese variety of broccoli has a smaller budding head, is leafier and more delicate in flavor than the one we are accustomed to eating in this country. It is often prepared with chicken or beef, or served separately as a vegetable.

It can be purchased fresh in Chinese stores and is rich in vitamins A and C, and pantothenic acid, one of the B complex.

Cabbage, Celery (Pai Tsai) A pale green vegetable with long compact leaves, celery cabbage grows somewhat like celery. It is excellent sliced in soup, or stir-fried with meats or vegetables.

Many supermarkets and specialty green grocers carry celery cabbage as a regular item. It's rich in vitamins C and A (see "Grow Your Own Chinese Vegetables").

Cabbage, Chinese (Bok Choy) This is a favorite Chinese green, a lovely contrast of chalk-white stems and deep green leaves. Well-known in *wonton* soup, it can be stir-fried with all kinds of meats, poultry and fish.

Look for Chinese cabbage in Chinatown groceries. Pick the younger, smaller stalks, not yet in flower, if possible. Chinese cabbage contains large amounts of vitamin C. (see "Grow Your Own Chinese Vegetables").

Chinese Cabbage

Cabbage, Green (*Gai Choy*) Chinese green cabbage grows in an elongated shape and has unusual, fan-shaped leaves. Its slightly bitter flavor is enhanced when used in *Bean Curd and Greens Soup*. Also try it stir-fried with meats, poultry or fish, or prepared sweet and sour.

Fresh green cabbage is available only in Chinatown. (see "Grow Your Own Chinese Vegetables").

Chinese Green Cabbage

Chestnuts, Fresh (*Fone Lut*) Fresh chestnuts are served with braised poultry and meat dishes and in sweet desserts.

To remove shell, add chestnuts to boiling water and cook for 20 minutes. Remove shells and inner skin.

Chestnuts are available during such a short season in the autumn that it may be tempting to freeze them. Freezing appears to break down the firm texture of chestnuts; they tend to crumble when thawed, and are difficult to prepare.

Chestnuts, Dried (*Loot Jee*) Imparting a sweet, deeply rich flavor to braised chicken and pork dishes, dried chestnuts make a convenient substitute when fresh chestnuts are out of season. They are usually sold shelled and skinned, a great time saver.

First, boil them for 15 minutes, then add the chestnuts to the braising liquid and cook for one and one half to two hours. Do not overcook them or they will disintegrate.

Curry (Gar Lay) A mixture of spices traditionally used in Indian cooking, curry has long been favored by the Chinese in meat and seafood dishes during the winter months.

Turmeric and nutmeg, two of the prime ingredients in curry, are thought by the Chinese to relieve pains in the limbs and dissolve blood congestions.

Use curry sparingly. You can buy it in any fine food shop and in most supermarkets.

Eggs, Ancient (Pay Don) The "black eggs" of China, or ancient eggs, are fermented several months in lime, wood ashes and salt, until they are translucently black and highly aromatic.

Their pungent delicacy is a banquet favorite, but we can enjoy them as an *hors d'oeuvre* with a dipping sauce, or with fresh eggs, either steamed or scrambled.

To prepare ancient eggs, pare off black outer coating with a knife. If coating is particularly hard, soak for 30 minutes in water, then scrape off the softened coating. Carefully crack the egg shell and remove it.

Ancient eggs will keep for several weeks at room temperature, and if refrigerated, three to six months. They are also known as preserved eggs, hundred-year-old eggs, thousand-year-old eggs, and century eggs.

Top, Ancient Eggs, Unpeeled.
Bottom, Sliced Ancient Eggs
Ready to Eat.

Five-Spice Powder (*Ng Heung Fun*) This is a very aromatic, delightful blend of the following spices; cinnamon bark, star anise, anise pepper, fennel and cloves. It is popularly used in meat, chicken, and especially duck dishes.

Both cinnamon and fennel are believed to improve digestion and appetite.

Ginger Root (*Sang Gueng*) Fresh ginger is a many-jointed, highly pungent root. Used frequently with fish to mask any odors, it is also added to soups and meats to impart a piquant flavor.

When a recipe calls for a slice of ginger, cut off a slice, about ⅛ inch thick, and remove the skin. Do not substitute ground ginger; the flavor is quite different.

When ordering ginger root, ask for a young, small root. Store it in any of the following ways:

1. Refrigerated in the vegetable crisper drawer.
2. In a cool, dry spot.

3. Peeled, and submerged in sherry.

4. In a plastic bag in the freezer. Do not defrost, but merely shave off a slice or two while the root is still frozen.

Traditionally, ginger is recommended by the Chinese to settle upset stomachs (see ginger broth), to treat colds, to strengthen the heart, and to relieve fever. Western physicians might do well to investigate a food-medicine that is so highly valued.

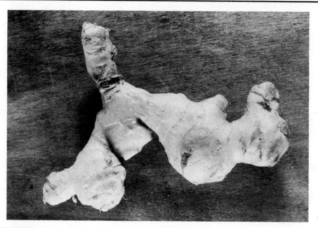

Ginger Root

Ginkgo Nuts (Bok Gwar) Available canned or dried, ginkgo nuts add an unusual, somewhat bitter flavor to meat and vegetable dishes.

Hair Seaweed (Faht Choy) Hair seaweed is found mainly in vegetarian recipes of Buddhist origin. When dry it has the appearance of thick black hair.

To prepare hair seaweed, boil it for three minutes, then drain and wash it thoroughly in cold water. Gently squeeze out the excess water. Hair seaweed is expensive, but it's rich in minerals.

Hoisin Sauce (Hoy Sin Jeung) A soybean-based sauce flavored sweet-pungent-mildly hot, *hoisin* accompanies Peking duck or is used to season some seafood dishes and other poultry dishes, such as diced chicken with nuts. It also can be used as a dipping sauce at the table for simply-cooked meats.

Buy *hoisin* sauce from gourmet food shops or by mail order from Chinatown. Once the can has been opened, store contents in a jar and refrigerate; keeps up to four months.

Use sparingly, since *hoisin* contains an artificial red food coloring, possibly harmful in large quantities.

Jellyfish (Hoy Git Pay) Savored for its crunchiness in cold appetizers, dried jellyfish is sold in clear plastic packages in Chinatown, or by mail order.

To use jellyfish, soak it in warm water for eight hours or overnight. Drain and rinse well. Shred it thinly.

Kohlrabi (Choy Gwoh) A member of the cabbage family, kohlrabi grows as an enlarged, bulbous stem, like a turnip, but just above ground. Peel, slice or dice kohlrabi and use it as you would bamboo shoots—in soups and stir-fried dishes or steamed with meats, poultry, fish or vegetables.

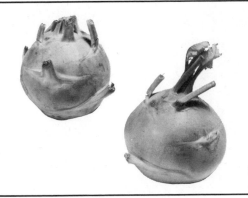

Kohlrabi

Fresh, large kohlrabi are sold almost exclusively in Chinese groceries. Smaller, more tender bulbs can be grown easily in home gardens or in a hothouse (see "Grow Your Own Chinese Vegetables"). Kohlrabi, also known as kale or cabbage turnip, is rich in vitamin C.

Lily Buds (Gum Jum) Known also as golden needles, lily buds are the dried buds of the tiger lily. Their flavor is somewhat acrid, but agreeable, in small quantities. Lily buds are cooked with meats, poultry or fish.

To prepare lily buds, soak them for 30 minutes in warm water. Nip off the hard ends. Cut them in half, or, for an elegant look, make a knot in the middle of each of the strands before cooking.

Dried Lily Buds

Longan (Loong Nan Gawn) Longans, or dragon's eyes, are related to the lychee, but their taste is not quite so perfumed. They are available dried or canned, to be served as a dessert or snack.

The Chinese claim that longans are stimulating to the mind and invigorating to the entire body.

Lotus Stem (Lien Ngow) Actually the underwater stem of the water lily, lotus stem resembles a large, fat sweet potato. Its interior contains linear air holes, which form an exotic geometric pattern when the lotus stem is sliced. Its texture is crisp, yet tender, when cooked. Lotus stem is excellent in soup or stir-fried with beef.

Fresh lotus stem should be purchased directly in Chinatown, since it is too perishable for shipping. It will keep in the refrigerator for about three weeks. Dried or canned lotus stem is available by mail order. The flavor of dried lotus stem is smoky and more intense than the fresh and its texture is not quite as crisp. But it is an acceptable substitute for the fresh lotus stem.

Soak dried lotus stem for 30 minutes in hot water, then parboil for about 45 minutes.

At Left, Pieces of
Dried Lotus Stem.
At Right, Fresh Lotus Stem

Lychee or Lichee (Ly Chee) Fresh lychee fruits have a juicy, translucent flesh covering a large brown pit. A leathery reddish shell, easy to remove, protects the fruit. The flavor is unbelievably delicate and perfumed. Lychee season is a short few weeks in June and July. The fruit is shipped from Florida and shows up in Chinese markets at a high price.

On Left, Canned Lichee Fruit.
On Right, Dried Lichee Fruit.

Organically-grown, fresh lychees may be ordered by mail from R. K. Trebel, Tropical Fruit Produce, R.3, Box 68, Estero, Lee County, Florida 33928. For the last five years, our family has thoroughly enjoyed Trebel lychees shipped on the branch. They will last three or four days refrigerated, but should be eaten as soon as possible to avoid loss of flavor.

Canned lychees are peeled and pitted, retaining most of their juicy texture. If you can't locate the fresh fruit, you should at least try the canned product, in spite of its sugar syrup. If you wish, place the fruit in a colander and rinse with cold water to drain off the syrup.

Dried lychees, resembling small prunes in a shell, are eaten out of hand just like any dried fruits and can be ordered by mail from some Chinese suppliers.

Lychees are thought by the Chinese to have a tonic quality. Their exquisite, sweet flavor is certainly a tonic to the spirit.

Melon, Hairy (Jeet Quar) A light green, small melon with fuzzy exterior, hairy melon is especially prized for its subtle flavor in soup. It can also be stir-fried, steamed or braised, but be careful not to overcook it.

Hairy melon is available fresh in Chinese stores.

Melon, Pleated (Si Gwa) Pleated melon (also known as ridged melon or Chinese okra) grows in the shape of a long cucumber, with sharp ridges. It has a refreshing taste in soup, and can be stir-fried. Peel off the sharp edges before using. Pleated melon can be found only in Chinatown.

Pleated Melon

Mushrooms, Cloud Ear (Wun Yee) This cultivated, dried fungus is known by several other names: tree fungus, brown fungus, and wood ears. When soaked, they expand greatly into earlike clumps of chewy texture, very delicate in taste.

The Chinese add cloud ears to many dishes (particularly soups and meat and vegetable mixtures) for their crunchy bite and dark brown contrast.

Soak cloud ears for 30 minutes in warm water, then wash them well. Cut off any hard sections. Cloud ears are very light weight, so buy them in small quantities.

They are appreciated by the Chinese for their apparent tonic quality. Chicken and cloud ear mushrooms, flavored with wine, was especially recommended to bring strength back to a new mother.

Cloud Ear
Mushrooms

Mushrooms, Dried Black (Dung Goo) Succulent black mushrooms figure in a great number of Chinese dishes—in soups and with all kinds of meats and fish. They lend themselves to all types of cooking methods, and their dark, firm flesh contrasts well with either white or green ingredients. Black mushrooms are cultivated in forest areas by inoculating logs with mushroom spores, which mature in about two years.

To reconstitute these dried mushrooms, soak them for at least one hour in warm water. Save the soaking liquid and add it to gravy or soup. This liquid has a rich deep flavor, so use it sparingly, or it will mask more delicate flavors.

According to *East Magazine*, modern Japanese research shows that black mushrooms are effective in lowering cholesterol levels in laboratory animals. High in vitamins B_2, C and D_2, the spores of black mushrooms have been found to help in controlling cancer and hardening of the arteries. Black mushrooms are fairly expensive, but are usually required in small quantities.

Black Mushrooms

Noodles, Cellophane (*Fun See*) Made from finely-ground mung beans, cellophane noodles become transparent when cooked. Always a great favorite with children, adults are also fond of these noodles, especially as served in soup, or stir-fried with meats, as spaghetti might be. Happily, the starch content of cellophane noodles is rather low, compared with that of wheat noodles.

Cellophane noodles are available in handy, two-ounce packages or in larger sizes; they can often be found in the gourmet section of department stores.

Before cooking cellophone noodles soak them in luke-warm water for 30 minutes and drain them. Other names for cellophane noodles are peastarch noodles, mung bean threads, shining noodles and transparent noodles.

Parsley, Chinese (*Een Sigh*) A flat-leaved parsley of more pronounced flavor than our familiar curly-leaved variety, Chinese parsley is used particularly in seasoning soups or meat balls and as a garnish for cold dishes.

Known also as cilantro or fresh coriander, this parsley can be grown in your own garden (see "Grow Your Own Chinese Vegetables"). It is high in vitamins A and C. Store in a plastic bag or in a jar, refrigerated up to one week.

Pepper, Szechwan (*Hwa Jo*) Common in the fiery-hot Szechwanese dishes, this pepper is more fragrant and somewhat less hot than our black peppercorns. Try filling a peppermill with Szechwan pepper for regular table use. Just a few grains will give a more spicy aromatic flavor to bland dishes.

Szechwan Peppercorns (enlarged)

Pinenuts (Cheung Che Yuen) These small, light beige nuts of the wild Western pine, *pinus edulis,* are usually prepared with chicken.

Pinenuts can be purchased at specialty nut shops and at some health food stores.

The Chinese believe that those who eat pinenuts tend toward a long life.

Pinenuts
(enlarged)

Purple Laver (Gee Choy) A thin, greenish-purple seaweed prepared in sheets, purple laver is best when it is served in rich meat, fish or poultry-based soups. Soak purple laver briefly for 15 minutes in warm water and rinse well. Drain and squeeze out excess moisture before using.

Frequently, purple laver can be purchased in gourmet shops or health food stores. It is well worth trying for its tangy sea taste and its rich store of minerals.

Purple Laver Seaweed

Red Dates (Hong Jo) Jujubes, or dried red dates, add a light, fruity sweetness to soups, braised dishes and some desserts. They have the appearance of a small, red, wrinkled peanut.

Red dates are popular in China as a restorative for the heart, lungs and circulation.

Sea Cucumber (Hoy Sum) One of the great Cantonese banquet delicacies, sea cucumber (also known as *beche de mer* or seaslug) is a soft but gelatinous shellfish, up to 12 inches long, found in the Indo-Pacific regions. It is usually served with chicken or pork and black mushrooms.

Long soaking is needed to soften the black, dried sea cucumber—fully 24 hours in warm water. The water must be changed several times and the shellfish cleaned well and simmered for four hours before it is used.

Occasionally, in a Chinese grocery, you may find pre-soaked sea cucumber in a barrel. This gourmet treat is expensive.

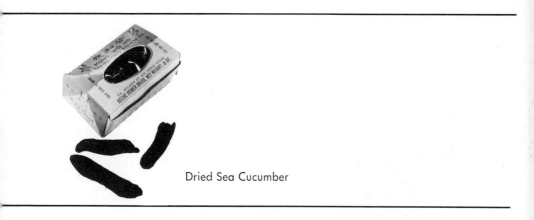

Dried Sea Cucumber

Seaweed (Chee Choy) See agar-agar, bird's nest, hair seaweed, and purple laver.

Sesame Oil (Jee Ma Jow) Chinese sesame oil is a highly aromatic flavoring made from toasted sesame seeds. It is not to be confused with the bland sesame oil usually purchased at health food stores. Just a few drops of this oil impart a distinctive, nutty taste to cold appetizers, such as agar-agar, seaweed and cucumber dishes. It is too strong to be used as a general cooking oil.

Sometimes the Chinese sesame oil can be located in gourmet shops, otherwise it must be ordered by mail. This is an expensive item, but is used in small quantities.

Sesame Paste (Jee Ma Jeung) Sesame paste is an aromatic, strongly-flavored seasoning, prepared from well-toasted sesame seeds, ground fine. It is used as a dressing on cold meats and vegetables, or as a sauce for noodles. Middle Eastern *tahini*, often available canned at health food stores, is a milder version made from untoasted sesame seeds. The Chinese in the United States frequently substitute peanut butter, which preserves the essential texture of the paste, although it differs somewhat in flavor.

Always stir sesame paste well before using it, to mix in the oil that floats to the surface.

Sesame seed products are excellent sources of protein, phosphorus and calcium.

Sesame Seeds (Jee Ma) Sesame seeds often serve as a garnish, particularly on cold appetizers. The Koreans, close neighbors of the Chinese, make extensive use of them, toasted and ground, as a flavoring in meat and vegetable dishes.

To toast sesame seeds, heat them in a frying pan at medium-low heat, stirring often, until they are golden, but not yet brown.

Sesame seeds can be found in almost all health food stores, and in many supermarkets.

They are rich in protein, lecithin and phosphorus and they contain almost twice as much calcium as there is in cheese, one of the highest sources.

Shark's Fin (Yu Chee) An important dish at most Chinese banquets, shark's fin is prepared from the chewy, cartilaginous back or tail fin. Usually served in a thick soup, sometimes teamed with crabmeat or chicken, it may also be presented with Chinese vegetables in a thickened sauce.

To use, soak dried shark's fin in warm water for 30 minutes. Then simmer in fresh water for two hours. This costly delicacy is high in protein, vitamins and minerals, especially calcium.

Dried Shark's Fin

Shrimps, Dried (Har May) Tiny, shelled dried shrimps are handy as a Chinese "convenience" food. They are useful for improving the flavor of soups and vegetable dishes.

To soften them for use, soak them in warm water for an hour.

Snow Peas (Soot Dow) One of the most beautiful of the Chinese ingredients, snow peas, also known as pea pods and Chinese peas, are the pods of the sugar pea, picked before the peas are formed inside. When stir-fried until barely cooked and still crunchy, they turn a light emerald green, most appetizing with white or dark ingredients. Snow peas are frequently used in soups, with all kinds of meat, poultry or fish or as a vegetable dish, often in combination with bamboo shoots and black mushrooms.

Snow peas are perishable and therefore must be bought in Chinatown. The price varies with the season, climbing as high as four dollars or more per pound in the winter.

319

It is not worth freezing snow peas, for the loss of crispness and color is too great.

This vegetable is ideal for growing at home (see "Grow Your Own Chinese Vegetables").

Snow peas are rich in vitamins A and C.

Soybean Sprouts (Da Dow Ngah) Although they are rarely served in Chinese restaurants, the sprouts of yellow soybeans are more flavorful and crisper than the usual mung bean sprouts, which are smaller and grow from tiny green seeds.

Soybean sprouts go best with hearty meats and rich soups. (Use the more delicate mung bean sprouts with fish and chicken). Before stir-frying, steam the sprouts for 12 to 15 minutes, covered, with two or three tablespoons of water.

Soybeans for sprouting can be purchased at health food stores, some supermarkets, and by mail order. Or grow your own! (See "Grow Your Own Chinese Vegetables").

Freshly sprouted soybeans are found at Chinese groceries, but cannot be mailed.

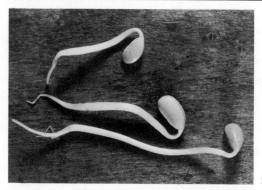

Soybean Sprouts

For several thousand years, the Chinese have depended upon soybeans as a main source of protein. The calcium content is nearly double that of milk. When soybeans are sprouted, they manufacture extra vitamin B complex and C as a welcome by-product. Most important to us is the action of soybeans in lowering cholesterol levels, reducing the chance of a heart attack.

Star Anise (Bot Gok) Star anise is an important spice, used when you braise meats and poultry with soy sauce. It is shaped like an eight-pointed star, reddish brown in color, and it is a major ingredient in the popular Chinese seasoning known as "five-spice." Chinese cooks often drop in a piece of star anise when making chicken stock, giving it a mild licorice flavor.

Star anise, also known as aniseed, is recommended by the Chinese to improve digestion.

Star Anise

Vinegar, Rice (*Bok Cho*) A mild, white vinegar resembling the taste of red wine vinegar, this flavoring seasons cold dishes and sweet-and-pungent mixtures.

Vinegar, Black Rice (*Hak Mi Cho*) A dark-colored liquid, black rice vinegar figures in meat dishes as well as in dipping sauces and dressings. A few drops may be added to dishes prepared with a fair amount of oil, counteracting any greasiness.

Walnuts (*Hop Ho*) Excellent stir-fried with chicken, walnuts also serve as a garnish for meat dishes.

Blanching is advisable before cooking to remove the walnuts' bitterness. To do that, put shelled walnuts in a saucepan, cover them with cold water, bring the water to a boil and cook for three minutes. Dry the walnuts well before using.

The Chinese believe walnuts invigorate the kidneys and stomach. They provide important amounts of magnesium, lecithin and un-saturated fatty acids. Their hard shells protect walnuts from insecticide residues.

Water Chestnuts (*Mar Tai*) The crunchiness of water chestnuts provides an important textural effect with meats and poultry in many stir-fried dishes. Fresh water chestnuts, available in China-town, are especially crisp and have a rich sweetness. Each bulb should be chosen carefully. Very firm ones are the best. Fresh water chestnuts may be frozen for a few weeks or refrigerated and used within a week. The brown outer husk must be peeled off before slicing.

Almost every supermarket stocks canned water chestnuts in their Chinese department. Once opened, they will keep several weeks if refrigerated. Cover them with water and change the water every other day.

A fine flour is made from water chestnuts, dried and ground. It serves as a thickener and a special ingredient in batter mixtures to improve the crust.

In Southern China many farmers cultivate their own water chestnuts in fish ponds.

Fresh Water Chestnut

Winter melon (Dung Quar) This is a very large melon with white, delicate flesh, most frequently used for winter melon soup. It is customary to buy winter melon by the wedge in Chinatown. Peel off the green skin and throw away the seeds before cooking. For a banquet, winter melon soup is sometimes steamed inside a whole melon.

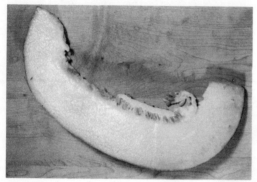

Slice of Winter Melon

Glossary

Bok choy—Chinese cabbage

Cha—tea

Char shew—roast pork

Chow—stir-fry

Congee—gruel or porridge made from rice or other grains

Dim sem—assorted steamed dumplings and hot snacks, customarily served at lunch

Ding—diced

Don—egg

Dow foo—soybean curd

Fan—rice

Gai—chicken

Har—shrimp

Kew—chunks

Lo mein—soft noodles

Loong har—lobster

Mein—noodles

Moo goo—white mushrooms

Ngow yuk—beef

Opp—duck

Pan (peen)—sliced

Red-simmer (red-cook)—cook in a soy sauce-flavored liquid

See—shred

Skins—dough casings for eggrolls or wontons

Soybean curd—custard-like white cakes made by precipitating soybean milk with an acidifying agent, like gypsum or vinegar.

Soong—mince

Stir-fry—cook on a high heat while stirring rapidly in a small amount of oil.

Sub gum—mixture

Tamari—long-fermented soy sauce sold in health-food stores

Tong—soup

Steaming, wet—cook covered on a rack over boiling water

Wok—cooking pan with rounded bottom

Wonton—small dumplings filled with meat or seafood

Wor—boneless

Ying—wet steam

Yu—fish

Bibliography

Chen, Philip, M.D. *Soybeans for Health, Longevity, and Economy.* S. Lancaster, Ma.: Chemical Elements, 1956.

Chu, Grace Zia. *Pleasures of Chinese Cooking.* New York: Simon and Schuster, 1962.

Miller, Gloria Bley. *The Thousand Recipe Chinese Cookbook.* New York: Grosset and Dunlap, 1970.

New York Academy of Sciences. "A Symposium on the Pharmacology and the Physiologic and Psychologic Effects of Tea," New York, 16 May 1955.

Ouei, Mimie. *The Art of Chinese Cooking.* London: W. H. Allen, 1963.

Shalleck, Jamie. *Tea.* New York: Viking Press, 1972.

Wallöfer, Heinrick, and Von Rottauscher, Anna. *Chinese Folk Medicine.* New York: Crown Publishers, 1965.

Yutang, Lin. *The Importance of Living.* New York: John Day Company, 1937.

Index

334

338

R

bean and
and.
egg.